Speak to me Softly

Speak to me softly, o' fine spotted steed,

On past days of glory, and valiant deed.

Come; speak to me softly of all that you've seen,

For, how can I know where you'll take me,

If I don't understand where you've been.

— *Frank Holmes*

Spotted **PRIDE**

The Appaloosa Heritage Series™

By Frank Holmes

SPOTTED PRIDE

Published by

LOFT
Enterprises, LLC
2767 Jeep Road
Abilene, KS 67410

Cover Design
Sandy Cochran
Fort Collins, Colorado

Cover Photo
Heaven Forbid
1982 Stallion
(Mighty Paul x Honkie Tonk)
Photo By KC Montgomery

Design, Typography, and Production
Sandy Cochran Graphic Design
Fort Collins, Colorado

Copy Editor
Dan Streeter
Hurst, Texas

Printing
Friesens Corporation
Altona, Manitoba, Canada

First Printing: July 2003

ISBN 0-9714998-3-7

DEDICATION

This book is dedicated to Laura Brest
—life-long friend and mentor—
She embodies the bold, visionary type of soul
that championed the breed.

INTRODUCTION

Having been a fan of the Appaloosa breed since the early 1930s, I am delighted to have been asked to write an introduction to *"Spotted Pride."*

Pride in the breed was a motivating factor when Claude Thompson of Moro, Oregon, incorporated the Appaloosa Horse Club (ApHC) in December of 1938; and pride was at the heart of my decision to join the Club in 1942 and register Toby II F-113 as my first Appaloosa stallion.

From the time of my appointment as ApHC Executive Secretary in 1947, I was fortunate to have worked with dedicated men and women who had that same kind of pride in the horse. Among them were such capable individuals as Dr. Francis Haines of Lewiston, Idaho; Bob Peckinpah of Quincy, California; and L. W. Moore of Hansen, Idaho.

For the past 56 years, I have also been fortunate to have had Iola Hatley as my wife and alter ego. Throughout the registry's formative years, Iola served in a crucial capacity as administrative secretary, bookkeeper and social hostess.

In this eagerly-awaited book, Frank Holmes has captured the essence of the passion that drove so many horsemen and -women to become involved with the breed, and to do all that was in their power to assure that it was preserved and perpetuated.

Because Frank's involvement with the breed dates back more than 40 years, and because he has first hand knowledge of a number of the horses and people that are portrayed on the pages that follow, you are certain to both enjoy and learn from the profiles he presents. By personally interviewing many of the pioneer personalities that

George and Iola Hatley, and Toby II F-113—photographed in the mid-1940s on the land that now houses ApHC headquarters.
Courtesy of George Hatley

owned, showed and promoted the breed's early-day champions, Frank has been able to successfully establish the colorful connection between the people and the horses.

I have been a proud participant in the Appaloosa story for more than 60 years and, during that time, I have seen the breed progress from near oblivion in the 1930s to a position of prominence within the livestock industry by the late 1970s.

In my case, the participation has been a labor of love, and it has enriched me beyond description.

I hope you enjoy *Spotted Pride*. It is bound to entertain you, inform you, and help you appreciate the special people and horses who established this extraordinary breed.

George G Hatley

BECAUSE OF THE PEOPLE

I received my first exposure to Appaloosas just as countless other people have over the years—through the pages of *Western Horseman* magazine.

It was June of 1961, and I was a 12-year-old Army brat, spending the summer on my Swedish grandparents' farm in northwestern North Dakota. We had made a 100-mile jaunt from the farm near Niobe to the regional shopping center of Williston. There, I plunked 50 cents on a drugstore counter for an issue of the magazine.

That single issue opened my eyes to a world of spotted horses that I never knew existed. In it, there were photos of such Hall of Fame horses as Joker B., Bright Eyes Brother and Rustler Bill. I was hooked.

Over the next 20 years, I devoured everything I could find about the breed. And I visited with the people—the pioneer breeders and exhibitors who were actually in the process of spreading the Appaloosa story throughout the land. People like Andy Moore, Clarence Danielson and Leroy Nelson in North Dakota; Laura Boggio Brest and Russell Brest in Montana; George Stephens and Art Stilke in Illinois; and Dick Southern, Mavis Peavy, Cecil Dobbin and Lane Hudson in Colorado.

To the last man (and woman), these dedicated Appaloosa people realized right off the bat that I was just a penniless kid and that the chances of making any money off me were slim to none. And yet they took me in. They plied me with stories and literature, they hauled me around to shows and sales, and they took me to visit other Appaloosa lovers.

Why?

I'd like to think that they saw something in me—a kindred spirit, maybe—or a passion for this special breed of horse. Or maybe they just thought I was in need of a little help.

Twenty-five years ago, a well-known Quarter Horse photographer and breeder asked me why I was so "wrapped up in Appaloosas." I thought for awhile before I answered, "It's because of the people."

On the following pages, you'll find the profiles of 24 Appaloosa stallions and one mare. You'll also find references to the men and women who bred these horses, used them in the course of their everyday lives, and showed and promoted them.

Great men and women—as colorful in every respect as the horses they championed.

And I need to make a very important point here.

For every Appaloosa profiled, for every pioneer Appaloosa man and woman mentioned, there are scores more who should have been given their due. Time and space simply wouldn't allow it.

So, here's to all of them—the horses and the people responsible for writing the history of the breed.

The Appaloosa story is a great one, long and involved and full of interesting subplots and tangents. And it is so for one overwhelming reason.

Because of the people.

Frank Holmes

ACKNOWLEDGMENTS

In actual time spent before the computer, *Spotted Pride* took six months to write. In terms of time spent being devoted to the breed, time spent visiting with breeders and exhibitors, and time spent poring over old magazines and photo albums, the book has been more than 40 years in the making.

I bought my first issue of *Appaloosa News* magazine in the spring of 1962. I picked it up at the Libertyville Saddle Shop in Libertyville, Illinois. Having always been interested in the history of the breed and curious about the men and women who championed it, I suppose I actually started doing the research that resulted in *Spotted Pride* on that long-ago day.

As is always the case, no man is an island and no book gets done without help.

I take this opportunity to recognize and thank the people who helped turn this effort into a reality.

Roger Klamfoth, CEO of the Appaloosa Horse Club, was instrumental in enlisting the full cooperation of his staff. Shonda Nelson, ApHC registrar, provided me with reams of registration information and production records; and Kelly Hastings, ApHC customer service representative, helped me resolve numerous historical issues.

Robin Hendrickson, *Appaloosa Journal* editor, cheerfully granted me access to her ApHC Hall of Fame files; and Tracy Early and Kara Vandenbark, *Journal* graphic artists, scanned literally hundreds of historical photos for me.

Stacey Garretson, ApHC museum director, tolerated several days of my rifling through her extensive photo collection.

I'd also like to pass along a note of thanks to the Sundance 500 International folks—Bonnie-Jean Newitt, Gala Argent, Lisa Banks and Sandy Dean—for their cooperation in ensuring that Sundance was among the horses profiled.

As has been the case in my past efforts, Randy Witte, publisher of *Western Horseman* magazine, graciously granted me access to his rich library of historical photos. As a long-time leader of the equine publishing community, Randy has a deep appreciation for historical efforts of this type. Furthermore, as a protégé of renowned *Western Horseman* publisher Dick Spencer III and an in-law of the Peavy family, he has always been doubly aware of the positive role both entities played in the development of the Appaloosa breed.

For the third book in a row, *Paint Horse Journal* Senior Editor Dan Streeter of Hurst, Texas, pulled double-duty as my copy editor, and Sandy Cochran of Fort Collins, Colorado, served as my graphic artist and book designer.

Finally, I thank Gene Carr of Hayti, South Dakota, and Robert Lapp of Eau Claire, Wisconsin, two men who played especially critical roles in assuring that this book was written.

Gene Carr—long-time friend, mentor and supporter—has always encouraged me to research and write Western horse history.

Robert Lapp—fellow historian and renowned "attention-to-detail" guru—provided me with invaluable research assistance and proofreading skills.

Without Gene and Bob's encouragement, I simply never would have tackled this project.

To the crew of LOFT—especially business manager Carol Plybon—thanks again for all your support and patience.

Finally, many thanks to my wife, Loyce, for graciously putting up with the long hours and daily distractions that seem to go hand-in-hand with a project of this nature.

Hey, gang…surely at some point practice will make perfect.

Frank Holmes

TABLE OF CONTENTS

Chapter 1

TOBY I

F-203

Toby I—seen here with Ardis Racicot of Sandpoint, Idaho—was one of the breed's first great performance stars.
Courtesy Appaloosa Museum & Heritage Center

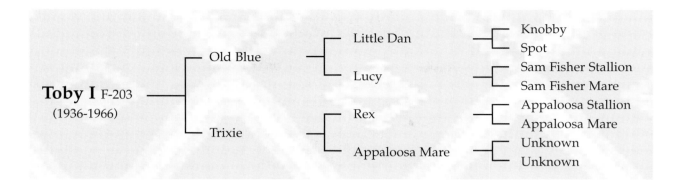

Toby I F-203
(1936-1966)

Old Blue
- Little Dan
  - Knobby
  - Spot
- Lucy
  - Sam Fisher Stallion
  - Sam Fisher Mare

Trixie
- Rex
  - Appaloosa Stallion
  - Appaloosa Mare
- Appaloosa Mare
  - Unknown
  - Unknown

Long before the Appaloosa Horse Club (ApHC) was founded in December of 1938, the breed was well established in the "Palouse Country" of southeastern Washington.

There, pioneer ranchers such as Guy Lamb of Central Ferry, Washington, and Floyd Hickman of Colfax, Washington, had been breeding Appaloosas in the region for decades. As a result, the blood of both men's horses contributed greatly to the registry's foundation gene pool.

Lamb's cornerstone Appaloosa stallion was Knobby, also known as The Lamb Horse. A 1918 stallion sired by an unnamed Appaloosa stallion and out of an unnamed Appaloosa mare, Knobby was a dark blue roan in color, with a white, spotted blanket over his hips. Unregistered and unshown, he was utilized strictly as a ranch horse and sire.

Floyd Hickman lived 25 miles "up-river" from the Lamb ranch. In the 1920s, he rode an Appaloosa mare named Spot down to be bred to Knobby. The following spring, Spot foaled a black, blanket-hipped colt who was named Little Dan.

Little Dan was kept by Hickman and used as a breeding animal. In time, Hickman bred the stallion to Lucy—a Sam Fisher-bred Appaloosa mare. Fisher, a Palouse Indian from Lyons Ferry, Washington, was yet another northwestern breeder whose horses influenced the registry's foundation gene pool.

The cross of Little Dan and Lucy produced Old Blue, Hickman's most noteworthy pre-registry Appaloosa stallion.

One of the most popular sires in the Palouse Country, Old Blue once bred 109 outside mares in a single season.

In 1935, Hickman bred Old Blue to an Appaloosa mare named Trixie. Sired by the Fisher-bred Appaloosa stallion Rex and out of a red roan Appaloosa mare, Trixie was a renowned Northwest relay-racing mount.

Toby I, a 1936 blue roan, blanket-hipped stallion, was the resulting foal.

For the first two years of his life, "Toby" was allowed to roam free and grow up naturally. When he was a 2-year-old, he was broke to ride.

At maturity, Toby stood 15.2 hands high and weighed 1,100 pounds. Used primarily as

Knobby, Toby I's great grandsire, antedated the Appaloosa registry but was responsible for several foundation lines.
Courtesy Appaloosa Museum & Heritage Center

Owned and exhibited by Harold Tibbs of Sandpoint, Idaho, Toby I was the Champion Performance Horse at the 1948 National Appaloosa Show in Lewiston, Idaho.

Courtesy Appaloosa Museum & Heritage Center

a Hickman ranch mount for the first years of his life, his breeder considered him to be the top stock horse he had ever ridden.

By all accounts, Toby I was a natural cow horse and adept at negotiating the steep river breaks. He was also reportedly so well trained that when it came time to load him in a pickup truck for work in outlying areas, he would jump up onto the truck bed from level ground.

In addition to his duties as a using horse, Toby also saw duty as a Hickman herd sire. Although it is probable that he bred a significant number of mares during this time, only a handful of the resulting foals were ever registered.

In 1946, Harold Tibbs of Sandpoint, Idaho, acquired the stallion.

"I didn't get Toby directly from Floyd Hickman," Tibbs says. "I bought him from Al Faulkner of Spokane, Washington, who had

owned him since the late 1930s or early 1940s.

"When America entered into World War II, Al joined up. Before he shipped out, he took Toby out to a friend's place. The friend was an elderly man who liked to ride. He couldn't get mounted up on Toby from level ground, so he taught the stud to side step over to a fence. Then he'd climb up on it and step over onto the horse's back."

When Faulkner came back from the war, he found he was no longer interested in horses. As a result, he kept Toby boarded at the McClellan Riding Stable near Dishman, Washington. Faulkner had very little to do with his horse, but did allow the stable's owners to use him as a riding and calf roping mount.

Shortly thereafter, Tibbs—who was very interested in horses—entered the picture.

"I had always been attracted to Appaloosas," he says. "My first one was

Toby II, owned and ridden by George Hatley of Moscow, Idaho, won the 300-yard race at the first National.
Courtesy Appaloosa Museum & Heritage Center

Chief Joseph F-92. I gave $175 for him and probably would have kept him for awhile if it hadn't been for a fluke kind of deal.

"I was up at a livestock show in Spokane, when it came over the loudspeaker that I was being paged. I got to the phone and a man was on the other end who wanted to know what I'd take for my Appaloosa stallion.

"I really didn't want to sell the horse, so I just figured to put a high enough price on him to discourage the guy. I told him I'd take $350.

" 'Well,' he said, 'that's a lot of money. I don't know if I want to go that high. But I'll tell you what. When you get back home, either your horse will be here, or a check for $350.'

"And, sure enough, when I got back, there was a check on the table and I was out a good Appaloosa that I really didn't want to sell."

In short order, however, the opportunity arose to acquire a second, and better, horse.

"In 1946," Tibbs says, "there was a classified ad in the Spokane paper offering a Canadian-bred Appaloosa stallion for sale. He was being stabled at Harold McClellan's, and I drove up to get a first-hand look at him. After I'd checked the Canadian horse out, Harold came up to me and said, 'You don't want this stud. You want this other horse that I've got boarded here.'

"The other horse was Toby. I liked him much better and wound up buying him for something like $350 or $400."

In April of 1946, Tibbs registered his new acquisition with the Appaloosa Horse Club as Toby I F-203. Having no safe place to keep

Toby I and Toby II then combined forces to take home the matched pair title.

Courtesy Appaloosa Museum & Heritage Center

After being sold to Ardis Racicot of Sandpoint, Idaho, Toby I saw extensive use as a pleasure and parade mount.
Courtesy Appaloosa Museum & Heritage Center

him, he boarded him at the local stable of W. C. "Fats" and Ardis Racicot.

"This was before I was married," Tibbs says. "I was working at an auto body shop at the time. I lived out at the Racicot place for a while and showed Toby in a lot of local saddle club shows and rodeos—in about every event that was offered.

"He was a top reining and roping horse, and so smart that you didn't have to teach him much. In fact, he always seemed to know more about things than I did."

In 1948, ApHC sponsored the first National Appaloosa Show in Lewiston, Idaho. Toby I was exhibited by Tibbs and Ardis Racicot at the hallmark event.

With Mrs. Racicot aboard, the 12-year-old stallion was named the Champion Ladies

Western Pleasure Horse. With Tibbs at the lead or in the saddle, he was named the get of sire winner, and the Champion Men's Western Pleasure Horse, Champion Matched Pairs (with Toby II), and the Champion Performance Horse.

All told, the 1948 National Show offered eight halter classes and seven performance events. Of the 15 first places that were awarded, Toby I and his descendants accounted for nine.

"Of course, that was the first National," Tibbs says, "and both Ardis and I had the advantage of being experienced show exhibitors. A lot of the other folks who attended had never shown before.

"It seemed like we won every class we entered, and it got a little embarrassing. In

Tobianna, a 1947 mare by Toby I and out of Diamond, was a top ranch mount and broodmare.

Courtesy Appaloosa Museum & Heritage Center

fact, I had Toby entered in the stock horse [reining] class, but I never took him in. I figured we'd won enough."

After the show, Tibbs continued to show Toby I on a limited basis and stand him to a few outside mares.

In 1954, he gave the stallion to Ardis Racicot. From that point on, Toby was used primarily as a personal riding mount. He was also exhibited by his new owner at numerous local horse shows, parades and social events.

In 1955, the pair won the parade class at the Washington State University Open Show. Three years later, at the age of 22, Toby placed third in the stock horse class at a Sandpoint, Idaho, horse show.

The colorful stallion's last public appearance took place in July of 1965, at a Girl Scout

Jamboree in Farragut, Idaho. There, at the age of 29, he was put on display by Mrs. Racicot.

As noted earlier, Toby I sired very few ApHC-registered foals. In fact, ApHC records reveal him to be the sire of only 47 offspring. Still, he managed to sire such noteworthy show horses and breeding animals as Toby II, Tobianna, Chief Spokane Garry, Chief Red Wolf and Rapid Lightning.

Toby II F-113, a 1939 stallion out of Dappal, was almost singularly responsible for the perpetuation of the line. Bred by Floyd Hickman and owned by George Hatley, he will be profiled in the following chapter.

Tobianna F-350, a 1947 mare out of Black Diamond, was bred by W. D. Lewis of Sandpoint, Idaho. Purchased as a weanling by Harold Tibbs, she was then re-sold to Harry Anderson of Eureka, Kansas.

Anderson, who personally made the trip to Idaho to take possession of the young Appaloosa filly, accompanied her on the four-day train ride to her new home. At several points during the trip, Tobianna was taken from the boxcar and allowed to get some exercise. Her unusual markings created an uproar, and large crowds would gather to get a look at her.

In the beginning, Tobianna was utilized as a ranch horse. Later retired to the broodmare band, she produced 17 foals and several of the Sunflower State's first noteworthy show ring stars.

Durango F-1694, a 1955 stallion by Buttons B. and out of Tobianna, was a top halter and performance horse. Retired to stud, he sired such horses as Toby's No-Wa-Che D.E., the Champion Junior Reining Horse at the 1973 National Show in Salem, Oregon, and Kiamichi Brave, a regional champion halter and performance horse.

Chief Spokane Garry F-447, a 1948 stallion by Toby I and out of Rosary, was bred by C. A. and Fern Schmidt of Chattaroy,

Washington. Kept by them and utilized as a breeding animal, he went on to become a noted regional sire.

Chief Red Wolf F-746, a 1949 stallion out of Princess Pat, was another of Toby I's early-day champions. Bred by Jesse Heffel of Kendrick, Idaho, he was named the Champion Yearling Stallion at the 1950 National Show in Lewiston.

Rapid Lightning F-1825, a 1957 mare out of Titania by Red Eagle, was one of her sire's most-accomplished show get. Bred by Earl Perin of Priest River, Idaho, she was a champion at halter many times, and was a top producer.

The Toby I and Titania cross was a potent one. In addition to Rapid Lightning, it also resulted in top show and breeding horses such as Kaniksu's Little Beaver, a 1958 geld-ing; Kaniksu's Chain Lightning, a 1962 mare; Kaniksu's Kiowa, a 1963 gelding; and Kaniksus Sheet Lightening, a 1966 mare.

Toby I passed away of natural causes on February 21, 1966—two months short of his 31st birthday. He was buried on the Racicot ranch where he spent the last two decades of his life.

Later that spring, the legendary stallion's final two registered get were born. They were the aforementioned Kaniksus Sheet Lightening and Toby's Chico, a 1966 mare out of Chico's Babe by Freel's Chico.

Toby I, who was foaled two years before ApHC was incorporated, possessed strong Appaloosa bloodlines on both sides of his pedigree. He lived up to his heritage by becoming one of the breed's first noteworthy performance horses and sires.

Rapid Lightning, a 1957 mare by Toby I and out of Titania, was a multiple grand champion halter mare.
Courtesy Appaloosa Museum & Heritage Center

Chapter 2

TOBY II
F-113

Toby II was a classic Palouse Country Appaloosa.
Photo by Henry Sheldon, courtesy George Hatley

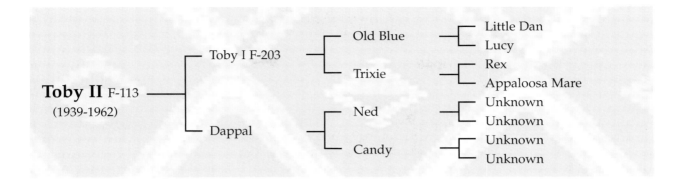

Toby II F-113
(1939-1962)
— Toby I F-203
  — Old Blue
    — Little Dan
    — Lucy
  — Trixie
    — Rex
    — Appaloosa Mare
— Dappal
  — Ned
    — Unknown
    — Unknown
  — Candy
    — Unknown
    — Unknown

(Note: Both Toby I and his son Toby II were commonly known as "Toby." In the following chapter, Toby I is referred to only as Toby I. Toby II is referred to as both Toby II and Toby.)

Toby II, a 1939 stallion by Toby I and out of Dappal, was his sire's first ApHC-registered get and his first show ring champion. Furthermore, as a consistent sire of top breeding sons, he was almost singularly responsible for the perpetuation of the line.

Toby II was bred by Floyd Hickman of Almota, Washington, and allowed to grow up wild and free on the Snake River breaks. Gathered up in the summer of 1941, the 2-year-old stallion was broke to ride by a Hickman ranch hand named Archie Hennigar.

Later that same year, Toby II was purchased by George Hatley of Moscow, Idaho, who, at that time, was a 17-year-old high school student with an entrepreneurial bent.

"I was born July 18, 1924, on the farm my grandfather homesteaded in 1877," he says. "The Hatley family had owned Appaloosas for years, so I was reasonably well-acquainted with them.

"All throughout high school, I was involved in the Future Farmers of America (FFA) program. I subscribed to the *Western Livestock Journal*—a California agricultural publication—and through it learned of an Appaloosa Horse registry that had been founded by Claude Thompson of Moro, Oregon. In 1941, I corresponded with Mr. Thompson and, as a result, began looking for a young Appaloosa stallion to purchase."

In time, Hatley's search took him to Floyd Hickman's ranch.

"Floyd's ranch was located 20 miles southwest of Pullman, Washington," Hatley says. "At the time, he was one of the best-known and most-respected horse breeders in the region. In addition to his Appaloosa stallions, he also stood a draft stallion and a Shetland pony.

"I went out to Floyd's place and I bought Toby II for $170, with money I had earned with my FFA cattle. Back then, my father had a 1939 Chevrolet pickup truck with stock racks. He loaned it to me to go get my new horse. We didn't own a horse trailer, but that didn't present a problem. Like his sire, Toby II was trained to jump up in the back of a pickup from level ground. We just hopped him up and headed for home."

Several months after acquiring the young

Owned for most of his life by ApHC Executive Secretary George Hatley of Moscow, Idaho, Toby II saw extensive duty as a "rough country" ranch mount.

Courtesy George Hatley

Shown by Hatley, Toby II earned Champion Stallion honors at the 1955 Washington State Horse Show in Pullman.
Courtesy George Hatley

Hickman-bred stallion, Hatley registered him with the Appaloosa Horse Club as Toby II F-113. The young horseman joined the club at the same time and was assigned ApHC membership no. 45.

After being acquired by Hatley, Toby II's use as a rough-country ranch horse continued. In this, he proved outstanding.

"By the time I got him," Hatley says, "Toby was very well-reined, and had a fast walk. He was also very intelligent and was imbued exceptional cow-sense.

"The Hatley ranch is located on the Snake River breaks. It's extremely rough country, covered with steep hills and dense thorn thickets. When we gathered cattle, they would sometimes hole-up in the thickets.

"If a cow had slipped off to hide, Toby would know that and he would not willingly leave the area. He would point, like a pointing dog. If you tried to rein him away, he'd shake his head. He didn't want to leave until he got that cow out."

In addition to his role as a ranch mount, Toby II was also utilized as a breeding animal.

"To begin with," Hatley says, "I didn't own a pickup or horse trailer of my own. So I used to just ride Toby around the country to mare owners who wanted to breed to him.

"During this time period, the federal government made top Thoroughbred stallions available to the public through the Remount program. The government only charged a $10 stud fee, so that was pretty much all I could charge.

"Toby bred quite a number of mares during the early to mid-1940s, but very few of the resulting foals were registered."

In the mid-1940s, while attending University of Idaho, Hatley met and married Iola Golden—a California girl with no experience with livestock. Had it not been for the young Idaho stockman's easy-going manner, that marriage might have had a harder time getting off the ground.

"In 1945 or 1946," George Hatley recalls, "there was a local sleeping sickness scare. The vet from Lewiston, Idaho, came up to vaccinate the horses, so the hired hand and I gathered up 20 head of mares. To corral them, we had to bring them down a lane. There was an open gate at the end of the lane, but someone had to stand in the lane and turn the horses into the corral.

"Iola and I weren't married yet, but she was visiting for the weekend. So I asked her to stand in the lane and wave and shoo the horses into the corral. With 20 head of horses thundering down the lane at her, instead of standing there, Iola dove under the fence. The horses escaped.

"I didn't say a word. I just got back on my horse and went to gather them back up.

"Twenty years later, Iola and I were at an Appaloosa sale in Lewiston. That same vet was issuing the health certificates. He took one look at Iola and said, 'Say, aren't you the girl who let all those horses escape 20 years ago?'

"She kind of hung her head in shame and replied, 'Yes, I am.'

" 'I never thought he'd marry you,' the vet said."

In time, however, Iola learned a little more about horses. And Toby II proved to be one of her very first mentors.

"I was just a city girl," Iola says. "But I wanted to learn how to ride, so George just put me up on Toby. He was really quite a horse; so nice to ride, with a soft, easy way of traveling. And he was always a perfect gentleman. As green as I was, even I realized Toby was a very unusual horse."

In 1946, George Hatley was appointed assistant secretary of the Appaloosa Horse Club. In 1947, he became the executive secretary. He would hold the latter position for 31 years.

As a result of becoming the head of the Appaloosa organization, Hatley made the conscious decision to not promote Toby II. He did, however, show him at the inaugural National Appaloosa Show.

"As a boy, I went to a country school where everyone rode a horse to school," Hatley says. "We didn't have facilities for organized sports but we'd have horse races over the noon hour. I never won a horse race and it was something I badly wanted to do.

"At the first National, we had a 300-yard race and I won it. That was quite an accomplishment for me, because I had this burning desire to sometime in my life win a horse race."

In addition to winning the race, George and

Toby II and Patti Murphy dressed up in Nez Perce Indian regalia to lead a circa 1950s Moscow, Idaho, May Day parade.
Courtesy George Hatley

Topatchy, a 1953 stallion by Toby II and out of Kathy, was the Champion Yearling Stallion at the 1954 National Show in Deer Lodge, Montana.

Courtesy Appaloosa Museum & Heritage Center

Toby II also teamed up with Harold Tibbs of Sandpoint, Idaho, and Toby I to win the matched pairs Western pleasure class.

All in all, the first National Show was a watershed event—for both the breed and the Hatley family.

"George and I were married in 1947," Iola Hatley says. "George decided we should have an all-Appaloosa show in Lewiston, Idaho, in 1948.

"The show was held on our first anniversary. George managed the show and announced it. I clerked it and handed out ribbons.

"So we worked all day on our very first anniversary. But we were just kids and we were having the time of our lives. Plus, I got to present George with a couple of first-place

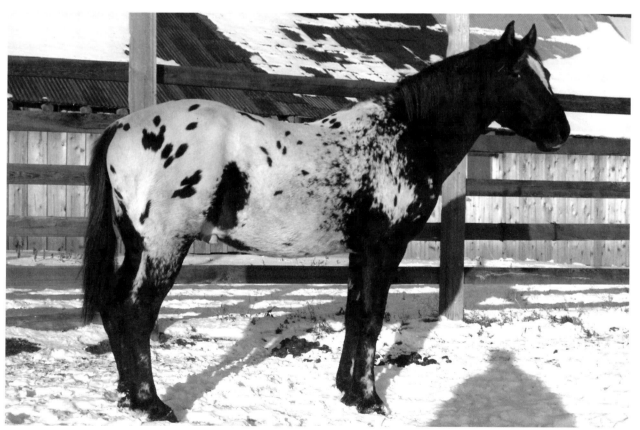

Doll's Toby, a 1960 stallion by Toby II and out of Riley's Purple Doll, was born in the Palouse Country and exported to South Africa.

Courtesy Appaloosa Museum & Heritage Center

ribbons."

In addition to being shown at the National Show, Toby II was also exhibited locally at halter. In 1948, he won the light horse division of the University of Idaho's Little International. He was also named the Champion Appaloosa Stallion at one of the early Washington State University horse shows.

Like his sire, Toby II was not heavily utilized as a breeding animal. The reason behind this fact had little to do with the colorful stallion's popularity. Rather, it had to do with the fact that his owner was too dedicated to building up the Appaloosa registry to devote much time to advertising and standing a stallion.

Despite the lack of promotion and numbers, however, Toby II did much to further the family name. Among his earliest noteworthy get were Toby III, Diamond Bell, Topatchy and Maumin Tosteen.

Toby III, a 1944 stallion out of Arrow, was bred by George Hatley. Gelded while young and used as a movie horse, Toby III sired only six foals. Of those, two—Chief Eagle and Toby IV—earned national halter titles.

Diamond Bell, a 1946 mare out of Trudy, was bred by Jesse Heffel of Kendrick, Idaho, and earned honors as the Champion 2-Year-Old Mare at the 1948 National Show.

Maumin Tosteen, a 1947 mare out of Asotin Annie, was the winner of the 1/4-mile race at the 1953 National Show in Quincy, California.

Topatchy, a 1953 stallion out of Kathy, was also bred by Hatley. The Champion Yearling Stallion at the 1954 National Show in Deer Lodge, Montana, he went on to become a top sire.

With a total of only 47 ApHC-registered foals, Toby II was known primarily as a sire of males, and contributed top-siring foundation sons such as Chief Handprint, Toby II's Patchy, Topatchy, Toby K, Doll's Toby and Polkadott Toby to the breed.

Chief Handprint, Toby II's Patchy, Topatchy

Chief Handprint, a 1950 stallion by Toby II and out of Lolo, was so named because of the unusual marking on his left flank.
Courtesy Appaloosa Museum & Heritage Center

and Toby K were all three-quarter brothers, sired by Toby II and out of daughters of Patchy F-416.

Doll's Toby and Polkadott Toby were full brothers—sired by Toby II and out of Riley's Purple Doll—and bred by Palmer Wagner of Garfield, Washington.

All six Toby II sons were heavily utilized as sires and were instrumental in introducing both the line and the breed to new fans in virtually every corner of the country.

Although he was not used heavily as a sire, that's not to say that Toby II was unappreciated or under-used in other aspects. In addition to being a life-long ranch mount, the foundation stallion also saw duty as a rodeo pickup horse and as a backcountry trail and bear-hunting mount. As a highly colored and well-dispositioned horse, he also saw considerable duty as a pleasure and parade mount.

Toby II passed away on September 26, 1962, as the result of a freak ranch accident.

A member of one of the Northwest's first prominent, post-registry lines, Toby II did much to enhance the family name and contribute to the development and spread of the breed.

Chapter 3

RED EAGLE
F-209

Red Eagle—"The Patriarch of a Strain"

Courtesy Appaloosa Museum & Heritage Center

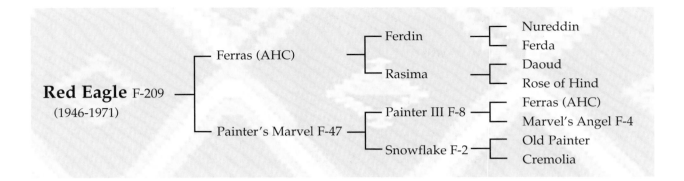

Red Eagle F-209
(1946-1971)

- Ferras (AHC)
  - Ferdin
    - Nureddin
    - Ferda
  - Rasima
    - Daoud
    - Rose of Hind
- Painter's Marvel F-47
  - Painter III F-8
    - Ferras (AHC)
    - Marvel's Angel F-4
  - Snowflake F-2
    - Old Painter
    - Cremolia

As the marquee stallion bred by the founder of the Appaloosa Horse Club, Red Eagle enjoys a singular position in the history of the breed.

Claude Thompson, a wheat farmer from Moro, Oregon, incorporated the Appaloosa Horse Club on December 30, 1938. His personal interest in the breed dated back to the mid-1920s, when he began a breeding program based on the Old Painter line.

Beginning with Babe F-1, a 1929 mare by Old Painter and out of June's mare, and Snowflake F-2, a 1929 mare by Old Painter and out of Cremolia, the first 17 horses to be accepted into the registry were all Thompson/Painter-bred.

In the early 1930s, looking to add more refinement to his herd, Thompson purchased an Arabian stallion named Ferras from the famed Kellogg Ranch of Pomona, California. The outcrossing contributed a number of outstanding individuals to the early registry.

In June of 1946, Thompson registered two weanling stallions with ApHC—Spotted Eagle F-208 and Red Eagle F-209.

Spotted Eagle, a 1946 stallion by El Zorro F-108 and out of Daybreak F-155, was the Champion 2-Year-Old Stallion at the 1948 National Show in Lewiston, Idaho, and the Champion Ladies Western Pleasure Horse at the 1949 National Show in Lewiston.

Sold to A. T. "Cap" McDannald of Houston, Texas, and utilized as a herd sire, the bay, blanket-hipped stallion went on to sire such top show horses as Captain Barry, Little Bird and Eagles 132.

Red Eagle, a 1946 stallion sired by Ferras (Arabian Horse Club #992) and out of Painters Marvel F-47, was kept by Thompson. A bay, blanket-hipped stallion whose forequarters roaned with age, Red Eagle was actually a double-bred Ferras descendant. Painters Marvel, his dam, was a 1940 mare by Painter III F-8 and out of Snowflake F-2. Painter III, in turn, was sired by Ferras and out of Marvel's Angel F-4 by Young Painter by Old Painter.

Red Eagle was bred by ApHC founder Claude Thompson of Moro, Oregon. The famous duo is seen here at a mid-1950s horse show.
Courtesy Appaloosa Museum & Heritage Center

Red Eagle was the Champion Aged Stallion and Reserve Grand Champion Stallion at the 1957 National Show in Canby, Oregon.
Courtesy Western Horseman

For the first several years of his life, Red Eagle was allowed to grow up naturally and free on the Thompson Ranch. Apparently a precocious yearling, he bred and settled Night Flower F-259, a 2-year-old mare by Ferras and out of Flash's Pepper F-63.

Titania F-604, a 1948 mare, was the result. Sold first to C. A. and Fern Schmidt of Spokane, Washington, and later to Earl Perin of Priest River, Idaho, Titania went on to become a top producer.

Bred five times to Toby I, she was the dam of two sons—Kaniksu's Little Beaver and Kaniksu's Kiowa—and three daughters—Rapid Lightning, Chain Lightning and Sheet Lightening.

Returning to Titania's sire and half-brother, Red Eagle was broke to ride

American Eagle, a 1951 stallion by Red Eagle and out of Dutchess, was the Champion 2-Year-Old Stallion and Grand Champion Stallion at the 1953 Nationals in Quincy, California.
Courtesy Appaloosa Museum & Heritage Center

as a young horse, was shown on a limited basis and then was pressed into duty as a herd sire.

Named the Champion Aged Stallion and Grand Champion Stallion at the 1951 National Show in Lewiston, the Thompson-bred stallion began attracting outside mares from both the Northwest and California.

American Eagle, Red Eagle's first ApHC-registered son, was bred by Con Ruff of Riverside, California.

A 1951 stallion out of Dutchess F-1110, American Eagle was the Champion 2-Year-Old Stallion and the Grand Champion Stallion at the 1953 National Show in Quincy, California. As a result of winning the 2-year-old halter class, "Eagle" was awarded the first Bear Step Katouche. Crafted by Cascade, Colorado, silversmith and ApHC Hall of Fame inductee Shatka Bearstep, the Katouche award was conceived as an incentive to breed and show top young Appaloosa stallions.

Retired to stud, American Eagle went on to become a legendary sire in his own right. Among his top show get were American Marvel, Malibu Chief, Mister Blue, Blue Chip, T's Kokatina, May Day J. and Villa Miss.

American Marvel, a 1955 mare out of Freckles Honey, was the earner of two national titles at halter. Malibu Chief, a 1957 stallion out of Malibu Queen, was the Champion Hunter and Reserve Champion Performance Horse at the 1962 National Show in Springfield, Illinois.

Mister Blue, a 1958 stallion out of Little Dutchess, was the earner of five national titles at halter and performance. In addition, he was the Co-Champion Performance Horse at the 1963 World Performance Playoffs in Las Vegas, Nevada. Blue Chip, a 1960 full brother to Mister Blue, was the earner of three national titles in performance.

T's Kokatina, a 1959 mare out of Punkinlight, was the Champion Weanling

Malibu Chief, a 1957 stallion by American Eagle and out of Malibu Queen, was the Champion Hunter at the 1962 National Show in Springfield, Illinois.
Courtesy Appaloosa Museum & Heritage Center

Filly at the 1959 National Show in Santa Barbara, California.

Finally, May Day J., a 1960 mare out of Too Mee, was the Champion Hackamore Horse at the 1963 National Show in Boise, Idaho, and Villa Miss, a 1961 mare out of Pixie, was the Champion Men's Western Pleasure Horse and Reserve Champion Performance Horse at the 1964 Nationals in Albuquerque, New Mexico.

Simcoe's Chinook—Red Eagle's second noteworthy son—and La Nina—his second noteworthy daughter—were foaled in 1952.

Simcoe's Chinook, out of Maize F-1643, was bred by Martin and Grace Forry of Goldendale, Washington. The Champion Weanling Stallion at the 1952 National Show in Quincy, California, "Chinook" went on to earn five additional national titles in performance and become a top sire.

La Nina, out of La Chiquita F-1109, was bred by Rhoma Cox of Riverside, California. A champion regional show mare, she became a top producer, as well.

Mister Blue (above), a 1958 stallion, and Blue Chip (below), a 1960 stallion, were full siblings by American Eagle and out of Little Dutchess. Between them, they amassed seven national and world performance titles.

Courtesy Appaloosa Museum & Heritage Center

Red Eagle's Peacock and Storm Cloud F., two more great Red Eagle sons, were foaled next.

"Peacock," a 1953 stallion out of Easter F-33, was bred by Claude Thompson (then living in Pomona, California). The Champion 3-Year-Old Stallion and Grand Champion Stallion at the 1956 National Show in Elko, Nevada, Peacock went on to become a top sire.

Among his best-known get was Blue Admiral, the earner of four world titles in performance.

Storm Cloud F., a 1954 stallion by Red Eagle and out of Maize, was bred by the Forrys. Retained by them as their cornerstone herd sire, he was the Champion Weanling Stallion at the 1954 National Show in Deer Lodge, Montana, and the Champion

3-Year-Old Stallion at the 1957 National Show in Canby, Oregon.

The 1957 Nationals amounted to a "Red Eagle Extravaganza."

Taken out of retirement and fitted for the show, 13-year-old Red Eagle was named the Champion Aged Stallion and Reserve Champion Stallion.

In addition, Simcoe's Koosah, a 1957 stallion by Storm Cloud F. and out of Morgan's Cheetah, was the Champion Weanling Stallion; Simcoe's Sarcee, a 1955 stallion by Simcoe's Chinook and out of Morgan's Cheeta, was the Champion 2-Year-Old Stallion; and Storm Cloud F. was the Champion 3-Year-Old Stallion.

All four of the above-mentioned Simcoe horses went on to make significant contributions to the breed. In doing so, they established the Forrys' Simcoe Stables as one of the premier Appaloosa breeding establishments of its day.

Several other top Red Eagle get were foaled during the Claude Thompson era.

Red Eagle's Prince, a 1956 stallion out of Princess Beryl F-85, was the Champion Hackamore Horse at the 1960 National Show in South Sioux City, Nebraska.

Simcoe's Frosty Eagle, a 1956 gelding out of Chica, was the Champion Trail Horse, Champion Ladies Western Pleasure Horse, Champion Hunter-Jumper and Reserve Champion Performance Horse at the 1967 National Show in Walla Walla, Washington.

Wanebe, a 1958 mare out of La Nina, was a champion regional halter mare and a top producer, as well.

Based solely on his accomplishments as a Thompson herd sire, Red Eagle was named the Champion Get of Sire winner at both the 1956 and 1957 Nationals.

Red Eagle's Peacock, a 1953 stallion by Red Eagle and out of Easter, was the Champion 3-Year-Old Stallion and Grand Champion Stallion at the 1956 National Show in Elko, Nevada.
Courtesy Appaloosa Museum & Heritage Center

Red Eagle's Prince, a 1956 stallion by Red Eagle and out of Princess Beryl, took the Champion Hackamore Horse title at the 1960 National Show in South Sioux City, Nebraska.
Courtesy Appaloosa Museum & Heritage Center

Storm Cloud F., a 1954 stallion by Red Eagle and out of Maize, was the Champion 3-Year-Old Stallion at the 1957 National Show in Canby, Oregon.

Courtesy **Western Horseman**

In the fall of 1956, Red Eagle changed hands. Various accounts state that he was sold first by Claude Thompson to movie director John Derek, who wanted him for a movie he was planning on filming in Mexico. When the movie failed to materialize, Derek reportedly sold the 12-year-old stallion to Thomas Clay of Riverside, California.

For the record, John Derek is not listed on any ApHC documents as having ever owned Red Eagle. Be that as it may, he is listed as being the stallion's owner in several 1956 and 1957 *Appaloosa News* show result reports.

To further complicate the issue, the show results of the 1957 National list Red Eagle's owner as Carson Shade of Riverside, California. As near as can be determined, Shade never owned Red Eagle, but was instead a Derek employee.

In the spring of 1958, Derek sold Red Eagle

to Clay and a transfer of ownership *between Claude Thompson and Clay* was duly recorded with ApHC.

As the owner of the 1001 Ranch—first located in California and then Nevada--Tom Clay immediately placed Red Eagle at the head of a broodmare band consisting mostly of foundation-numbered Appaloosa mares.

According to ApHC records, the first crop of 1001 Ranch-bred Red Eagle foals hit the ground in 1958 and the last in 1970.

After being acquired by Clay, Red Eagle was utilized as a sire in a decidedly different manner. Less emphasis was put on the production of show horses and more was put on the production of top pleasure mounts and breeding animals.

Red Eagle Jr. and Red Eagle's Guild of 1001 were exceptions to the rule.

"Junior," a 1959 stallion out of Bonita of

1001, was sold to Rick and Don Nord of Melrose, Iowa. A top sire, he contributed such champion get as 7C Red Eagle's Pride and Count Brown Eagle to the breed.

"Guild," a 1959 stallion out of Heart Shot, was shown by the 1001 Ranch and was a regional champion halter horse. Sold first to Sue and Bob Pabst Jr. of Woodbury, Connecticut, and later to John Baker of Hickory, Pennsylvania, he became a top sire, as well.

Red Eagle's last foal crop, numbering seven, hit the ground in 1970. By this time, Clay had apparently gotten tired of trying to think up horse names. The last of the Red Eagles—three stallions and four mares—were registered as numbers, i.e. "1001-139."

Red Eagle lived for several years after he was retired from breeding. He passed away on May 17, 1971, at the age of 25. His death was attributed simply to old age.

Bred as he was by the Appaloosa Horse Club's founder, Red Eagle was a standard bearer. As a national champion stallion, a two-time national champion get of sire winner, and the sire of such top sons as American Eagle, Simcoe's Chinook, Red Eagle's Peacock and Storm Cloud F., the Claude Thompson-bred stallion carried his banner well.

Red Eagle was inducted into the ApHC Hall of Fame in 1988.

Simcoe's Chinook, a 1952 stallion by Red Eagle and out of Maize, was a national champion halter, cutting, roping and reining horse. In addition, at the 1955 National Show in Colorado Springs, Colorado, the well-mannered stallion carried young Billy Jack Johnson to victory in the Children's Pleasure Horse class.

***Courtesy* Western Horseman**

Chapter 4

APACHE
F-730

Apache, seen here after being named the Grand Champion Stallion at the 1954 National Show in Deer Lodge, Montana, compiled the greatest national show record of his era.

Courtesy Appaloosa Museum & Heritage Center

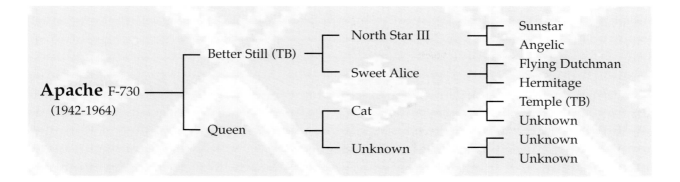

```
                                        ┌─ North Star III ──┬─ Sunstar
                    ┌─ Better Still (TB) ┤                  └─ Angelic
                    │                   └─ Sweet Alice ─────┬─ Flying Dutchman
Apache F-730 ───────┤                                       └─ Hermitage
  (1942-1964)       │                   ┌─ Cat ─────────────┬─ Temple (TB)
                    └─ Queen ────────────┤                  └─ Unknown
                                        └─ Unknown ─────────┬─ Unknown
                                                            └─ Unknown
```

From the outset, the founding fathers of the Appaloosa Horse Club touted the breed as being "the world's best rough-country stock horse."

Apache, a 1942 stallion by Better Still (TB) and out of Queen, served as a classic example of all that description entailed.

Apache was bred by Orvil Sears of Elba, Idaho. Like a number of other foundation Appaloosas, the stallion was a by-product of the U.S. Government's Remount Service program. Founded in 1908, the Remount program made top Thoroughbred stallions available to horse breeders throughout the West, with the goal of producing an improved strain of U.S. Cavalry mounts.

In the process, the initiative also turned out a steady stream of top-notch ranch horses, polo ponies and breeding stock.

Better Still (TB)—Apache's sire—was a Remount stallion that stood during the 1940s at the Malta, Idaho, ranch of John Hitt.

Queen—Apache's dam—was a second-generation offshoot of the Remount program. According to owner Sears, she was a top individual in her own right.

"Queen was an Appaloosa mare that I traded for in the late 1930s from Howard Haller and Jenks Telford of Albion, Idaho," he says. "She was a 7-year-old when I got her and basically white in color. I was told she had black spots over her hips when she was younger, but by the time I got her they had mostly faded away.

"Cat, Queen's sire, was a John Hitt-bred horse. He was sired by the Remount stallion Temple (TB) and out of an unknown mare. Like Queen, he was a white horse with black spots over his rump.

"Cat was well-known in these parts. In the 1930s, John Hitt used to produce rodeos and race meets throughout the southern half of the state. Cat was one of his top race and calf roping horses. And John also used him as a rodeo pickup horse. That stud was so well-broke that John would take his bridle off and pick up those bronc riders using just a neck rope.

"Queen when well-broke by the time I got her," he continues. "And she was cow-savvy; you could do anything with her. And she could run. For a quarter of a mile, she was stout.

Apache's dam, Queen (left), was a top ranch and race mount. In this shot, twin sisters Mrs. Edris Sears, on Queen, and Mrs. Edith Carlson, on Stagamuck, prepare to lead a county fair parade.
Courtesy Orvil Sears

A top ranch mount, Apache was bred, owned and trained by Orvil Sears of Elba, Idaho.   ***Courtesy Orvil Sears***

"We had an ol' track out here in the sage-brush. We'd run Queen there, or run her up the road. It didn't make any difference. We'd pass the hat and run for $10, or maybe $7.50.

"I even let John take her up to Sun Valley, Idaho. He put on a rodeo and race meet up there every weekend for the dudes. He'd enter Queen in the flat races and relay races, and got along real well with her."

In 1941, Sears took Queen to the court of Better Still. The following summer, she foaled a chestnut, blanket-hipped colt.

"After the colt was born," Sears says, "we started calling him 'Appy.' And that's all we really ever called him. After he got a little age on him, we tacked an 'Ol' on the front of it."

Sears broke Appy to ride as a 3-year-old.

"In 1944," he says, "a bunch of us fellas got together and formed a sheriff's posse. There were 52 of us to begin with—from Malta, Elba, Burley and all points in-between.

"We built a rodeo arena on the outskirts of Elba, with a 1/2-mile track around it. And that's where I broke Appy to ride. He never was any trouble; he just always seemed to want to do the right thing."

As was to be expected, as soon as he had his young Appaloosa stallion well-started under saddle, Sears began training him for the track.

"Outside of the 'posse' arena," he says, "the only other place I trained Appy to run was out at the ranch. It was located around 1-1/2 miles west of town, in the foothills of the Independence and Cash peaks. It was pretty hard ground, but great for building up a horse's lungs and legs. Because he learned to run on that type of ground, Appy always loved a hard track"

In the fall of 1946, the Sears Appaloosa was given his first real opportunity to showcase his speed.

"The Eastern Idaho Fair was held every fall in Blackfoot," Sears says. "They always held a five-day pari-mutuel race meet during it.

"Most of the races were for Thoroughbreds and Quarter Horses, but the seventh race each day was

A legendary racehorse, Apache is shown here with jockey Johnny Schooley in the irons at a mid-1940s pari-mutuel race meet in Pocatello, Idaho.

Courtesy Orvil Sears

A versatile performance horse, Apache was named the Champion Stock Horse (reining) at the 1956 National Show in Elko, Nevada. In this shot, Kay McKelvey of Estes Park, Colorado, presents the Western Horseman *Trophy to Lana and Orvil Sears.*

***Courtesy* Western Horseman**

The earner of 21 national titles in halter, performance and racing, Apache was honored in a special ceremony at the 1963 National Show in Boise, Idaho. Bob Peckinpaugh, Edris Sears and Orvil Sears are at Apache's head, while former jockey Tinker Hutchison is in the irons.

Courtesy Appaloosa Museum & Heritage Center

open. That's the one I'd put Appy in. And he had to take on some pretty stiff competition. He'd run against Thoroughbreds, half-Thoroughbreds, and sons and daughters of such foundation Quarter Horse sires as Midnight Jr. and Ding Bob.

"But he always held his own. I'd race him five days in a row, and he just seemed to get stronger as the week wore on. We never won a race, but we ran second and third pretty consistently.

"We competed in that race meet in 1946, 1947 and 1948. And in-between, we raced at county fairs and rodeos at places like Oakley, Rupert, Burley, Filer and Salmon, Idaho."

In the late 1940s, Sears began hearing about a registry for Appaloosa Horses that was headquartered in the northern part of the state. He also heard that a National Show for the breed was being held in Lewiston, Idaho. As a result, he made plans to register his stallion and attend the show.

"I registered Appy in 1949, when he was 7," he says. "Up until that time, people had a bunch of different names for him. They'd call him 'the Appaloosa,' 'Apple Juice' and 'Apple Jack.'

"When it came time to register him, we decided to name him Apache. It was the closest thing to Appy that we could come up with."

That same year, the newly named Apache made his ApHC debut at the association's second National Show, held in Lewiston.

There, he won what would be the first of four straight titles in the 1/8-mile race and three straight titles in the 3/8-mile race. Sears—weighing in at 180 pounds—was the horse's jockey.

"Appy could run long or short," he says. "It didn't matter to him. But he loved the 3/8-mile distance. That race was generally run around one turn, and that's where he shined. He could go into the turn lapped on the horse ahead or a length behind. If the lead horse lugged out at all, Appy would shoot in toward the rail. When they came out of the turn, he'd be three lengths in the lead."

Over the course of four years—from 1949 through 1952—Apache would go on to win 10 straight national race titles. In 1950 and 1951, he returned to Lewiston where he successfully defended his 1/8th- and 3/8th-mile titles. In 1952, he journeyed to the 5th National Show in Quincy, California. There, he raced to victory in the 1/8th-mile race, the 1/4-mile race and the 1/2-mile race.

Apache did not compete at the 1953 National Show in Quincy. He did, however, return to the racing wars at the 1954 Nationals in Deer Lodge, Montana. Only one race—a 1/8th-mile affair—was held that year. Entered in it, Apache emerged the winner over a a 12-horse field that included Peter K., Callico Babe N., and an up-and-coming 2-year-old stallion named Chief of Fourmile.

After skipping the 1955 National Show, Apache made the trip to Elko, Nevada, in 1956. There, the now-14-year-old met defeat for the first time.

Entered in the 1/2-mile race, he finished second to Chief of Fourmile—who was 10 years his junior. Entered in the 3/8th-mile race, he avenged his lone national racing loss

Flake, a 1949 gelding by Apache and out of Trix, was the Champion Cutting Horse at the 1959 National Show in Santa Barbara, California. He is seen here with owner/trainer Orvil Sears Jr. competing in a 1959 Great Falls, Montana, contest.

Courtesy Appaloosa Museum & Heritage Center

by posting a victory over Chief of Fourmile.

Apache's final National Show race tally stood at 10 firsts and one second.

But the Orvil Sears-bred speedster was more than a one-event horse.

At the 1949 National Show, he was named the Reserve Champion Performance Horse. At the 1950 Nationals, he was awarded the *Western Horseman* trophy for his first-place finish in the stock horse (reining) class. In addition, he was named the Champion Cutting Horse and the Reserve Champion Performance Horse.

At the 1951 Nationals, Apache won the rope race, calf roping and cutting with Sears in the saddle, and the ladies' Western pleasure with Edris Sears—Orvil's wife—aboard. Those four victories, coupled with his two

racing wins, were enough to earn him the Champion Performance Horse title.

At the 1952 National Show, the versatile stallion won his second Champion Stock Horse title. That victory, together with his three racing wins, earned him his third Reserve Champion performance title.

At the 1954 National Show, Apache was named the Champion Aged Stallion and Grand Champion Stallion. The double win, so it was rumored, was due to the fact that he had suffered a minor riding injury earlier in the year that had necessitated a lay-up from all ranching, showing and racing duties. As a result, he was fatter than usual and in "near halter shape."

Also named the show's Champion Rope Race Horse and, as previously noted, winner

Apache King S., a 1959 stallion by Apache and out of Mapeline, won 28 of his 36 race starts and set Appaloosa world records at six distances. Owner/trainer Joe King of Peck, Idaho, is seen at the speedy stallion's head.

Courtesy Western Horseman

Chicaro, one of Apache's top sons, was a 1956 stallion out of Calico Babe N. He won the 3/8th-mile race and the 1/2-mile race at the 1960 National Show.

Courtesy Appaloosa Museum & Heritage Center

of the 1/8th-mile race, he earned his fourth Reserve Champion performance title.

At the 1956 Nationals—the sixth and last such event he would compete in—Apache won his third stock horse title, his 10th flat race, and his fifth Reserve Champion performance award.

Apache was retired from national competition after the Elko show. His final record was a sterling one, and one that few horses would ever match.

In all, Apache won one National Grand Championship at halter, one National Champion performance award, five Reserve National Champion performance awards, and 21 individual national titles in halter, performance and racing.

As if that weren't enough, throughout his incredible National Show career, the durable stallion was utilized by his owner on a full-time basis as a ranch mount.

Then, on the weekends, it was play day, rodeo and racing time.

"Come the weekend, we used Ol' Appy for everything," Sears says. "At the open shows and play days, I'd ride him in our club's precision drill team. Then I'd put him in the barrel race, flag race and any other speed event that was offered. In the rodeos, I'd use him for calf roping, heading and heeling, flag racing and relay racing.

"And we flat raced him everywhere.

"Back in those years, I traveled with a group of local horsemen," he continues. "Dick Anderson from Albion was the best-known. He'd been back to Madison Square Garden. Dick was always gettin' us in a match race.

"We was up to Pocatello one time, and there was an ol' boy there—he was a state patrolman—who had a black horse he wanted to match.

My Ole Still, a 1962 stallion by Apache and out of Blossom, posts a victory in a 1964 stakes event at Centennial Race Track in Denver, Colorado. Seen with the speedy stallion in this shot are (from left) Ben and Dorothy Johnson, Claire Johnson Diers, Dick Southern, Linda Johnson Kukal, Ken Ochs and (in the background) a very mischievous-looking Thomas Southern. **Courtesy Ben Johnson**

"Dick said to him, 'We've got three horses here. We'll match you for $100. You can pick any one of the three to run agin'.

"I'll be damned if he didn't pick Ol' Appy.

"Now, we had just pulled up and I didn't even have time to tack my horse up right. But we had us a race, anyway. And he even made us go the wrong way.

"We won that race easy and, after we got done, the patrolman come up to me and said, 'Hell Almighty, do you know you run that horse with a spade bit in his mouth?'

"I just laughed. Appy didn't care what kind of bit he was wearin'. He just loved to run."

As if his careers as a show, rodeo and race horse weren't enough, Apache also saw full-time duty as a sire. In this endeavor, too, he proved outstanding.

Flake, a 1949 gelding out of Trix, was the first of Apache's get to achieve national recognition. Bred by rancher Henry Ottley of Elba, Idaho, he was acquired in the mid-1950s by the Sears family.

"It must have been in 1955 or 1956 when we got Flake," Orvil Sears Jr. of Pullman, Washington, says. "I was in high school at the time and wanted a cutting horse that I could take to the high school rodeos.

"Flake was well-broke when we got him. He was a lightly muscled, Thoroughbred-looking horse—very quick and agile, and very independent. He was not the kind of a horse that you could just walk up to and put a bridle on. Sometimes it would take me a half-a-day to catch him.

"But once I got him caught, he usually was-

Apache Double, a 1969 stallion by Double Reigh (TB) and out of Run Around by Apache, recorded 18 firsts and three seconds from 21 lifetime starts. In addition to setting 14 world or track records, the Apache grandson sired the race earners of more than $2 million.   **Courtesy George Hatley**

n't any trouble. And he was as 'cowy' as any horse I was ever around.

"Back then, I didn't know much about cutting horses. But there was a trainer named Glen Parke over around Malta. We took Flake up for one lesson with Glen. He showed us how to teach him to sidepass with draw reins, and we just went on with it from there.

"We began competing on Flake in high school rodeos in the mid-1950s and continued on with him in Appaloosa and National Cutting Horse Association competition."

With the teenaged Sears in the saddle, Flake was the Champion Cutting Horse at the 1959 National Show in Santa Barbara, California. Placing behind him at the prestigious event were such top horses as Simcoe's Sarcee, Quanah and Simcoe's Chinook.

Two years later, the talented pair teamed to win the Reserve Champion Cutting Horse title in a field of 35 entries at the 1961 National Show in Fort Worth, Texas.

Sandwiched in-between were a number of top showings in NCHA contests. At the 1960 Montana State Fair in Great Falls, Flake placed second to Vegas Boy in the open cutting. Third place in the contest went to the legendary Poco Lena.

After the event, Poco Lena's owner, B. A. Skipper of Longview, Texas, commented that the Apache son was "one of the smoothest, natural cutting horses I have had the pleasure of seeing perform."

Flake passed away as a result of colic on October 18, 1961.

In addition to Flake, Apache sired a number of other early Northwest champions.

Apache II, a 1951 stallion out of Randall's Silver, was bred by H. M. Randall of Craigmont, Idaho. Sold to Lew Ferguson of Helmville, Montana, he went on to sire such top individuals as Miss Apache.

Miss Apache, a 1966 mare out of a sorrel mare, was bred by Obert Nyland of Wolf Point, Montana. Sold to Ward and Alice Fenton of Meyers, Montana, she became a champion halter and performance horse and a 1992 ApHC Hall of Fame inductee.

Minidoka Belle, a 1957 mare out of Minidoka Lark, and Mitzi, a 1957 mare out of Ma, were grand champion halter horses.

Minidoka Minnie, a 1958 mare out of Speckald, won the 1960 Idaho-Oregon-Nevada (ION) race futurity, and Sizzle Britches, a 1958 stallion out of Babe of the Hoodoos, was a champion halter horse and race winner, as well.

Apache Patch, a 1960 stallion out of Kathy, and My Ole Still, a 1962 stallion out of Blossom, were also race winners and top sires. In addition, two Apache sons and one grandson—Chicaro, Apache King S. and Apache Double—achieved special fame as racehorses and sires.

Chicaro, a 1956 stallion out of Callico Babe N., was bred by Alan Newby of Kuna, Idaho. Shown at the 1959 National Show in Santa Barbara, he won both the 3/8-mile race and the 1/2-mile race.

Retired to stud, he went on to sire such champion show and race horses as Count Chic, Chic Supreme, Chic Appeal and Madam Chic.

Apache King S. was a locally bred champion.

"In 1958," Orvil Sears says, "I bred a half-Thoroughbred mare named Mapeline to Appy. She was owned by Dale Smith—a neighbor of mine—and I never did charge him any stud fee. Apache King S. was the resulting foal."

Sold to Joe and Marie King of Boise, Idaho, Apache King S. went on to become a top racehorse. The winner of the 1/2-mile race and the 910-yard ION Derby held during the 1963 National Show in Boise, Idaho, "King"

won 28 of his 36 starts and set Appaloosa world records at six distances.

Retired to stud, he sired such horses as Daiquiri-Bar, the Champion 2-Year-Old Filly at the 1971 National Show in Las Vegas, Nevada.

Apache Double, a 1969 stallion by Double Reigh (TB) and out of Run Around, by Apache, was bred by George and Iola Hatley of Moscow, Idaho. Trained for racing by Joe King, he recorded 18 firsts and three seconds from 21 lifetime starts. A bronze medallion race winner, he set 14 world or track records. In addition, he was also the Reserve Champion Aged Stallion at the 1975 National Show in Santa Rosa, California.

Retired to stud, he went on to become the all-time leading sire of racing Appaloosas and the only Appaloosa to sire the winners of more than $2 million.

By the early 1960s, the Apache line of halter, performance and race horses was generally acknowledged to be one of the breed's best. In recognition of that fact, a special retirement ceremony to honor Apache was held at the 1963 National Show.

Apache was paraded past the grandstand by Orvil and Edris Sears. The 21-year-old stallion was decked out in full racing regalia and Tinker Hutchison, the man who had ridden him to many of his victories, was in the irons.

It was a fitting tribute to one of the breed's best.

Then, less than a year later, tragedy struck.

"It was in the spring of 1964," Orvil Sears says. "Appy was 22 years old, but he was doin' so good. He was always healthy, nothing wrong with him.

"I went out in the corral one day and there he stood, head down. I knew something was wrong. I thought he had colic, so I called the vet and he came out and examined him. After he got through, he said, 'We better operate on him.' So I loaded him up and took him to town.

"After we got him opened up, we could see it was serious. His bowels had ruptured. So we put him to sleep.

"They helped me load him back on my pickup truck, and I brought him home.

"I had arthritis in my wrist, but I dug a hole with a pick and shovel, anyway.

"Ya' know, a horse takes a pretty fair-sized hole. My wrist was killin' me, but I got 'er done. And I buried him up there on the ranch.

"You know, Ol' Appy never was the head of any great promotional program," Sears continues. "We bred a ton of mares to him, but there weren't very many high-powered ones among them.

"We started out standing him for $10. Then we upped it to $25. When he died, we had two Thoroughbred mares here from California to be bred to him. We was gettin' $1,000 apiece for them.

"At one time, this country was full of his sons and daughters. Every rancher for miles around had a horse sired by him. And there weren't any dinks; they were all good horses.

"It was a sad day when we lost Appy, but, hell, we had a lot of fun with him. We knew he wasn't going to live forever.

"We just hoped he would."

Over the course of his long and illustrious performance career, Ol' Appy attracted a legion of fans—pioneer and newcomer alike. After the stallion's death, Orvil Sears removed Apache's shoes and sent one each to four of his staunchest admirers—Bob Peckinpah, W. H. "Hutch" Hutchinson, Mable Woodward and George Hatley.

Apache F-730 was inducted into the ApHC Hall of Fame in 1986—one of the first two horses to be so honored.

Apache F-730 is seen here on the Sears Ranch near Elba, Idaho, where he spent his entire life.
"We knew he wasn't going to live forever, we just hoped he would." —Orvil Sears

Chapter 5

SUNDANCE
F-500

Sundance F-500, seen here in a 1949 photo with Peggy Davis, founded an enduring line of leopard Appaloosas.
Courtesy Harry Edwards

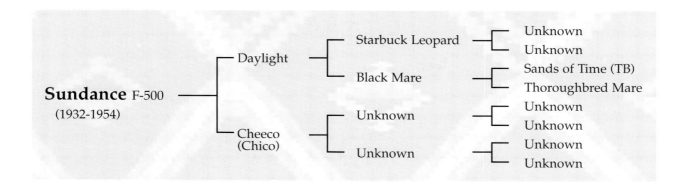

Sundance F-500 (1932-1954)	Daylight	Starbuck Leopard	Unknown
			Unknown
		Black Mare	Sands of Time (TB)
			Thoroughbred Mare
	Cheeco (Chico)	Unknown	Unknown
			Unknown
		Unknown	Unknown
			Unknown

Like the Palouse Country, the Rocky Mountain region was home to several Appaloosa lines that antedated the ApHC studbooks. The Sundance horses—one of the breed's first prominent leopard strains—was one of these.

Sundance, a 1932 stallion by Daylight and out of Cheeco, was bred by Phil Jenkins of Fort Collins, Colorado.

Daylight, a 1928 or 1929 stallion by Starbuck Leopard and out of a Thoroughbred mare by Sands of Time (JC), was bred by Charles Cummings of Evergreen, Colorado.

Cheeco (a.k.a. Chico), a minimally colored Appaloosa mare of unknown breeding, was purchased by Jenkins in 1929 out of a band of mustangs that had been recently captured in the Four Corners region of Colorado, Utah, Arizona and New Mexico. In later years, Jenkins recalled Cheeco as "a black mare covered with even blacker dapples, very well-made, with plenty of speed." Various accounts list the mustang mare as standing 14.2 hands high and weighing in the vicinity of 800 pounds.

Jenkins had acquired Cheeco with the intention of breaking her to ride. After experiencing some initial difficulties in doing so, he enlisted the aid of an older cowboy named Lafe Green. Cheeco responded well to the seasoned ranch hand's efforts and, in due time, became a top ranch mount.

From 1928 to 1940, Phil Jenkins ran horses in Estes Park, Colorado, in the summer, and worked on ranches in Colorado during the winter.

In 1931, he pastured his mares on the Doride Ranch east of Kersey, Colorado, in the northeast corner of the state. Sharing the pasture with the Jenkins horses was the Charles Cummings-owned red leopard Appaloosa stallion Daylight. In May of 1932, Cheeco foaled a red leopard Daylight colt.

Reverting to her wild days, the mustang mare had slipped away and gave birth up on

In this circa 1935 photo, Sundance is seen with breeder Phil Jenkins of Estes Park, Colorado, in the saddle. Mrs. Jenkins is on the right, mounted on a few-spot leopard mare.

Courtesy Sundance 500 International

This photo of Sundance was taken on the ranch of his last owner—P. S. "Doc" Edwards of Fort Morgan, Colorado.
Courtesy Harry Edwards

Mount Chiquita, about 10 miles west of Estes Park. Jenkins located the pair when the foal was around 1 week old. He immediately named the colt Sundance as tribute to the youngster's "snow-white body covered with a thousand blood-red spots."

Sundance grew up to be a 15-hand-high, 1,000-pound horse. In addition to being a working cowboy, Jenkins had a talent for training trick horses. Consequently, he taught Sundance a variety of tricks. Among the feats that the young stallion mastered were untying a handkerchief, counting, walking up stairs, answering questions with nods of his head, lying down and playing dead, jumping hurdles, rearing, and racing while carrying no rider. In addition, he was also utilized as a ranch horse and sire.

In a biography of Sundance, written by Jenkins, the loud-colored leopard was described as being "intelligent enough to learn any trick, gentle enough for a child, willing to do any job from elk hunting to calf roping, speedy enough to rope a coyote or do the half-mile in 49:7, plenty of cow savvy, plus prepotency to pass this on to his get, as well as the spots on a large percent of his foals."

Jenkins further credits Sundance with paying off the mortgage on a ranch the horseman purchased near Orchard, Colorado.

By 1937, Jenkins had a pasture full of Sundance foals. Consequently, he agreed to sell the then-5-year-old stallion to John Whisanad of Orchard, Colorado.

Whisanad was an agent for the U.S.

Government's Remount program and, while owned by him, Sundance was used as a rehabilitation stallion. During this period, he was hauled to mares throughout the Rocky Mountain region in an open-topped, open-sided trailer.

In 1947 or 1948, Whisanad traded Sundance and two of his sons to P. S. "Doc" Edwards of Woodrow, Colorado, for some cattle.

Edwards and his wife, Gladys, were schoolteachers who also farmed and raised cattle and horses. The nickname "Doc" was given to Edwards due to the fact that he was a highly respected local "country vet."

Shortly after purchasing Sundance, Edwards became acquainted with Ben Johnson of Loma, Colorado. Johnson had gotten into the Appaloosa business several years earlier through the acquisition of a Sundance daughter named Leopard Lady F-167.

It was Johnson, who was an Appaloosa Horse Club national director at the time, who convinced Edwards to register Sundance with ApHC. He did so in July of 1948. Sundance was assigned the number F-500, and his son Woodrow Shiek was given F-502.

Even though Sundance was now registered, Edwards made no attempt to promote him. The stallion was, instead, used as a saddle horse, working ranch horse and parade mount. Few mares were bred to him during this period of his life.

Harry Edwards—Doc and Gladys' son—currently resides near Greeley, Colorado. He was a young boy during the Sundance era but remembers the stallion well.

"My recollections of 'Sunny' are that he was a kind and friendly horse," he says. "We kept him in a small pasture near the house, and all I had to do to catch him was call his name. I could ride him bareback with even a string around his neck, and he'd take me wherever I wanted to go.

"Sunny was the center of attention around our place. People came from all over to see him, and they marveled at the tricks that Phil Jenkins had taught him.

"We had a lot of horses on the place back then, and I had my pick of them when it came time to go gather the milk cows. It was always a treat to use Sunny."

During his lifetime, Sundance no doubt

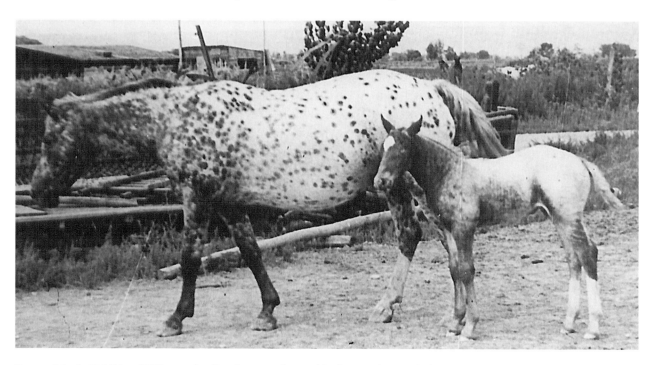

Leopard Lady F-167, a 1937 mare by Sundance and out of Lady, was her sire's first ApHC-registered daughter. Owned by Ben Johnson of Loma, Colorado, "Lady" was the cornerstone matriarch of a great Appaloosa line.

Courtesy Ben Johnson

Rocking Chair Porter F-574, a 1942 mare by Sundance and out of an unknown mare, was bred by Guy Porter of Woodrow, Colorado.
Courtesy Harry Edwards

sired many get. Only 13 of those foals, however, were registered with ApHC. Of these, Stardust F-50, Leopard Lady F-167, Woodrow Shiek F-502, Rocking Chair Porter F-574, Sundust F-1335, Black Leopard F-1569, Sunshine F-1290 and Mi Wacon F-1892 were especially instrumental in perpetuating the line.

Stardust, a 1939 stallion out of Cheeko, was bred by Howard Mayfield of Estes Park, Colorado. The stallion sired three ApHC-registered foals, including Dilly A T-542.

Bred and owned by Fred Kanady of Plainview, Texas, Dilly A was the dam of Little Red Leopard and Jagady— two of the Lone Star State's earliest show champions.

Sunspot Revel F-1904, a 1957 stallion by Revel Junior F-1728 and out of Rocking Chair Sun Dance F-587, did much to enhance the Sundance name. The loud-colored leopard is seen here with breeder Ralph Cannon of Elizabeth, Colorado, at his head, and renowned trainer Monte Foreman in the saddle.
Courtesy Appaloosa Museum & Heritage Center

Little Red Leopard F-3432—a 1955 stallion by Red Leopard T-541—went on to sire The Great Hot Shot, the Champion Stock Horse at the 1963 National Show in Boise, Idaho. Jagady F-3431—a 1956 stallion by Red Leopard—went on to found the highly-accomplished Jagady's Gold line of halter and performance horses.

Leopard Lady, a 1937 mare by Sundance and out of Lady, was bred by Otto Borches of LaSalle, Colorado. The cornerstone mare of Ben Johnson's breeding program, Leopard Lady will be discussed in detail in a subsequent chapter.

Woodrow Shiek, a 1944 stallion out of Stockings, was bred by John Whisanad of Orchard, Colorado. Owned by Doc Edwards and utilized by him as a working ranch mount for years, "Shiek" sired Bambi E. F-2497.

Bambi E., a 1954 stallion out of P.V.F.'s Butterfly, was bred by Doc Edwards. Sold to Lee Warne of Onida, South Dakota, "Bambi" became a champion halter and performance horse, as well as the founder of the highly successful "Sully" line of horses.

Rocking Chair Porter, a 1942 mare by Sundance and out of a bay Porter mare, was bred by Guy Porter of Woodrow, Colorado. Sold to E. P. Deahl of La Junta, Colorado, Rocking Chair Porter went on to produce Rocking Chair Sun Dance F-587.

Rocking Chair Sun Dance, a mare by Fox (Colorado Ranger Horse Association #10), was bred by Deahl. Sold to Ralph and Joyce Cannon of Elizabeth, Colorado, Rocking Chair Sun Dance produced Sunspot Revel.

Sunspot Revel, a 1957 stallion by Revel Junior F-1728, was kept by the Cannons and developed into one of the Rocky Mountain region's first great show and breeding stallions. Retired to stud, the loud-colored red leopard became a top sire.

Sundust F-1335, a 1941 sorrel and white mare by Sundance and out of Rosalie F-21, played a pivotal role in seeing to it that the

Sunshine F-1290, a 1950 mare by Sundance and out of Ratina F-405, was the Champion 3-Year-Old Mare and Grand Champion Mare at the 1953 National Show in Quincy, California. Breeder Ben Johnson is at the halter.

Courtesy Ben Johnson

Sundance line lived on.

In 1940, pioneer Appaloosa breeder Otis Barber of Glenrock, Wyoming, hauled his cornerstone mare Rosalie down to be bred to Sundance. Sundust was the resulting foal. Phil Jenkins liked Sundust well enough to buy her and breed her to Iben Hilal, his imported Arabian. Frosty-Ann F-1336, a 1948 red roan mare, was the resulting foal.

Sold to Lola Parks of Miles City, Montana, Frosty-Ann became the great-granddam of Wego Melody. Under the ownership of Gene Miles of Wichita, Kansas, Wego Melody went on to found what is without a doubt the first family of Appaloosa racehorses.

Inducted into the ApHC Racing Hall of Fame in 1988 on the strength of her production record, Wego Melody is the dam or granddam of such horses as:
- We Go Charge, a 1966 mare by Diamond Charge (QH)—ApHC Racing Hall of Fame 1998.
- We Go Easy, a 1973 mare by Easy Jet (QH)—ApHC Racing Hall of Fame 1991.
- Easy We Go, a 1977 stallion by Easy Jet

Woodrow Shiek, a 1944 stallion by Sundance and out of Stockings, was bred by Doc Edwards.

Courtesy Sundance 500 International

(QH)—ApHC Racing Hall of Fame 1992.

• Scooter Bug B, a 1972 stallion by Lady Bug's Moon—ApHC Racing Hall of Fame 1993.

• Some Kinda Easy, a 1982 stallion by Easy We Go—ApHC Racing Hall of Fame 2000.

• Three Chicks, Jr., a 1967 stallion by Three Chicks (QH)—AAA-rated race-horse and grand champion halter horse.

In addition to being the cornerstone matriarch behind the Wego Melody line, Sundust was responsible for yet another branch of the family tree.

Bred to her sire in 1946, Sundust produced Black Leopard F-1569, a 1947 stallion. Bred by P. C. Jenkins of Douglas, Wyoming, Leopard went on to make positive contributions as a herd sire in Wyoming and Illinois.

Bambi E. F-2497, a 1954 stallion by Woodrow Shiek and out of P.V.F.'s Butterfly, was also bred by Edwards. Sold to Lee Warne of Onida, South Dakota, "Bambi" founded the well-known "Sully" line of halter and performance horses.

Courtesy Appaloosa Museum & Heritage Center

Among his top sons were Sunbeau #1493 and Popo Aggie T-2957.

Sunshine, a 1950 mare by Sundance and out of Ratina F-405, and Mi Wacon, a 1950 mare by Sundance and out of Linda's Smokey F-1121, were bred by Ben Johnson. Kept by Johnson, Sunshine became the only one of her famous sire's get to earn a national title when she was named the Champion 3-Year-Old Mare and Grand Champion Mare at the 1953 National Show in Quincy, California.

Sold to Mary Ann Fox of Shelbyville, Indiana, Mi Wacon went on to become one of the Midwest's premier producers. Among her most noted produce are Patchy Jr.'s Baldy, Patchy Jr.'s Mi-Ta-Inga, Patchy Yamini's Mi Thega, Patchy Yamini's Mi Gina and Patchy Topa.

As far as Sundance—the head of the line—goes, he remained in Doc Edwards' posses-sion until 1954. By this time, the family had moved to a new home near Fort Morgan, Colorado. As befitted a horse of his stature, Sundance was accorded his own private, irri-gated grass/hay field.

One day, after eating too much of the wet hay, he became sick and died of colic.

Foaled as he was seven years before the incorporation of the Appaloosa Horse Club, and destined to live out his life before the breed gained a firm hold in the Rocky Mountain region, Sundance still managed to exert a positive influence.

Through the programs of pioneer ApHC breeders such as Ben Johnson, Ralph Cannon, Lee Warne and a host of others, the blood of the red leopard stallion was preserved and perpetuated throughout the land.

In recognition of that fact, Sundance was inducted into the ApHC Hall of Fame in 1988.

Here's a great shot of a pair of Sundance-bred leopard champions. Taken at the 1964 Five-Club Regional show in Jackson, Michigan, featuring Mary Ann Fox, Patchy Yamini's Mi Thega—a 1960 mare by Patchy Yamini and out of Mi Wacon—and Pe Je's Mon-Te-Ca, "Mi Thega's" 1964 colt by Pe Je.

Courtesy Mary Ann Fox

Chapter 6

PATCHY
F-416

Patchy F-416—the breed's first National Champion Stallion and National Champion Performance Horse.
Courtesy Appaloosa Museum & Heritage Center

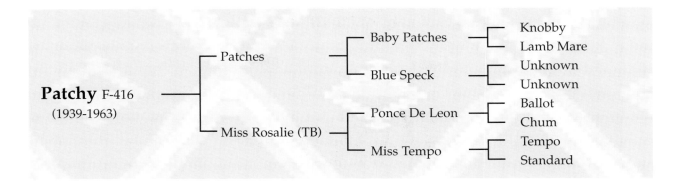

Patchy F-416
(1939-1963)

Patches
— Baby Patches
— Knobby
— Lamb Mare
— Blue Speck
— Unknown
— Unknown

Miss Rosalie (TB)
— Ponce De Leon
— Ballot
— Chum
— Miss Tempo
— Tempo
— Standard

Patchy holds the singular honor of being the first Appaloosa to be a national grand champion stallion and a national champion performance horse.

A 1939 stallion by Patches and out of Miss Rosalia (JC), Patchy was bred by Herb Babcock of Ewan, Washington.

Patches, a 1935 stallion by Baby Patches and out of Blue Speck, was bred by Guy Lamb of Central Ferry, Washington.

Miss Rosalia, by Ponce De Leon and out of Miss Tempo, was royally bred, tracing to such well-known speed sires as Hampton, Voter, Ballot and Hermit.

Patchy changed hands several times as a foal. At the age of 10 days, he was purchased by Lester Riley of Central Ferry, Washington. Shortly thereafter, he was acquired by Guy Lamb of Central Ferry.

Lamb kept Patchy several years and broke him to ride. By the pioneer horseman's own account, the stallion was hard to break and showed a rare talent when it came to bucking.

In time, Lamb sold Patchy to Herb Camp of LaCrosse, Washington. The stallion continued to have the reputation of being "cold-backed," but was utilized as a ranch horse and sire anyway.

In the spring of 1948, Patchy came to the attention of ApHC Executive Secretary George Hatley of Moscow, Idaho. Hatley had scheduled an all-Appaloosa horse show in Lewiston, Idaho, later that year and was determined to get as many quality Appaloosas to show at it as possible.

With that in mind, he paid a trip to the Camp Ranch. In May of 1948, at Hatley's suggestion, Camp registered his black, blanket-hipped stallion with ApHC as Patchy F-416. Hatley also convinced Camp to show Patchy at the 1948 National Show in Lewiston. Exhibited at halter there, the 9-year-old was named Champion Aged Stallion and Grand Champion Stallion.

While at the show, Patchy came to the attention of Ben Johnson of Loma, Colorado. Johnson had gotten into the Appaloosa business by accident several years earlier with the acquisition of a foundation mare from his older brother's estate. Johnson liked Patchy, but was not in a position to buy him. Two years later, he was.

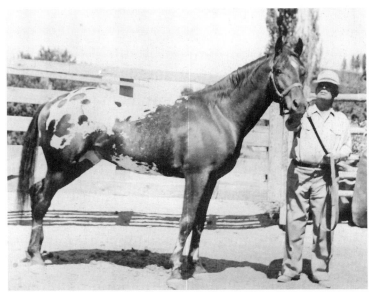

Patchy was registered as a 2-year-old by Herb Camp of LaCrosse, Washington.

Courtesy Ben Johnson

This classic photo of Patchy was taken in a Camp Ranch corral shortly after he had been separated from his broodmare band so he could be delivered to new owner Ben Johnson at the 1950 National Show in Lewiston, Idaho.

Courtesy Ben Johnson

"In 1950," he says, "I heard that Herb Camp might consider selling Patchy. I contacted him to find out if that was true. He told me it was and that he was asking $500 for him.

"I told him, 'If you can bring him to the National in Lewiston, and if he's in the same shape that he was two years ago, I'll take him.' "

Camp delivered Patchy to the show and Johnson took possession of him. What's more, Johnson showed the 11-year-old stallion in performance.

"Patchy was well-broke when I got him," he says. "He had a good rein on him and was a seasoned ranch horse.

"Up until right before the show, though, he had been out running with a band of mares. He wasn't too

Lolo F-462 (left) and Kathy F-895 (right) were two of Patchy's first ApHC-registered get. Bred by Herb Camp and sold to George Hatley, both mares went on to become top producers.

Courtesy George Hatley

happy about being separated from them, so the first thing he tried to do when I got on him the evening before the show was try to buck me off. But I never did let him get his head down. I just kept turning him around and backing him up until he settled down.

"The next day, we placed second in the calf roping, third in the cutting and fourth in the men's Western pleasure."

Johnson did not show Patchy at the 1951 National Show. He opted, instead, to take him to the 1952 Nationals in Quincy, California.

In his coverage of the show that appeared in the October-November 1952 issue of *The Horse Lover's Magazine*, W. H. Hutchison gave a full account of Patchy's efforts at the show:

"Patchy was entered in 11 of the 13 working events, missing only the Ladies' and Children's Pleasure classes.

"Ben rode most of the events himself, relinquishing in the 1/2-mile race and Most Colorful Mount to Tom Redheart, Lapwai, Idaho.

"Patchy took first in Men's Western Pleasure, Most Colorful Mount and the Parade class; second in Matched Pairs (with Toby III), Rope Race, Nez Perce Stake Race and 1/2-mile race; and fourth in the 1/8- and 1/4-mile races to score the most points and walk off with the High-Point Performance Horse trophy.

"The feat was the more remarkable as Patchy is 13 years old, a working range stock horse at home, and still looks like he could swallow his head and give Ben a ride."

In claiming his high-point performance title, Patchy became the first Appaloosa stallion to earn the aforementioned distinction of being a national grand champion stallion and a national champion performance horse. The following year, he added even more luster to his already shiny reputation when he was

Exhibited by Ben Johnson, Patchy was the Champion Performance Horse at the 1952 National Show in Quincy, California.
Courtesy Ben Johnson

named the Champion Get of Sire winner at the 1953 National Show in Quincy.

Shortly thereafter, he was retired from the show ring and switched to a full-time career as a working ranch horse and herd sire.

"There's been a lot of talk over the years about Patchy being a 'bronc,' " Johnson says. "He did have an independent streak; there's no doubt about that. If he hadn't been ridden for a while, the first time he was saddled up he liked to bounce the stirrups. But he wasn't a mean horse; he wasn't hard to handle. And I should know. Patchy and I covered a lot of miles and worked a lot of cattle together.

"Back then," he continues, "I did whatever it took to make a living. I operated a dairy, ran some beef cattle and farmed.

"I raised sugar beets, and after the harvest there'd always be some beets left. I'd feed them to the horses and they all loved them …

Blitz, a 1944 stallion by Patchy and out of Lavina, was bred by Herb Grieb of Hatton, Washington. Sold to the Bixby Ranch of Long Beach, California, Blitz was the Champion Aged Stallion and Reserve Champion Stallion at the 1953 National Show in Quincy, California.

Courtesy Appaloosa Museum & Heritage Center

Cojo Mapachi, a 1955 stallion by Blitz and out of Blue B., was a regional champion halter horse and Bixby Ranch sire.

Courtesy Appaloosa Museum & Heritage Center

except Patchy. He loved apples but he wouldn't have anything to do with sugar beets.

"I used to take a couple of slices of apple, put a slice of sugar beet between them and feed it all to Patchy. He'd chew away on it and, pretty soon, here would come the sugar beet slice out … and I couldn't find a tooth mark on it.

"He had a lot of personality."

Even before he was retired from the show ring, Patchy had begun to establish himself as a top-notch sire. While still in the Northwest, he sired such top show get as Chico, Kathy, Gypsy and Blitz.

Chico, a 1948 stallion out of Peaches F-635, was bred by Herb

Camp of LaCrosse, Washington, and was the Champion Weanling Stallion at the 1948 National Show in Lewiston, Idaho.

Kathy, a 1948 mare out of Rocksey F-636, was also bred by Herb Camp. Sold to George Hatley, she was the Champion Weanling Filly at the 1948 National Show. Retired to the broodmare band, she produced such notable show and race horses as Topatchy, Apache Patch and Double Patch.

Gypsy, a 1946 mare out of a Lamb mare, was bred by Guy Lamb. Shown by her breeder, she was the Champion Aged Mare and Grand Champion Mare at the 1951 National Show in Lewiston, Idaho.

Blitz, a 1944 stallion out of Lavina II, was bred by Bert Grieb of Hatton, Washington. Sold first to George Brookings of Sedro Wooley, Washington, and then to the Bixby Ranch of Long Beach, California, Blitz was the Champion Aged Stallion and Reserve Grand Champion Stallion at the 1953 National Show in Quincy.

In addition, the loud-colored stallion was the Champion Nez Perce Stake Racing Horse at the 1956 National Show in Elko, Nevada, and the Champion Rope Race Horse at the 1959 Nationals in Santa Barbara, California.

After being relocated to the Rocky Mountains, Patchy continued to turn out champions.

Keeko, a 1955 mare out of Sunray F-1277, was bred by Ben Johnson. Shown by him, she was the Champion Weanling Filly at the 1955 Estes Park, Colorado, show—the first organized Appaloosa show ever held in Colorado—and the Champion Weanling Filly at the 1955 National Show in Colorado Springs, Colorado.

Sold to Mary Ann Fox of Shelbyville, Indiana, Keeko became the Champion Produce of Dam winner at the 1974 National

Patchy's Geronimo, a 1954 gelding by Patchy and out of Fleet, was bred by J. F. Cherveny of Grand Junction, Colorado. Purchased by Ben Johnson for his daughter Claire, "Geronimo" became a top all-around show horse.
Photo by George Phippen, courtesy Claire Johnson Diers

Keeko, a 1955 mare by Patchy and out of Sunray, was the Champion Weanling Filly at the 1955 National Show in Colorado Springs, Colorado.

Photo by Clarence Coil, courtesy Ben Johnson

Show in Shelbyville, Indiana.

Patchy Jr., a 1952 stallion by Patchy and out of Leopard Lady F-167, was also bred by Johnson. The earner of nine national halter and performance titles, he will be profiled in the following chapter.

By the late 1950s, Johnson had dramatically cut back on his use of Patchy in the breeding shed. In 1959 and 1960, only four of the stallion's foals made their way into the ApHC registry.

The reasoning behind Johnson's move was simple—the focus of his program had been shifted to Patchy Jr. As a result, Johnson

agreed to sell half-interest in Patchy to fellow ApHC board of directors member Don Imboden of Sioux City, Iowa.

Patchy was transported from Colorado to Iowa prior to the 1960 breeding season.

While in residence at the Imboden farm, the stallion's daily care was entrusted to Don's wife, Jimmie. By all accounts, Patchy was quiet and easy to handle. What's more, as soon as he heard the kitchen door slam each morning—a sign that his morning feeding was in the offing—he would greet his caretaker with a loud whinny.

Patchy sired three full foal crops for the

Imbodens. Of the 35 foals born during this era, 1961–1963, most were relegated to use as breeding animals.

On the morning of March 17, 1963, Jimmie went out to the barn as usual to feed Patchy. Noticing that he failed to greet her in his usual manner, she immediately sensed that something was wrong.

She found the 24-year-old living legend dead in his stall, apparently the victim of a heart attack. Patchy was buried on the farm, with a marker erected over his final resting place.

"I still owned a half-interest in Patchy when he died," Ben Johnson says. "In fact, I was due to go back to Iowa and pick him up on April 1, 1963. Don had used him for several years and it was supposed to be my turn.

"Don told me later that it broke Jimmie's heart when Patchy died. She'd been the one to care for him every day and she'd gotten attached to him."

Patchy, one of the breed's earliest and brightest stars, made his mark upon the breed as a halter horse, a performance horse and a sire. In recognition of his accomplishments in all three areas, he was one of the first two horses to be inducted into the Appaloosa Hall of Fame in 1986.

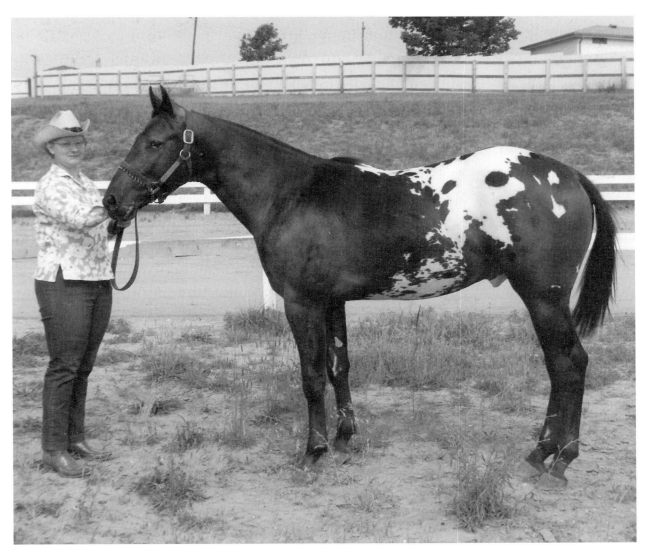

Sold to Mary Ann Fox of Shelbyville, Indiana, Keeko became a medallion-earning producer. Seen here is Lemme Go Patchy, a 1970 stallion by Lemme Go Boy (QH) and out of Keeko.

Courtesy Mary Ann Fox

Chapter 7

PATCHY JR.
F-1380

Patchy Jr., the Champion 3-Year-Old Stallion and Grand Champion Stallion at the 1955 National Show in Colorado Springs, Colorado, was a successful blend of two foundation families.

Photo by Clarence Coil, courtesy Ben Johnson

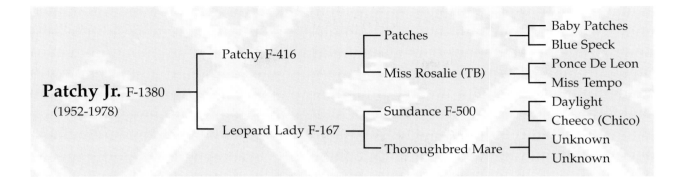

				Baby Patches
		Patches		Blue Speck
	Patchy F-416			Ponce De Leon
		Miss Rosalie (TB)		Miss Tempo
Patchy Jr. F-1380				Daylight
(1952-1978)		Sundance F-500		Cheeco (Chico)
	Leopard Lady F-167			Unknown
		Thoroughbred Mare		Unknown

Patchy Jr. F-1380 was a rare blend of two foundation families. It was a mix that worked and that had a positive impact on the breed.

Patchy Jr., a 1952 stallion by Patchy F-416 and out of Leopard Lady F-167, was bred by Ben Johnson of Loma, Colorado. As noted in the previous chapter, Johnson had gotten in the Appaloosa business by accident.

"My older brother Raymond was working as an assistant park ranger in Estes Park, Colorado," he says. "In the fall of 1939, he was killed in a car accident. Raymond was a pretty good hand with a horse. He had rodeoed a little and, when he died, he had a calf-roping mare and a 2-year-old Appaloosa filly. In settling his estate, it was decided that I would get the filly."

The filly, as it turns out, was very well bred. That fact notwithstanding, she came into the world under some rather unusual circumstances.

"In the spring of 1936," Johnson says, "my brother was working for our uncle Otto Borchers of Gilcrest, Colorado. While he was there, he had occasion to see Sundance F-500 at John Whisanad's place near Orchard.

"Raymond was very impressed with Sundance; so impressed that he 'borrowed' one of uncle Otto's Thoroughbred mares and took her to Jenkins to be bred. While he did pay Jenkins the stud fee, Raymond just kind of forgot to tell Uncle Otto what he'd done.

"Before long it became apparent what had happened. That precipitated a running, two-year battle

between Uncle Otto and Raymond. Most of it was good-natured, and it was finally resolved when Raymond gave up $125 of his wages for full ownership of the filly.

"That was back in the days when $25 would buy a well-broke saddle horse, so the filly did not come cheap."

In 1940, Ben Johnson was working at a tire store in Grand Junction, Colorado. While attending a Saturday night dance, he spotted Dorothy Eastman, a student nurse. He promptly asked her for a date and they were married a few months later.

The newlyweds moved onto a piece of rental property where they raised beans, corn, alfalfa and a few hogs. In time, that property was exchanged for a place of their

Leopard Lady F-167, Patchy Jr.'s dam, was a top ranch and pleasure mount, and a foundation producer.

Courtesy Ben Johnson

This is a great head-and-shoulders shot of Patchy Jr. and breeder/owner Ben Johnson, taken by renowned trainer and long-time friend Monte Foreman.

Courtesy Ben Johnson

own and a life of "doing whatever it took to make a living." Sugar beets were added to the row crop mixture and cattle were added to the livestock list.

And then there was the matter of the red leopard Appaloosa.

Several years after acquiring the filly, Ben and Dorothy were visiting Ben's uncle. There, Ben happened upon a copy of the Billings, Montana-based horse magazine *Bit and Spur*. In it was an article about the newly formed Appaloosa Horse Club. Johnson read the article and began corresponding with club founder Claude Thompson of Moro, Oregon.

In 1945, Johnson joined ApHC and received membership number 76. At the same time, he registered his Appaloosa mare as Leopard Lady F-167.

As noted earlier, Leopard Lady was sired by Sundance F-500 and was out of a Thoroughbred mare. While the mare's exact breeding is not documented, Phil Jenkins is officially on record as saying she was "a gray mare of Dan Lord breeding."

Owned for the rest of her life by Ben Johnson, Leopard Lady became an integral part of the Johnson family and the cornerstone matriarch of his Appaloosa breeding program.

" 'Lady' was 2 when I brought her home," he says. "From the very beginning, she was just one of those horses that wanted to do everything that was asked of her.

"Anyone could ride her. My son Jerry was 6, my daughter Linda was 4 and my daughter Claire was 2. She'd work well for Jerry, she kind of took care of Linda and she'd poke along with Claire. She worked the way a person could ride.

"In 1943, I bred Lady to an Appaloosa stallion named Nuggett. I got a roan Appaloosa filly with speckles over her rump that I later registered as Miss Sundance F-235. And that's when I got the Appaloosa bug."

Although Leopard Lady was used too extensively as a ranch and pleasure mount to be allowed full-time broodmare status, she did produce three additional foals.

Bred to Barrendo Red F-150—Johnson's first Appaloosa stallion—she produced Bald Eagle F-508, a 1948 stallion, and Sunray F-1277, a 1949 mare.

Bred to Patchy F-416 (see previous chapter), she produced a 1952 blue roan, blanket-hipped colt.

When the colt was 2-1/2 months old, "Lady" died of acute colic at the age of 15.

"We named Lady's last foal The Uncompahgre Kid," Johnson says. "After awhile, we decided that name was too hard to pronounce. When we registered him with ApHC in July of 1952, we changed the name to Patchy Jr."

Raised as an orphan foal, Patchy Jr. quickly became as much a part of the Johnson family as his dam had been. When it came time to break him to ride, Johnson was delighted to learn that, disposition-wise, he took after his mother.

"Patchy—the sire of Patchy Jr.—had an independent streak," Johnson says. "From time to time, he liked to bang the stirrups together. If he thought he could buck you off, he'd try.

"Patchy Jr., on the other hand, had none of that orneriness in him. Disposition-wise, he was as calm and

In addition to being the earner of seven national halter and perform-ance titles, Patchy Jr. was also a top-notch ranch horse.
Photo by George Phippen, courtesy Ben Johnson

The Johnson Appaloosa program was very much a family affair. Seen here is Patchy Jr. and Linda Johnson (now Kukal), Ben and Dorothy's eldest daughter, after winning the ladies Western pleasure class at the 1963 Golden Spike National Livestock Show in Ogden, Utah.
Courtesy Ben Johnson

Patchy Jr. and Claire Johnson (now Diers) are seen here competing in the Indian costume class at a show in Spanish Fork, Utah.

Courtesy Ben Johnson

The Patchy/Johnson family relationship extended to the next generation. Seen here is Gordy and Claire Diers' daughter, Audra, competing in the Nez Perce stake race on the Patchy Jr. daughter Give Or Take.

Courtesy Claire Diers

willing as Leopard Lady. I broke him myself and logged a lot of hours on him in some pretty rough country. He never did even offer to give me any trouble."

In 1953, the Appaloosa movement breached the Continental Divide with the formation of the Colorado-based Mountain and Plains Appaloosa Horse Club (MPApHc) regional. Ben Johnson was installed as its first president.

That same year marked Patchy Jr.'s debut as a show horse.

Named the Champion Yearling Stallion at the 1953 National Show in Quincy, California, he followed that up by earning Champion 2-Year-Old Stallion and Reserve Champion Stallion honors at the 1954 National Show in Deer Lodge, Montana.

In March of 1954, *Western Horseman* magazine spotlighted the Appaloosa breed.

Largely as a result of the publicity generated by that single issue, the decision was made to hold the 1955 Naional Show in Colorado Springs, Colorado.

The first MPApHC show was held in July of 1955 in Estes Park, Colorado. There, Patchy Jr. was named the Champion 3-Year-Old Stallion and Reserve Champion Stallion.

Two months later, he topped that by being named the Champion 3-Year-Old Stallion and Grand Champion Stallion at the 1955 National. Then, in 1956, he earned Grand Champion Stallion honors at the Colorado State Fair in Pueblo.

Not strictly a halter horse, however, Patchy Jr. also excelled in performance.

"Due to the fact that I was busy trying to make a living and raise a family," Ben Johnson says, "I didn't show Patchy Jr. as

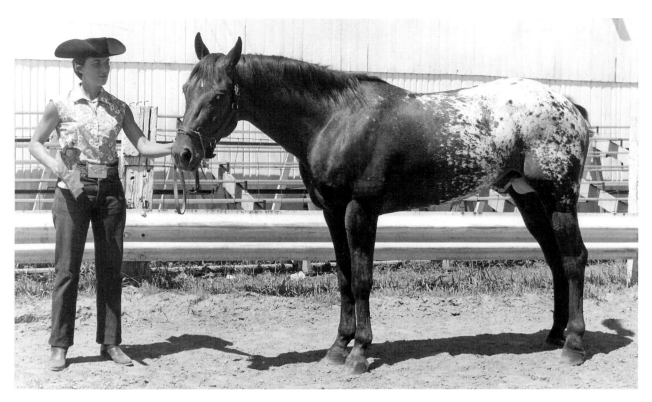

Shavano, a 1955 stallion by Patchy Jr. and out of Blossom F-1678, was his sire's first ApHC-registered get. Sold to Harold Tyner of Tipton, Indiana, Shavano became a top show horse and sire.

Courtesy Ben Johnson

much as I should have. Still, he did well in a wide variety of events."

Shown by Ben, Linda and Claire Johnson, Patchy Jr. competed and won in English pleasure, Western pleasure, trail, Camas Prairie stump race, Nez Perce stake race and the native costume class.

On the national level, he was named as the Champion Trail Horse at the 1957 National in Canby, Oregon.

On one occasion, the versatile stallion even filled in as a racehorse.

"In 1962," Johnson says, "they had an all-breed race meet in Grand Junction. In order to fill the Appaloosa race, I entered Patchy Jr.

"He was a 10-year-old at the time, but he still finished fourth, 3-1/2 lengths behind the winner. Dawndee and Frae—a couple of Utah mares—placed first and second in the race, and they were seasoned racehorses."

Shown at halter and performance in a number of shows, Patchy Jr. was named the

Appaloosa Champion of Champions at the 1958 Colorado State Fair, and the Champion of Champions at the 1959 Grand Junction, Colorado, all-breed show.

The athletic ability and innate willingness of Patchy Jr. was apparent to all who came in contact with him. As a result, he attracted a legion of fans. Among them was Laura Boggio Brest of Capitan, New Mexico.

"I was attending the 1955 National in Colorado Springs," she says. "Ben Johnson had Patchy Jr. there and asked me if I'd like to ride him. At first I thought, 'Why would I want to get on that little horse?' But I did, and I can remember that ride to this very day.

"Patchy Jr. was one of the best-broke horses—with one of the lightest mouths—that I have ever been on. From that day forward, I had a new-found respect for both him and Ben."

Brest's opinion was shared by a number of other top horsemen.

Renowned Colorado trainer and clinician Monte Foreman of Elbert, Colorado, said that Patchy Jr. had more athletic ability than any horse he had ever seen. Dr. DeBelle—a noted French horseman from Caen, France—was in Colorado in 1964 to deliver a medical paper. He made a special trip to Grand Junction to see Patchy Jr. After riding him, DeBelle remarked that the stallion would have made a wonderful dressage horse.

By the time he was retired in 1964, Patchy Jr. had amassed more than 30 halter and performance championships, and accumulated more than 200 trophies and ribbons.

All that was left for the talented performer to do was to reproduce himself.

Patchy Jr.'s first three foal crops hit the ground in 1955, 1956 and 1957. Totaling but eight, they nevertheless included several of his best-known offspring.

Shavano, a 1955 stallion out of Blossom F-1678, was bred by Ben Johnson. Sold to Harold Tyner of Tipton, Indiana, he became an outstanding show horse and sire.

Patchy's Jr. Lila Gleska, a 1956 mare out of Gipsy, was also bred by Johnson. Sold to Jo Warren of Langley, British Columbia, Canada, she was the Champion Yearling Filly of the 1957 National Show in Canby, Oregon. Retired to the broodmare band and bred to Warren's Red Dog—a direct son of Patchy Jr.—she went on to produce such top horses as Warren's Wardance, Warren's Tribal Dance and Warren's Raindance. In addition, she was a 1993 inductee into the Appaloosa Horse Club of Canada Hall of Fame.

Patchy Jr.'s Wanonshe, a 1956 stallion out of Blossom; Patchy Yamini, a 1957 stallion out of Wibluta; and

Patchy Yamini, a 1957 stallion by Patchy Jr. and out of Wibluta F-1680, was also bred by Johnson. Sold to Evan Runion of Rushville, Indiana, "Yamini" did his part to further the family name.

Courtesy Ben Johnson

Patchy Yamini's Mi Thega, a 1960 mare by Patchy Yamini and out of Mi Wacon, was the Champion Weanling Filly at the 1960 National Show in South Sioux City, Nebraska. Owner Mary Ann Fox is seen at "Mi Thega's" halter.

Courtesy Mary Ann Fox

Patchy Jr.'s Shaun-Tonga, a 1960 stallion by Patchy Jr. and out of Rudy Johnson's Lady, was the Champion Aged Stallion and Grand Champion Stallion at the 1964 National Show in Albuquerque, New Mexico. Seen here with the third-generation champion are Ben Johnson and Claire Diers.

Courtesy Ben Johnson

Patchy Jr.'s Baldy, a 1957 stallion out of Mi Wacon; were all bred by Johnson and all went on to become top show horses and sires.

During the next two decades, Patchy Jr. turned out a consistent stream of all-around champion halter and performance horses.

Patchy Jr.'s Mi Ta Inga, a 1958 mare out of Mi Wacon, was the Champion Ladies Most Colorful Mount and Rider (costume class) at the 1960 National Show in South Sioux City, Nebraska. Ladyfinger, a 1961 mare out of Colon, was the Champion Junior Reining Horse at the 1965 National Show in Sacramento, California.

Patchy Jr.'s Shaun Tonga, a 1960 stallion out of Rudy Johnson's Lady, was the Champion Aged Stallion and Grand Champion Stallion at the 1964 National Show in Albuquerque, New Mexico.

In addition, Swan Lake Patchy, Patchy Jr.'s Mokena, Warren's Red Dog, Oo-Wow-Ee, Patchy Jr.'s Yampah, Junior Blue Koo-bay, Patchy Jr.'s Royalty, Patchy Jr.'s Cayenne and Happiness Is were all top regional halter and performance champions.

Patchy Jr. was named as the Premier Sire of Performance Horses at the 1960 National in South Sioux City, Nebraska, and the Champion Get of Sire winner at the 1964 National in Albuquerque, New Mexico.

Give Or Take, a 1972 mare by Patchy Jr. and out of Sue Duster (QH), was a special mare for a variety of reasons.

"I learned to ride on a son of Patchy named Patchy's Geronimo," Claire Johnson (now Mrs. Gordy Diers) of Delta, Colorado—says. "He was my constant companion and friend at home, and my show ring partner when we went to town.

"Give Or Take filled that same role in our daughter Audra's life. I know I might come across as being prejudiced when I say this, but I believe that Give Or Take was the best mare Patchy Jr. sired and perhaps the best horse.

"Beginning in 1977, Give Or Take was Audra's lead-line horse. And then she became her youth showmanship and horsemanship horse; her open pleasure, trail and jumping horse; and her barrel racing and pole bending horse. And she had enough speed to beat AAA-rated racehorses in the latter two events.

"Plus, she was a top ranch mount and Audra's best friend. It was more than a 10-hanky day, when we had to put her down in 1999 at the age of 27."

Patchy Jr. suffered a mild heart attack in 1974. In the summer of 1978, he suffered a severe attack. After recovering sufficiently to breed and settle several mares, he died on October 20, 1978.

Patchy Jr. was never heavily promoted as a public breeding stallion, nor was he heavily bred at home. As a result, he sired only 100 ApHC-registered get. Despite this, his legacy as one of the breed's greatest foundation sires is an established fact.

He was living testimony to both the genetic strength of his forebears and the intuitive knowledge and skill of his breeder.

Happiness Is, a 1965 stallion by Patchy Jr. and out of Ellie's First (TB), was a top halter and race horse. Sold to Dr. Norman Shealy of Brindabell Farms, LaCrosse, Wisconsin, he went on to become a top sire.

Photo by Johnny Johnston, courtesy Ben Johnson

Chapter 8

CHIEF OF FOURMILE
F-2219

Chief of Fourmile was a three-time National Champion Performance Horse and one of the breed's first promotional icons.
Courtesy Appaloosa Museum & Heritage Center

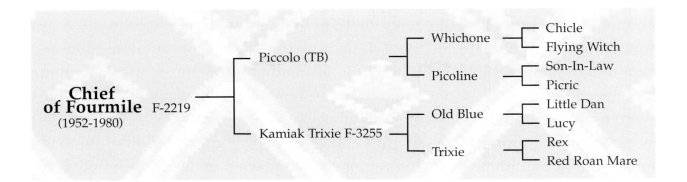

Chief of Fourmile F-2219 (1952-1980)	Piccolo (TB)	Whichone	Chicle
			Flying Witch
		Picoline	Son-In-Law
			Picric
	Kamiak Trixie F-3255	Old Blue	Little Dan
			Lucy
		Trixie	Rex
			Red Roan Mare

In the early 1950s, an Appaloosa colt was foaled in the Northwest who would have a profound impact upon the breed. Although he was left as a stallion and headed several high-profile breeding programs during his life, his main contributions to the breed would not be as a sire. They would be, instead, as a performance horse and promotional icon.

His name was Chief of Fourmile.

Chief of Fourmile, a 1952 stallion by Piccolo (TB) and out of Kamiak Trixie, was bred by Lester Brown of Pullman, Washington.

Piccolo, a stakes-winning grandson of Chicle*—and thus a cousin to the famous Quarter racing sire Chicaro (TB)—was owned by Washington State University in Pullman. As a 3-year-old, Piccolo had met the celebrated Seabiscuit in four races, defeating him twice.

Kamiak Trixie F-3255, a 1932 mare sired by Old Blue and out of Trixie, was bred by Floyd Hickman of Pullman. A full sister to Toby I F-203, Kamiak Trixie was steeped in the blood of some of the Northwest's most renowned Appaloosas (see Chapter 1).

Chief of Fourmile—the most famous of several full siblings by Piccolo and out of Kamiak Trixie—was foaled on June 13, 1952. Jet-black in color, with a big white blanket full of haloed spots, he attracted attention at an early age.

George Hatley, pioneer Appaloosa breeder and long-time ApHC executive secretary, was among the first to view the classically marked colt.

"I was living in town—in Moscow,

Idaho—at the time," Hatley says, "but I traveled back and forth to the family farm on a regular basis. Lester Brown happened to live on the road that I used.

"I got my first glimpse of Chief of Fourmile when he was just a few days old. Kamiak Trixie was a nicely marked red roan mare with dark red spots over her hips. With "Chief" being jet-black in color with a big white blanket, they made what I called an eye-popping pair."

At some point between Chief's birth and his 2-year-old year, Lester Brown gave the colt to his son-in-law, Roy Parvin of Pullman. George Hatley did not forget about the horse

Bred in the Northwest and sold as a 2-year-old to Gus Oettermann of San Antonio, Texas, Chief of Fourmile was named the Champion Aged Stallion at the 1956 National Show in Elko, Nevada. Long-time Oettermann trainer Bill Pearson is seen at the halter.

Courtesy Appaloosa Museum & Heritage Center

Exhibited at the first International Appaloosa Show in San Antonio, Texas, in February of 1956, "Chief" was named as the Champion 4-Year-Old Stallion and Reserve Grand Champion Stallion.

Courtesy Appaloosa Museum & Heritage Center

and eventually had the opportunity to see him again.

"As near as I can recall," Hatley says, "it was in May of 1954 when Roy Parvin and I happened to be at the WSU veterinary clinic at the same time. He knew that I was connected with the Appaloosa Horse Club and asked me out to see Chief of Fourmile.

"Roy had broke Chief to ride and had him in good shape. I encouraged him to register him and bring him to the 1954 National in Deer Lodge, Montana."

Registered with ApHC as Chief of Fourmile T-373 (later F-2219), the 2-year-old stallion was indeed exhibited by Parvin at the association's seventh National Show.

Shown at halter, he placed second to Ben Johnson's great all-around champion Patchy Jr. Entered in the 220-yard race, he placed second to Orvil Sears' legendary Apache. Though his winnings were modest, Chief was touted as one of the show's top juvenile stars and he attracted enough attention to get sold.

"Gus Oettermann of San Antonio, Texas, attended the seventh National," George Hatley says. "He was just getting interested in Appaloosas at the time, and he singled out Chief of Fourmile as the one horse at the show that he wanted. In December of 1954, he gave Roy $1,000 for him.

"That kind of price for an Appaloosa horse was unheard of up to that time. It certainly was a transaction that the Appaloosa Horse Club was proud of, and it served as an omen for great things to come."

Oettermann, a German-born industrialist, owned Indian Lakes Ranch near Boerne, Texas. On it, during the mid- to late-1950s, he assembled one of the greatest sets of Appaloosa horses ever seen up to that time.

Fellow pioneer Appaloosa breeder and exhibitor Laura Brest of Capitan, New

Mexico, knew both Chief of Fourmile and Gus Oettermann well.

"I was Laura Boggio at the time of the Deer Lodge National," she says. "My husband, Matthew, and I were living in Clyde Park, Montana, and we attended the show. In fact, I won the ladies' Western pleasure class there on a mare named Dark Shadow.

"Chief of Fourmile was a big hit at the show. The thing that I recall most about him, other than his loud black and white color, was that he was a big colt—much bigger than most of the Appaloosas of that day and time.

"Matthew and I became good friends with Gus Oettermann. He used to come to our place and buy Appaloosa horses. He was a wonderful, honest man, who loved the breed with a passion."

After purchasing Chief of Fourmile, Oettermann turned him over to resident trainer Bill Pearson to be made ready for the upcoming 1955 show season. One of the stallion's chief competitors throughout the year was J. D. Davis's well-known stallion, Quanah F-706. And, though Quanah was a great one, Chief more than held his own when pitted against him.

Shown at the 1955 National Show in Colorado Springs, Colorado, Chief of Fourmile was entered in 10 of the show's 12

While owned by Oettermann's Indian Lakes Ranch, "Chief" was ridden by John Mullins of Elba, New York, to victory in the Nez Perce stake race at the 1958 International Appaloosa Show in San Antonio, Texas.
Courtesy Appaloosa Museum & Heritage Center

At the Indian Lakes Ranch Dispersal Sale, held October 22, 1960, Chief set a new record for an Appaloosa sold at auction when he was purchased by C. D. Leon of Sapello, New Mexico, for $10,000. Shown here with the famous stallion are (from left) Bill Pearson, Jim Trammell, auctioneer Cecil Dobbin and Leon.

Courtesy Appaloosa Museum & Heritage Center

performance events. He emerged as the winner in the rope race, Nez Perce stake race, the 3/8-mile race and the 1/2-mile race, and was the second-place finisher in ladies' Western pleasure and matched pairs (teamed with Buttons B.).

Those placings were enough to also earn him the eighth National Show's Champion Performance Horse title.

In February of 1956, Chief was shown at the first International Appaloosa Show in San Antonio. With Gus Oettermann at the halter, he was named the Champion 4-Year-Old Stallion and Reserve Grand Champion Stallion (to Quanah). In the 4-year-old stallion class, he defeated such top horses as Poteet B., Revel Jr. and Simcoe's Chinook.

In February of 1957, at the second International Appaloosa Show, Chief was named the Champion Aged Stallion over such early-day stars as Buttons B., Apple and Whistle Britches.

Next up for Chief was a return to the National Show to defend his performance crown. Shown by Bill Pearson at the 1956 Nationals in Elko, Nevada, the talented performer was named the Champion Aged Stallion and was the first-place finisher in the rope race and trail classes.

Entered in the straightaway racing competition, we won the 1/4-race over Apache and Joker B., and finished second to Apache in the 3/8-mile race. For the second year in a row, he was named the National Show's Grand Champion Performance Horse.

Named the show's Champion Aged Gelding and Grand Champion Gelding was Kamiak Prince, a 1949 gelding by Piccolo and out Kamiak Trixie—and thus a full brother to Chief.

Another highlight of the 1956 show season took place in New Orleans, Louisiana. There,

Chief of Fourmile and Quanah met head-to-head in a thrilling battle for all-around working horse honors. At stake was a hand-tooled trophy saddle.

Chief finished first in trail, Camas Prairie stump race, most colorful mount and rider (Indian costume), and matched pairs (with Dawn); and third in Western pleasure.

Quanah countered by finishing first in Nez Perce stake race and rope race, second in Western pleasure and third in stock horse (reining).

By show's end, Quanah had accumulated 15 points and the all-around title. Chief had finished second, 1/2 point behind.

Oettermann chose not to haul Chief of Fourmile to the 1957 National Show in Canby, Oregon. Chief was, however, entered in the 1958 Nationals in Hutchinson, Kansas.

This National Show was another noteworthy one for the big, spotted stallion. Exhibited by Clif Proctor, Chief of Fourmile placed first in English pleasure, the Nez Perce stake race, and the 1/2-mile race. Those victories, coupled with a third-place finish in the 3/8-mile race, were enough to earn the stallion an unprecedented third National Champion Performance Horse title.

Back home in Boerne, the team of Gus Oettermann and Chief of Fourmile made a major contribution of another type to the Appaloosa breed.

Oettermann commissioned renowned Western artist Orren Mixer to paint oil portraits of both Chief of Fourmile and his mares and foals, and Kaw-liga F-1725, another top Indian Lakes herd sire.

The paintings—especially the one of Chief and his harem—were used in advertisements that appeared in such leading horse magazines as *Western Horseman*, *Horse Lover's* and *Appaloosa News*. They were also made available to the general public as 6-by-9-inch color postcards at a cost of $1 each, or three for $2.50.

The impact of the paintings and the postcards cannot be overstated. Though of specific horses, they served as positive images for the entire Appaloosa breed and attracted hundreds—if not thousands—of new fans.

As far as Chief of Fourmile himself was concerned, the 1958 National Show marked the end of one stage of his life and the beginning of another. That year, he was retired from show competition and used solely for breeding.

As the senior sire of Oettermann's Indian Lakes Ranch, Chief of Fourmile stood at the head of a top-flight program. Despite this, he made relatively few contributions as a breed-

Sirdar, a 1957 stallion by Chief of Fourmile and out of Debbie, was bred by Gus Oettermann. Sold to Selma Johnson of Houston, Texas, he went on to become a top show horse and sire.

Courtesy Appaloosa Museum & Heritage Center

ing animal.

That's not to say he had no champion offspring.

Sirdar, a 1957 stallion out of Debbie F-2870, was a top show horse and sire. Chief of Four Mile's Nugget, a 1957 mare out of Texanna, was a top producer and the dam of Hawk's Domino Dancer—the high-selling horse at the 1962 National Sale. Fourmile Princess, a 1959 mare out of He-Topa F-2220, and Chief of Fourmile II, a 1960 stallion out of He-Tanga, were top show horses, as well.

The cross of Chief of Fourmile and Little Red Chick F-1445 was an especially productive one. Roblene's Son of Fourmile, a 1957 stallion; Doby, a 1958 stallion; and Chief Running Bear S., a 1960 stallion; were all top show or breeding stallions.

Neither these nor any other Chief of Fourmile get, however, ever excelled at the National or World Show level.

On April 20, 1959, Gus Oettermann passed away. Virginia, his widow, continued to run Indian Lakes Ranch for more than a year. Then, on October 22, 1960, she held a dispersal sale at the ranch. With Cecil Dobbin of Colorado Springs, Colorado, presiding as auctioneer, and such Appaloosa dignitaries as George Hatley in attendance, 20 lots were sold for an all-time high average of $2,485.

Chief of Fourmile—the sale headliner—set an new record for an Appaloosa sold at auction when he elicited a final bid of $10,000 from C. D. Leon of Sapello, New Mexico.

With Quanah already in residence at his Pendaries Ranch, the addition of Chief of

Chief of Fourmile II, a 1960 stallion by Chief of Fourmile and out of He-Tanga, was sold in the Indian Lakes dispersal sale to an Indiana syndicate for $2,300. The syndicate members were (from left) Robert Smith of Rochester, William Carter and Bernard Minear of Warsaw, Clarence Baldwin of Hammond and Harold Tyner of Tipton.

Courtesy Appaloosa Museum & Heritage Center

Fourmile left Leon the owner of two of the highest-profile Appaloosas in the country. He had been campaigning Quanah in performance for two years. In preparation for the first World Performance Playoffs, to be held in November of 1961 in Sedalia, Missouri, he also put Chief of Fourmile back in training.

At that watershed event—the forerunner of the World Championship Show—Chief was named the Champion Nez Perce Stake Racing Horse. He was retired from competition after the show.

C. D. Leon kept Chief of Fourmile for only two years. While ApHC records show Leon to be Chief's sole owner from November 3, 1960, through July 8, 1963, he reportedly syndicated the well-known stallion. Members of the combine were listed as Selma Johnson of Houston, Texas; Joe Stroube of Corsicana, Texas; Elvin Blevins of Wynnewood, Oklahoma; and Francis Johnson of Hutchinson, Kansas. Whatever his actual ownership structure, Chief resided exclusively at Leon's Pendaries Ranch.

As was the case at Indian Lakes, Chief of Fourmile sired only a few notable horses while in New Mexico. Pine's Mr. Fourmile, a 1962 stallion out of Pendaries Miss Tonkawa, and Sage Acre's Fourmile, a 1962 stallion out of Utah Queen, both went on to become good sires.

On July 6, 1963, Leon sold Chief of Fourmile at a Pendaries Ranch reduction sale for $20,000 to Earl Boyles of Winchester, Kentucky. In December of 1966, the stallion sold again, this time to Steven Dobbs of Escalon, California.

It was at this point in his life that Chief was reportedly neglected to the point of near starvation. He also suffered a reproductive disorder that rendered him nearly impotent. As corroborating evidence, ApHC records reveal that there were no Chief of Fourmile offspring registered from 1968 through 1976.

The cross of Chief of Fourmile and Little Red Chick F-1445 produced several top individuals. Including Chief Running Bear S., a 1960 stallion.

Photo by Chuck Bearden

On June 9, 1975, the then-23-year-old stallion changed hands for the seventh and final time, when he was sold to Tom and Robert Ludwig of Waterford, California. The pair nursed Chief back to health and even succeeded in returning him to sound breeding shape. Between 1977 and 1980, 47 Chief of Fourmile foals were registered.

Chief of Fourmile passed away in June of 1980, at the age of 28. The following spring, his final two foals were born. They were 4Mile Debutant, a mare out of Fourmile Brite Star, and Fourmile's Last, a stallion out of Peacock's Blondy.

Throughout his long life, Chief of Fourmile was a celebrity. First as a heralded performance horse, then—courtesy of the Orren Mixer painting—as an Appaloosa "poster child," and finally as a living legend.

He wore all three mantles well, and the Appaloosa breed benefited greatly as a result.

Chief of Fourmile was inducted into the ApHC Hall of Fame in 1988 and further honored in 1999 as a Breyer commemorative-edition model horse.

Chapter 9

MANSFIELD'S COMANCHE
F-3096

Mansfield's Comanche—founded of one of the Southern Plains' first great Appaloosa families.

Courtesy Ed Roberts

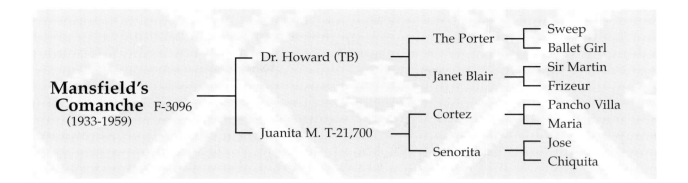

Mansfield's
Comanche F-3096
(1933-1959)

- Dr. Howard (TB)
  - The Porter
    - Sweep
    - Ballet Girl
  - Janet Blair
    - Sir Martin
    - Frizeur
- Juanita M. T-21,700
  - Cortez
    - Pancho Villa
    - Maria
  - Senorita
    - Jose
    - Chiquita

As the Appaloosa movement spread southward and eastward during the late 1940s and early 1950s, a family of spotted horses was discovered on the vast grasslands of the Texas Panhandle that would have a great impact on the breed. They were known as the Comanche horses.

At first glance, the Panhandle would seem an unlikely spawning ground for Appaloosas. It was, after all, the stronghold of the Quarter Horse. Not only did the region contain a vast number of pioneer Quarter Horse breeders, but the American Quarter Horse Association's (AQHA) national headquarters was located within its boundaries, in Amarillo.

A short distance to the west of Amarillo—near Vega, Texas—there was a stronghold of a different type. This was the 60,000-acre

Alamosa Ranch, owned and operated by Jack Mansfield.

Mansfield had become an Appaloosa breeder by accident in the early 1930s, when he and a partner purchased the Indio Ranch in Eagle Pass in South Texas. The ranch came stocked with more than 500 horses. Many of those horses were Appaloosas, and they had been there for longer than anyone could remember. Although the exact origin of the spotted horses was not known, it was always assumed that they came from somewhere in Mexico.

Mansfield was quick to realize that, wherever the Appaloosas came from, they were top ranch mounts and worth keeping. In 1939, he moved his ranching operations—including the best of the Appaloosas—from Eagle Pass to the Panhandle.

For most of his life, "Comanche" lived the unfettered life of a range stallion on the Jack Mansfield ranch of Vega, Texas.
***Courtesy* Western Horseman**

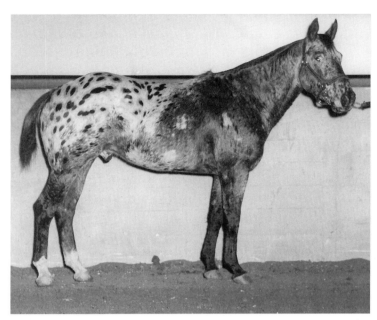

Comanche Jr., a 1954 gelding by Mansfield's Comanche and out of UXA 11 Mansfield, was the Reserve Champion Gelding at the 4th International Appaloosa Horse Show, held in 1959 in San Antonio, Texas.

***Courtesy* Western Horseman**

Key among the horses that made the trip north was a dark blue roan stallion with a big white blanket and black spots. He was known first as Comanche, and then later as Mansfield's Comanche.

Mansfield's Comanche was a 1933 stallion sired by Dr. Howard (TB) and out of Juanita.

Dr. Howard—a descendant of Kentucky Derby winner Ben Brush—was a government Remount stallion that stood at Billy Anson's famous Head of the River Ranch near Cristoval, Texas. Anson, one of the founders of the Quarter Horse breed, was using the Thoroughbred on his stock horse mares to get offspring that were suitable for use as either light carriage horses or as polo ponies.

Juanita was a 1930 or 1931 mare sired by Cortez and out of Senorita. Cortez was by Pancho Villa by Little Joe by Traveler. Senorita is listed as being by Jose and out of Chiquita.

When Juanita was an aged mare, Mansfield sold her to Lloyd Ortiz, a Trinidad, Colorado,

barber and Appaloosa fancier. It was while she was owned by Ortiz that the foundation mare came to the attention of pioneer Appaloosa breeder and showman Riley Miller of Justiceburg, Texas.

"It was in the mid- to late 1950s when I saw Juanita" he says. "I had known Lloyd Ortiz for a number of years and had bought some horses from him.

"Juanita was certainly well past 20 when I saw her. Still, she was an above-average individual. She stood maybe 15 hands high and was very Thoroughbred-looking in her appearance. She was a nice-headed, nice-necked mare with a long, clean throatlatch.

"Juanita had a prominent set of withers, but was a little long-backed, as I recall. She had a small blanket over her hips and was speckled all over—marble-colored as I recall.

"Lloyd told me he was trying to get her in foal, but wasn't having any luck. Soon afterwards, he sold her to J. E. Baker of Oklahoma City, Oklahoma. As far as I know, neither man ever got a live foal from her."

Baker wound up being Juanita's last owner. She died of a heart attack on his place west of Oklahoma City on July 20, 1962.

Mansfield's Comanche spent his entire life on the Mansfield Ranch. Contrary to some published accounts, he was broke to ride. Joe Wheeler, a Mansfield hand, broke Mansfield's Comanche and used him on the ranch. After it was determined that the stallion had enough intelligence and working ability, and the right disposition to merit being used as a breeding animal, he was retired from riding.

From that point on, the stallion's sole purpose was to produce ranch horses for use by the cowboys who worked on the Mansfield spread. He was turned loose on the range with a band of mares and allowed to roam free year-round.

As was the generally accepted practice at the time, most of the ranch hands preferred to ride geldings. The fillies that Mansfield's Comanche sired were therefore relegated to duty in either his broodmare band or another band headed up by one of his sons.

This resulted in an intensely line-bred family of horses, with fathers being bred to daughters and brothers to sisters. The horses produced by these crosses were even bred to each other in some instances.

This seemingly haphazard manner of horse breeding resulted in one of the genetically strongest Appaloosa families the breed has ever known.

By the time the Appaloosa world in general became aware of the Jack Mansfield Appaloosas, Mansfield's Comanche was an aged stallion.

Old Pay Day, a 1946 stallion by Mansfield's Comanche and out of Lucine, founded his own family of show and breeding horses.
Courtesy Appaloosa Museum & Heritage Center

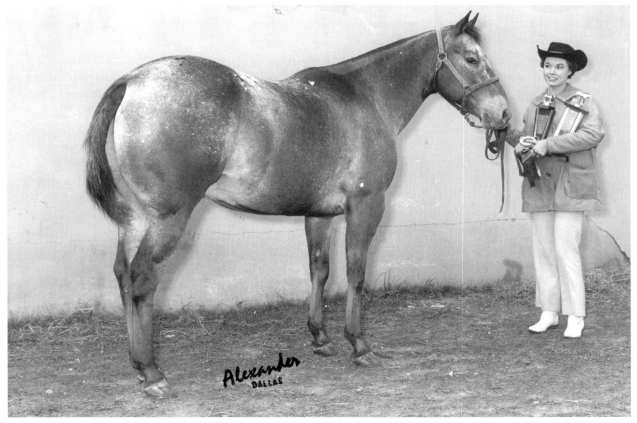

Pay Day's Double Trouble, a 1953 gelding by Old Pay Day and out of Seven X (QH), was a top halter gelding. During one stretch, "Double Trouble" was shown 33 times and recorded 26 wins.
Courtesy Appaloosa Museum & Heritage Center

Manzy Maid, a 1946 mare by Mansfield's Comanche was one of her sire's top-producing daughters.

ApHC registration file photo

Few of his early get had found their way into the registry, and fewer yet had made any inroads as show horses.

Two exceptions to this rule were High Dice and Comanche, Jr.

High Dice, a 1948 gelding out of Leopard Rose by Mansfield's Comanche, was sold to L. G. Hooper of Plainview, Texas. Fitted for halter and exhibited by Hooper, High Dice stood grand at several early-day West Texas Appaloosa shows.

Comanche, Jr., a 1954 gelding out of UXA 11 Mansfield, was sold to L. S. Johnson of Canyon, Texas. He, too, was turned into a grand champion halter horse.

The main contribution of this first generation of Mansfield's Comanche horses would be as prolific sires and dams.

Double Six Domino, a 1943 stallion out of Susan by Mansfield's Comanche, was the eldest of the first generation horses to be registered. One of the most influential stallions of the entire line, he will be profiled in the following chapter.

In addition to "Domino," such Mansfield's Comanche sons as Caliente and

Commanche's Equal made noteworthy contributions to the breed.

Caliente, a 1951 stallion by Comanche and out of Leah by Comanche, sired Squaw Ann and Caliente Jr.

Squaw Ann, a 1955 mare out of Pat's Pocahontas, was the Champion Produce of Dam winner at the 1964 National Show in Albuquerque, New Mexico. Among her top produce were Humdinger's Maharani Ann, winner of the junior cutting class at the 1967 World Champion Playoffs in Sweetwater, Texas, and the senior cutting class at the 1973 World Champion Playoffs in Jackson, Mississippi.

Caliente Jr., a 1960 stallion out of Kiowa Lady, was also a national champion sire. Among his top get were Caliente's Baldy and Caliente Revel, both bred by Mike and Ruby Blair of Erie, Kansas.

"Baldy," a 1963 gelding out of Lucky, was the Champion Performance Horse at the 1971 National Show in Las Vegas, Nevada. "Revel," a 1967 stallion out of Revel Ann, was the Reserve Champion Performance Horse at the 1971 National Show, and the Champion Performance Horse at the 1972 National Show in Columbus, Ohio.

Commanche's Equal, a 1952 stallion by Mansfield's Comanche and out of Loma, was a unique member of the Comanche clan.

To begin with, he was not colored like a typical Comanche horse. Listed on his registration papers as dark brown in color, "Equal" was in reality a dark, smutty-colored dun. Where the dun color came from remains a mystery. The generally accepted theory is that his dam, Loma, was sired by Sheik P-11—the great Coke Roberds-bred and Matador Ranch-owned foundation Quarter Horse sire.

Given the timeframes and locales involved, this is a plausible explanation.

In its heyday, the Matador Ranch encompassed more than one and a half million acres. Most of its holdings were located southeast of Amarillo—in Floyd, Motley, Cottle and Dickens counties.

There was also a division of the ranch known as the "Upper Matador" or "Alamositas Division." It covered 270,000 acres of land that was once part of the XIT Ranch. Situated on the south side of the Canadian River, it adjoined the Alamosa Ranch.

As the story goes, Sheik—the palomino AQHA sire—and Leopard Rose—the Mansfield's Comanche daughter—wound up on the same side of the river at some point. Equal's dam, Loma, was said to be the result.

Wherever the dun gene came from, Commanche's Equal consistently passed it on and contributed a number of palomino and buckskin champions to the breed.

Equal was born on the Alamosa Ranch, and while still a youngster was injured in a cattle guard accident. Sold first to Cal Barton of Paul's Valley, Oklahoma, and later to Jake and Bob Snipes of Clovis, New Mexico, he went on to sire such champions as Comanche's Dawn, Dubonnet, Gold Strikes Equal and Silver Strikes Equal.

Comanche's Dawn, a 1960 mare out of an unregistered bay mare, was the Champion Yearling Filly at the 1961 National Show in

Hawk Eye, a 1955 stallion by One Eye Geronimo and out of Manzy Maid, was the 1958 National Champion 3-Year-Old Stallion. ***Courtesy Appaloosa Museum & Heritage Center***

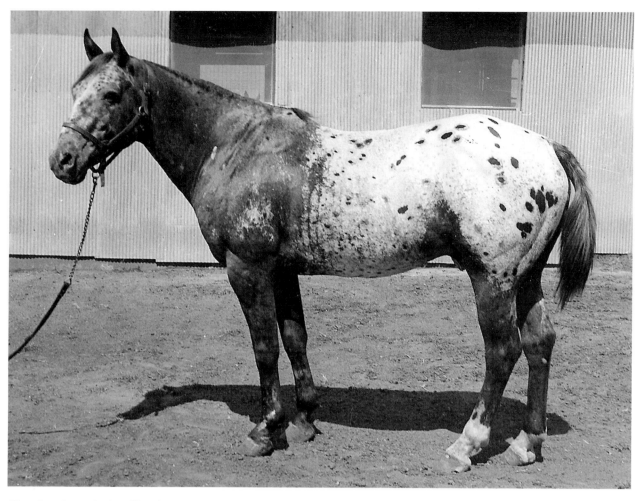

Cherokee A., a 1946 stallion by Mansfield's Comanche and out of Leopard Rose, sired a number of winning halter, performance and race horses.

Courtesy Western Horseman

Fort Worth, Texas.

Dubonnet, a 1959 mare out of Sorrel Sue, was the Champion Calf Roping Horse at the 1967 World Champion Playoffs.

Gold Strikes Equal, a 1963 stallion out of Whirling Ex (TB), was the winner of the 1965 World Wide Futurity in Albuquerque and the 1966 Mountain and Plains Senior Stakes in Denver, Colorado. He was a three-time winner of the 870 Handicap in Denver and went on to become a top halter and speed sire.

Silver Strikes Equal, a 1965 stallion out of Whirling Ex, was the Champion 3-Year-Old Stallion and Grand Champion Stallion at the 1968 National Show in Oklahoma City, and the Champion Aged Stallion and Grand Champion Stallion at the 1971 National Show in Las Vegas. He was also the Champion English Pleasure Horse at the 1971 National Show.

In addition to the above-mentioned stallions, such Mansfield's Comanche sons as Old Pay Day, Cherokee A., and Oklahoma also made notable contributions to the breed.

Old Pay Day, a 1946 stallion out of Lucine, was owned by Elvin Blevins of Wynnewood, Oklahoma. He sired such early-day champions as Wood's Pay Day, Mojave W and Pay Day's Double Trouble.

Cherokee A., a 1946 stallion out of Leopard

Rose, sired such top show winners as High Spot, Chief of Swan Lake and She'll Do.

Oklahoma, a 1952 stallion out of Pett M, was sold to Howard Thompson of Shawnee, Oklahoma. The stallion sired such halter and racing champions as Chiquita Steak, Kiamichi Jr. and Ghost of Comanche.

Ghost of Comanche, a 1962 stallion out of Smokey Babe, was the 1965 World Champion 3-Year-Old Race Colt. Retired to stud, he sired What's Up Ghost, a 1988 inductee into the ApHC Racing Hall of Fame, and Ghost's Gayla, the Reserve Grand Champion Mare at the 1971 National Show.

Several additional Mansfield's Comanche sons—such as Depression Argo, Comanche Rondo, Speckled Butt, Fieldman, Panhandle Scout and Kelley's Comanche Kid—were also utilized as breeding animals.

And then there were the Mansfield's Comanche daughters. Of the famous stallion's 53 ApHC-registered get, 34 were mares.

Manzy Maid, a 1946 mare out of an unknown mare, was the dam of Hawk Eye, the 1958 National Champion 3-Year-Old Stallion and Most Colorful Mount and Rider at the Hutchinson, Kansas, event.

Theda, a 1950 mare out of Leopard Lady, was the dam of the aforementioned Chief Of Swan Lake. Likewise, Tiger Lily, a 1950 mare out of Speckled Lady, was the dam of High Spot.

Susie Q., an unregistered full sister to Double Six Domino, was the dam of many-time grand champion Kelley's Sonny Boy.

Comanche's Dot, a 1953 mare out of Leah (also a full sister to Double Six Domino), was the 1964 Oklahoma Appaloosa Horse Club High-Point Produce of Dam winner.

There were a number of other Mansfield's Comanche daughters that excelled as producers. Some—like Tesuque Molly, Tawana, Valencia and Manfielda—were named.

Others—like Mansfield's Comanche Nos. 1 though 12—weren't.

Named or unnamed, all made positive contributions to the breed.

By the time the 1960s rolled around, the Mansfield's Comanche family was firmly entrenched as one of the breed's best. So popular was the line that, in 1962, an organization promoting the bloodline was formed.

Known as the Mansfield's Comanche Breeders, the group began placing full-page ads in *Western Horseman* magazine and the Appaloosa News. In addition to spotlighting the Mansfield's Comanche line and the men and women who featured it, the ads spread the Appaloosa message, as well.

The group also handed out year-end halter and performance awards and, in 1962 and 1963, held Mansfield's Comanche-bred consignment sales in Fort Worth.

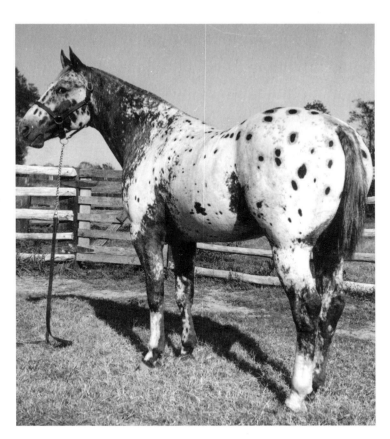

Chief of Swan Lake, a 1956 stallion by Cherokee A. and out of Theda, went on to become one of Louisiana's first great halter and performance stars.

Courtesy Appaloosa Museum & Heritage Center

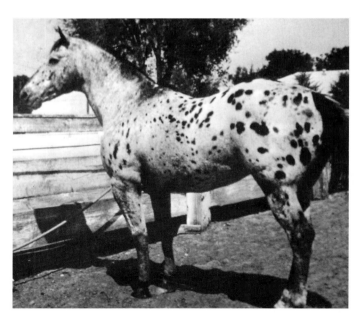

Commanche's Equal, a 1952 stallion by Mansfield's Comanche and out of Loma by Sheik P-11, was responsible for a unique family of dun and palomino horses.

Courtesy Appaloosa Museum & Heritage Center

As far as the fountainhead of the line went, Mansfield's Comanche passed away in the fall of 1959, at the age of 26. His death was at first attributed to lightning but was later amended to be of unknown causes.

Mansfield's Comanche was not registered with ApHC during his lifetime, but in 1960, Elvin Blevins—who had based his entire breeding program on the famous sire's blood—submitted a posthumous registration application.

On May 7, 1960, Mansfield's Comanche was issued registration number F-3096.

Un-registered and un-shown for his entire life, Mansfield's Comanche must nevertheless be acknowledged as one of the breed's foremost foundation sires.

In recognition of that fact, he was inducted into the ApHC Hall of Fame in 1988.

Comanche's Dawn, a 1960 mare by Commanche's Equal and out of a bay mare, was shown by breeder-owner Cal Barton of Paul's Valley, Oklahoma, to Champion Yearling Filly honors at the 1961 National Show in Fort Worth, Texas.

Courtesy Appaloosa Museum & Heritage Center

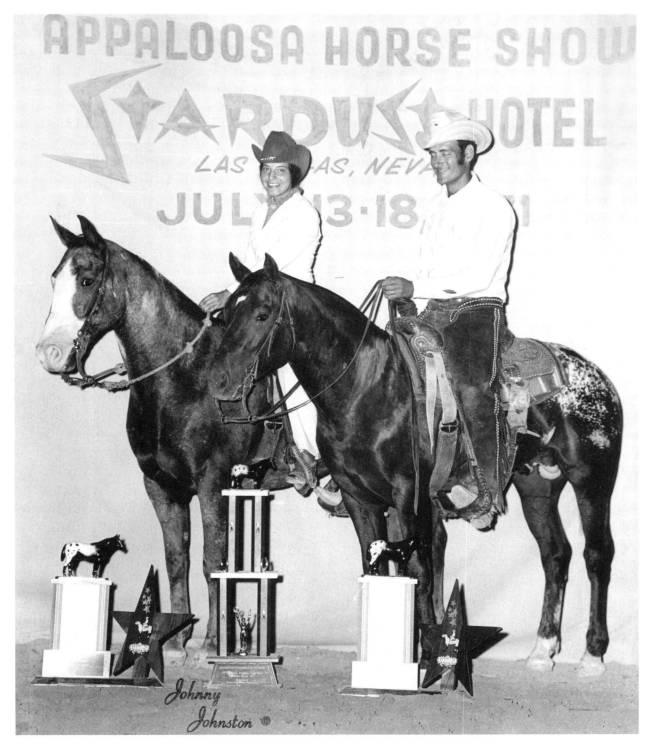

Caliente's Baldy (left), a 1963 gelding by Caliente Jr. and out of Lucky, was the Champion Performance Horse at the 1971 National Show in Las Vegas, Nevada. Caliente's Revel, a 1967 stallion by Caliente Jr. and out of Revel Ann, was the Reserve Champion Performance Horse at the same show. "Baldy" was ridden to his title by Debbie Bloom of Waverly, Kansas, while "Revel" was exhibited by Chet Bennett of Independence, Kansas.

Courtesy Appaloosa Museum & Heritage Center

Chapter 10

DOUBLE SIX DOMINO
F-2646

Double Six Domino was the eldest registered son of Mansfield's Comanche and a legendary sire in his own right.
ApHC registration file photo

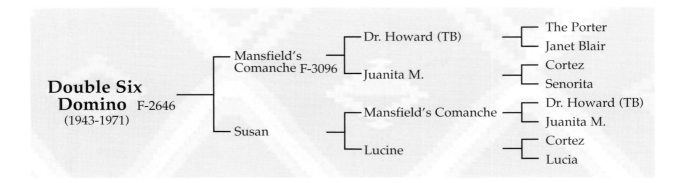

Double Six
Domino F-2646
(1943-1971)

Mansfield's
Comanche F-3096
— Dr. Howard (TB) — The Porter
— Janet Blair
— Juanita M. — Cortez
— Senorita

Susan
— Mansfield's Comanche — Dr. Howard (TB)
— Juanita M.
— Lucine — Cortez
— Lucia

As noted in the preceding chapter, the Mansfield's Comanche line played a major role in the development of the Appaloosa—particularly in the Southern Plains region. Much of the family's earliest contributions can be attributed to a stallion known initially as "Domino," then as "Pete Smith's Domino," and finally as Double Six Domino.

Double Six Domino, a 1943 blue roan stallion sired by Mansfield's Comanche and out of Susan by Mansfield's Comanche, was bred by Jack Mansfield and foaled on his Alamosa Ranch near Vega, Texas.

In or around 1948, the stallion was acquired by Pete Smith of Tatum, New Mexico. The circumstances surrounding the acquisition remain unclear, but one distinct possibility was that Mansfield deemed the colorful stallion to be unsuitable for use as a range stallion. During the first 11 years of "Domino's" documented breeding career—from 1949 through 1959—he was known to be semi-infertile and sired only 22 registered get.

Despite this fact, such top Domino sons as Whistle Britches, Buttons B., One Eye Geronimo and Arapahoe Riley were born during this era.

Whistle Britches, a 1949 red dun, blanket-hipped stallion out of Freckles H., was bred by Pete Smith and sold as a yearling to Elvin Blevins of Tatum.

At the same time he bought "Whistle," Blevins also purchased an Appaloosa broodmare named Bluebird B., who was in foal to

Domino. The following spring, the mare foaled a blue roan, blanket-hipped colt.

One year later, Blevins registered both of his young stallions with ApHC—the red dun 2-year-old as Whistle Britches T-71 (later F-2492), and the blue roan yearling as Buttons B. T-70 (later F-1681).

Whistle Britches was eventually sold to Carl Miles of Abilene, Texas. Under Miles' ownership, the loud-colored stallion was developed into a top reining horse and sire. Among his better-known get are Little Britches, the Champion Yearling Filly at the 1955 National Show in Colorado Springs, Colorado; Navajo Britches, the Grand

Poteet B., a 1952 stallion by Buttons B. and out of Golden, is seen after being named Grand Champion Stallion at the 1957 Mountain and Plains Appaloosa Horse Club show in Estes Park, Colorado. Owner W. C. "Pete" Smith of Tatum, New Mexico, is at the halter.
Courtesy Western Horseman

Cooterville Echohawk, a 1956 stallion by Poteet B. and out of Cooterville Blue Rock, is seen here being held by owner Merle McDole of McDade, Louisiana. "Echohawk" was named after the renowned Pawnee Indian artist Burnett Echohawk.

***Courtesy* Western Horseman**

Champion Stallion at the 1958 National Show in Hutchinson, Kansas (see the following chapter); Yellow Jacket, the Champion 3-Year-Old Stallion at the 1962 National Show in Springfield, Illinois; and Quill, the Champion Senior Cutting Horse at the 1966 National Show in Syracuse, New York.

In the early 1950s, Blevins moved from Tatum, to Wynnewood, Oklahoma. Making the trip with him were Buttons B., Bluebird B. and a select group of young brood stock. Over the course of the next two decades, Buttons B. would go on to become a grand champion halter and performance horse,

foundation sire and the winner of the get of sire class at the 1958 National Show in Hutchinson, Kansas.

Among "Button's" top get—all bred by Blevins—were Poteet B., Quavo B. and Tequila.

Poteet B., a 1952 stallion out of Golden, was sold to Pete Smith. One of the top halter stallions of his day, Poteet B. earned honors as the Grand Champion Stallion at the 1957 Mountain and Plains Appaloosa Horse Club show in Estes Park, Colorado.

Retired to stud, he sired such champions as Poteet Baby Doll, the Champion Yearling Filly at the 1960 National Show in Santa

Barbara, California, and Cooterville Echohawk, the Champion Aged Stallion at the 1961 National Show in Fort Worth, Texas.

Quavo B., a 1956 stallion out of Sacaweista, was a top halter and cutting stallion and the Champion 2-Year-Old Stallion at the 1958 National Show in Hutchinson. Retired to stud, he sired Beau Quavo, the Champion 2-Year-Old Stallion at the 1961 National Show.

Tequila, a 1954 mare out of Miss Blue McCue (QH), was the Champion Aged Mare at the 1958 National Show.

Although not as well-known as their two older brothers, One Eye Geronimo, a 1951 stallion by Double Six Domino and out of Bobbie, and Arapaho Riley, a 1952 stallion by Domino and out of a Quarter Horse mare, were also top sires.

"Geronimo" sired Hawk Eye, the Champion 3-Year-Old Stallion at the 1958 National Show, and "Arapahoe" sired Dandy Domino, the Champion Junior Cutting Horse at the 1963 National Show in Boise, Idaho.

Getting back to Double Six Domino—the patriarch of the clan—the period of his life from 1951 through 1953 is shrouded in mystery. In or around 1951, he was sold to Ronald Corn of Roswell, New Mexico. Shortly thereafter, Corn apparently suffered a financial setback that resulted in a Roswell

Dominette, a 1957 full sister to Whistle Britches, was one of the Southwest's top halter mares. She is shown here after being named the Grand Champion Mare at the 1960 International Appaloosa Show in San Antonio, Texas.
***Photo by Zintgraff Photographers, courtesy* Western Horseman**

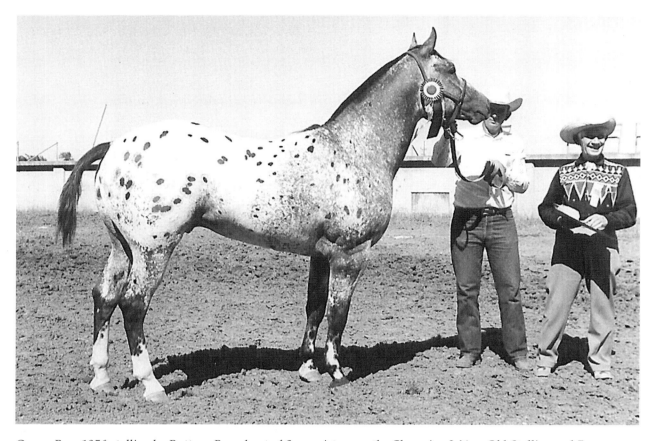

Quavo B., a 1956 stallion by Buttons B. and out of Sacaweista, was the Champion 2-Year-Old Stallion and Reserve Grand Champion Stallion at the 1958 National Show in Hutchinson, Kansas. Seen with the winning stallion is breeder Elvin Blevins and Bear Step Katouche award originator Shatka Bear Step.

Courtesy Western Horseman

Beau Quavo, a 1960 stallion by Quavo B. and out of Turner's Squaw, was a national champion halter horse and top cutting competitor.

Courtesy Western Horseman

bank gaining control of Domino. Reportedly under-nourished and used sparingly at stud, he sired just one foal in 1953 and two in 1954.

In 1953, the 10-year-old, still-unregistered stallion wound up in the hands of Elvin Blevins. Transported to Blevins' Beau Cheval Ranch near Wynnewood, he promptly got into a fight with his son Buttons B. and was severely injured as a result.

In early 1955, Domino was purchased by Harmon Scales of Lubbock, Texas. Scales bred him to several mares and registered him with ApHC as Double Six Domino T-679 (later F-2646).

From that point on, Double Six Domino's fortunes took a turn for the better.

His next two foal crops were still small—three in 1956 and three in 1957—but among their number were three of the stallion's most famous get.

Tick Tock, a 1956 mare out of a "bay mare," was bred by Scales. Sold to Jim Wild of Sarcoxie, Missouri, she was the Champion 3-Year-Old Mare and Reserve Grand Champion Mare at the 1959 National Show in Santa Barbara, California.

Double Five Domino, a 1956 stallion out of a "Scales Mare," was also bred by Scales. Sold to Alvin Davis of Brownfield, Texas, "Double Five" went on to become one of the Lone Star State's most versatile performers

and the Reserve Champion Cutting Horse at the 1961 World Champion Playoffs in Sedalia, Missouri.

Davis, who currently resides in Lubbock, remembers Double Six Domino well.

"Harmon kept 'Domino' and a few mares on a place just east of town," he says. "I remember the horse as being medium in height—15 hands or a little under—and very beautifully colored. He was the same nice shade of blue as Joker B., and had a big white blanket, full of dark, haloed spots.

"He was a nice-headed horse, but lacked the heavily muscled conformation and refined bone that Joker B. had. Still, there's no getting

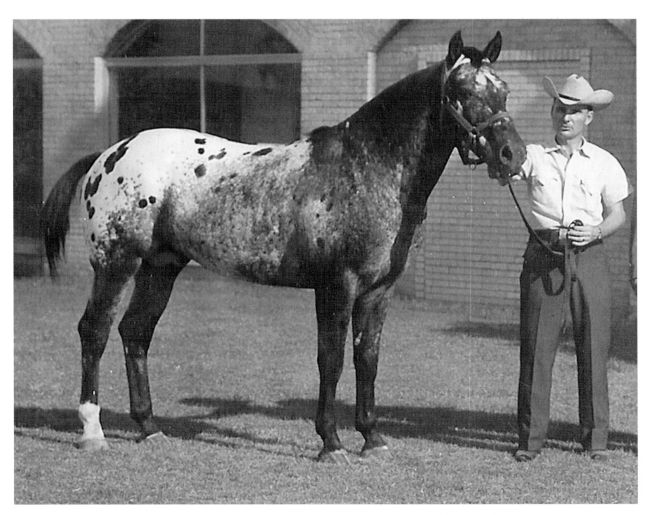

Double Five Domino, a 1956 stallion by Double Six Domino and out of a black Scales mare, was one of his sire's most versatile get. While owned by Alvin Davis of Lubbock, Texas, "Double Five" was the Reserve Grand Champion Cutting Horse at the 1961 World Champion Playoffs in Sedalia, Missouri, and a winner in six performance events.

Courtesy Appaloosa Museum & Heritage Center

Here's a "Double Six" of a different persuasion. Dom Leo Bar, a 1963 stallion out of Kathy Bar (QH), was a top race-horse and the winner of the 1966 World Wide Derby.

Courtesy Appaloosa Museum & Heritage Center

around the fact that he was a top sire.

"Double Five Domino was one of the first foals that Harmon raised from the old horse," he continues. "He was a good-looking black horse with a big white blanket. Conformation-wise, he was quite an improvement over his sire. Working ability-wise, he was one of the best.

"I was busy trying to make a living in those days, so I was never able to campaign 'Double Five' to the extent he deserved. Still, with at least six different riders in the saddle he managed to win his share in no less than six performance events."

In 1956, looking to bolster Domino's brood-mare band, Scales bought Freckles H., Whistle Britches' dam, and Freckles Dun, her 1952 daughter.

The Double Six Domino and Freckles H. cross was a particularly successful one. In addition to Whistle Britches, it produced

Dominette, the Champion Weanling Filly at the 1957 National Show in Canby, Oregon; Split Britches, a 1958 stallion; and Mr. Jacob, a 1959 stallion.

At the 1959 Nationals, both "Domino" and "Freckles" earned championships of their own—he in the get of sire class and she in the produce of dam class.

Double Six Domino also crossed well on Freckles Dun, an in-bred daughter of Whistle Britches and Freckles H. Among the top show and breeding horses to come from this mating were Copper Domino, a 1959 stallion, and Freckles Domino, a 1960 mare.

By the late 1950s, Double Six Domino's fertility had improved somewhat. His 1959 foal crop was the largest to that point, numbering five and including the likes of Reigning Beauty.

"Beauty," a leopard mare out of Yellow House Lady, was bred by Dr. Jo Ann Dillard of Duncan, Oklahoma. Trained for roping and reining by ex-rodeo great Slim Whaley of Velma, Oklahoma, the loud-colored mare was one of the top halter and performance horses of her era.

Domino's 1960 crop also numbered six and included the aforementioned Freckles Domino, Domino's Double Bubble and Charlo.

"Double Bubble," a mare out of Sugar Bubbles, was a grand champion halter horse and the high-selling mare at the 1961 National Sale. Charlo, a stallion out of Patsy Ola, was a top halter and race horse, and

Tick Tock, a 1956 mare by Double Six Domino and out of a bay Scales mare, was a national champion at halter. She is seen here with Stanley Lewis after earning Grand Champion Mare honors at a 1959 Texas Appaloosa show. ***Courtesy Jim Wild***

Reining Beauty, a 1959 mare by Double Six Domino and out of Yellow House Lady, was one of the Sooner State's top performance horses during the mid- to late 1960s. ***Courtesy Western Horseman***

Ike Domino, a 1964 stallion by Double Six Domino and out of Don's Brownie Miss (QH), was the Champion Aged Stallion and Reserve Grand Champion Stallion at the 1970 National Show in Huron, South Dakota.
Photo by Johnny Johnston, courtesy Appaloosa Museum & Heritage Center

the sire of such top show and race horses as Charlo II and Double J. Domino.

In 1960, Scales sold half-interest in the then-17-year-old Double Six Domino to Bill Tyson and C. W. "Spud" Hawkins of Higgins, Texas. Two years later, he allowed the two men to purchase the remaining half-interest.

Tyson and Hawkins stood Double Six Domino at their facilities in the northeastern Texas Panhandle from 1961 through 1967. At an age when most stallions were being retired from breeding, Domino was just coming into his own.

Between 1961 and 1965 the aged Appaloosa sired 126 registered foals. That number

equated to more than half of his 24-year total and included such champions as Striking's Domino Easter Bunny, Domleo Bar, Ike Domino, Deea's Double Deuce, Duke Domino, Domino's Candy Man, Domino's Red Dog, Domino's Dena B. and Coop Domino.

"Easter Bunny," a 1963 mare out of Striking, was the Champion 3-Year-Old Mare at the 1966 National Show in Syracuse.

Domleo Bar, a 1963 stallion out of Kathy Bar (QH), was a top racehorse and the winner of the 1966 World Wide Derby.

Ike Domino, a 1964 stallion out of Don's Brownie Miss (QH), was the Champion Aged

Stallion and the Reserve Grand Champion Stallion at the 1970 Nationals in Huron, South Dakota.

Deea's Double Deuce, a 1963 gelding out of Dena B (TB), was the Champion Timed Calf Roping Horse at the 1979 World Championship Show in Oklahoma City, Oklahoma.

Duke Domino, Domino's Candy Man, Domino's Red Dog, Domino's Dena B. and Coop Domino were grand champion halter horses, as well.

As the 1960s drew to a close, Domino remained a popular—and fertile—sire. His 1966, 1967 and 1968 foal crops averaged 15 and included such halter and performance champions as Domino's Blackfoot and Domleo Bars Sister.

In April of 1968, the then 25-year-old living legend sold for a sixth and final time to George and R. M. Dryden of Marianna, Florida. For the Drydens, Domino sired four foal crops. He passed away of natural causes on May 5, 1971, at the age of 28.

Viewed from a historical perspective, Double Six Domino was the quintessential late bloomer.

Unregistered and the sire of only nine foals through the age of 11, he blossomed into one of the most popular and prolific sires of all-time. The family of halter, performance and race horses that he founded went on to compete and win at every level and its influence extended into virtually every corner of the country.

In recognition of his contributions, Double Six Domino was inducted into the ApHC Hall of Fame in 1988.

The winner of the get of sire class at the 1959 National Show in Santa Barbara, California, Double Six Domino was the leading sire of show horses in Oklahoma in 1964 and 1965. Seen here is "Domino's" winning entry at the 1963 Ardmore, Oklahoma, show, comprised of (from left) Reining Beauty, Duke Domino and Domino's Candy Man.
Photo by John Williams, courtesy Western Horseman

Chapter 11

NAVAJO BRITCHES
F-2709

Navajo Britches was a national grand champion halter stallion, and a leading halter and race sire. .
Courtesy Appaloosa Museum & Heritage Center

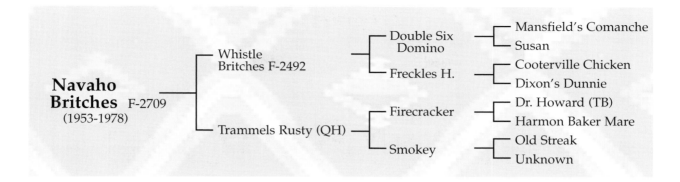

Like so many of the top Appaloosa horses surfacing throughout the Southwest in the early to mid-1950s, Navajo Britches was a descendant of Mansfield's Comanche.

As noted in Chapter 11, Double Six Domino, a 1943 stallion by "Comanche" and out of Susan, was one of the first members of his clan to leave the Jack Mansfield ranch of Vega, Texas.

Purchased from Mansfield by Pete Smith of Tatum, New Mexico, in the late 1940s, "Domino" was immediately placed at the head of Smith's foundation Appaloosa broodmare band. Among the top individuals in that band was Freckles H, a 1944 mare by Cooterville Chicken and out of Dixon's Dunnie.

Whistle Britches, a 1949 stallion by Double Six Domino and out of Freckles H, was the first of several full siblings that would impact the breed. The dun, blanket-hipped stallion initially stood alongside his sire on the Smith ranch. Among his first top show get were Little Britches and Navajo Britches.

Little Britches, a 1954 mare out of Cooterville Yellow Mex (also known as Chicken's Sister), was sold to Cal Barton of Paul's Valley, Oklahoma. Shown by him at halter, she was the Champion Yearling Filly at the 1955 National Show in Colorado Springs, Colorado.

Navajo Britches, a 1953 black (dark dun) stallion out of Trammel's Rusty, was bred by Pete Smith's cousin, Ned Smith of O'Donnell, Texas. From the

top side of his pedigree, "Navajo" inherited color and conformation. From the bottom side, he inherited speed.

Trammel's Rusty was foaled about 1928. Purportedly bred by the Trammel family of Sweetwater, Texas, she was sired by Firecracker and out of Smokey by Old Streak.

Firecracker has been listed as being by Harmon Baker and out of a "9 R" mare. Pre-eminent Quarter Horse historian Bob Denhardt, in his book Foundation Sires of the American Quarter Horse, records the stallion's bloodlines as follows:

"Firecracker. (Young Dr. Howard). Firecracker was a sorrel foaled in 1929 who

A 1953 stallion by Whistle Britches and out of Trammel's Rusty (QH), Navajo Britches was bred by Ned Smith of O'Donnell, Texas. This is a rare shot of Ned and "Navajo" taken in the fall of 1953.

Courtesy Rube Smith

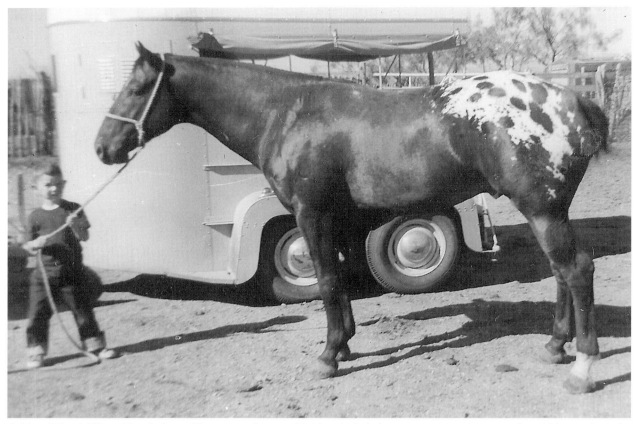

Sold to Riley Miller of Justiceburg, Texas, as a 2-year-old, Navajo Britches went on to earn more than 100 grands and firsts at halter. That's young Ben Miller at Navajo's lead.

Courtesy Riley and Mary Miller

died in 1940. He was by Dr. Howard (TB) and out of a Harmon Baker mare. He was bred by Mrs. William Anson of Cristoval, Texas, (or Lea Aldwell) and owned by Roy Headrick, Ramon L. Rasberry, and Marshall Pryor, all of Sweetwater, Texas."

(Note: As a son of Dr. Howard, Firecracker was a paternal half-brother of Mansfield's Comanche.)

Denhardt goes on to provide detailed information on Old Streak—Trammel's Rusty's maternal grandsire. He details his bloodlines as follows:

"Streak. This stallion was by Snake Bit Horse by Little Joe by Traveler, and his dam was by Hickory Bill by Peter McCue. His second dam was by Traveler. He was bred by George Clegg of Alice, Texas, and owned by J. D. Hudgins of Hungerford, Texas, and then by Cecil K. Boyt of Devers, Texas."

Trammel's Rusty, then, was an exceptional-ly well-bred mare. Owned for most of her life by Ned Smith, she was used extensively by him as a match-racing horse.

A dark, or "smutty," dun in color, "Rusty" ran throughout the Southwest during the mid- to late 1930s. Because of her tremendous worth as a breadwinner, she was not bred until she was 18.

In 1953, at the age of 25, Rusty produced Navajo Britches. The following year, she produced a solid full sister. In 1955, at the age of 27, she was struck and killed by lightning.

Navajo Britches—Rusty's most-accomplished foal—was kept by Smith until he was two. He was then sold to Riley Miller of Justiceburg, Texas.

"Navajo Britches was broke to ride by the time I bought him," Miller says. "In fact, Jim Smith, Ned's son, had even done some calf roping off of him.

"I gave Ned $1,000 for 'Navajo.' A year or

so later, I sold him to O. B. Haley of Abilene, Texas, for $2,000. I thought that was a good price at the time."

As it would turn out, Haley was in fact purchasing Navajo Britches for Carl Miles of Abilene. In 1957, the 4-year-old stallion was transferred to the latter man's ownership. Miles also owned Whistle Britches by this time, and he began showing both horses throughout the Southwest.

Jim Trammel, a well-known West Texas trainer, showed "Whistle" in performance. Gordon Davis, another top hand, exhibited both Whistle and Navajo at halter. When it was necessary to show both horses at the same time, Davis would task Bill Hudlow of Shawnee, Oklahoma, with leading the younger stud.

Panderita, a 1958 mare by Navajo Britches and out of a Quarter Horse mare, was a champion halter and cutting horse.

***Courtesy* Western Horseman**

Arapaho Britches, a 1959 stallion by Navajo Britches and out of Dorwin's First Lady (TB), was the Champion Yearling Stallion and Most Outstanding Individual Under 2 Years of Age at the 1960 National Show in South Sioux City, Nebraska.

***Courtesy* Western Horseman**

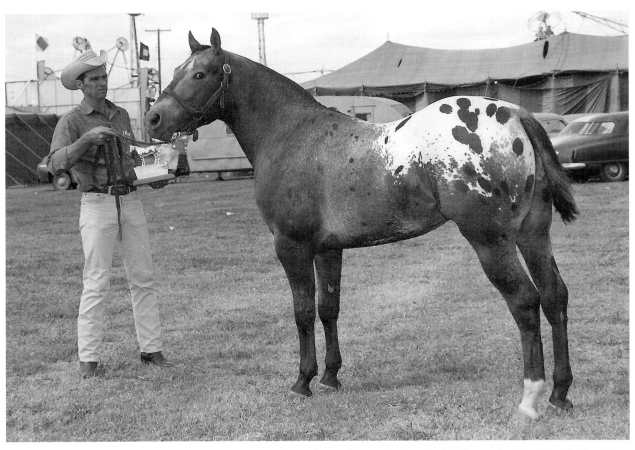

Navajo Britches, Jr., a 1958 stallion by Navajo Britches and out of Lucy Lockett R. (QH), was bred by Carl Miles. The stallion was purchased by Bill Hudlow to serve as a junior show horse and sire.

Courtesy Appaloosa Museum & Heritage Center

Nava Patrice, a 1961 mare by Navajo Britches Jr. and out of Mrs. Dillon, was a champion halter mare and top producer.

Photo by Alexander, courtesy Western Horseman

Hudlow was new to the Appaloosa game, but he took a liking to Navajo and started trying to talk Miles into selling him the blanket-hipped stud. Finally, after a year of trying, he bought Navajo in March of 1958.

Hudlow wasted little time in enhancing Navajo Britches' already-successful show career. In August of 1958, he took him to the National Show in Hutchinson, Kansas. There, Navajo Britches earned dual honors as the Champion Aged Stallion and the Grand Champion Stallion.

The next show for Hudlow and Navajo was later that fall at the Big "D" Show in Dallas, Texas. Once again, Navajo went grand over a field of such early-day greats as Rustler Bill, Hawkeye, Quavo B, Cooterville Echohawk and Vanguard D.

Hudlow continued showing Navajo Britches until 1962, when the stallion was retired from halter at the age of 9. He had won more than 100 firsts and grands during that time and was the high-point halter stallion for Oklahoma every year that he was shown.

While still owned by Miles, Navajo was campaigned in roping by Don Rutledge, an RCA cowboy from Abilene, Texas. In 1962, with an 18-year-old high school boy named Jim Moore tossing the loops off of him, Navajo won the Mansfield's Comanche Breeders Association High-Point Roping Horse award.

As great a show horse as Navajo Britches was, however, he made his most significant

contribution to the breed as a sire.

Wohelo, a 1956 mare out Wilde Figure 5, was his first registered get and his first champion. Owned by G. C. Wilson of Goldthwaite, Texas, she was named a grand champion halter mare at 6 months of age. In 1960, she was the top aged halter mare of Texas. In addition, she was also a winning cutting horse.

Panderita, a 1958 mare out of an unnamed Quarter Horse mare, was sold to Carl Miles. Under his ownership, she was the 1961 Texas High-Point 3-Year-Old mare. And, like Wohelo, she, too, was a champion cutting horse.

Arapaho Britches, a 1959 colt by Navajo Britches and out of Dorwin's First Lady (TB), was the first of his sire's get to be campaigned by Hudlow. With Hudlow at the lead shank, "Arapaho" was named the Champion Yearling Stallion and Most

Bridgett Britches, a 1962 mare by Navajo Britches and out of A's Indian Lady, was the Reserve Grand Champion Mare and Champion Ladies Western Pleasure Horse at the 1964 National Show in Albuquerque, New Mexico.

Courtesy Western Horseman

Boogie Britches, a 1961 stallion by "Navajo" and out of Ginger Girl F., was the winner of the 1963 World Wide Futurity and the 1964 World Wide Derby in Albuquerque, New Mexico.
Courtesy Appaloosa Museum & Heritage Center

Outstanding Individual Under Two Years of Age at the 1960 National Show in South Sioux City, Nebraska. In winning the latter honor, Arapaho defeated Pateeka, the show's Grand Champion Mare.

In reminiscing about Arapahoe Britches' prestigious win, Hudlow recalls the circumstances surrounding the colt's relocation to California right after the show.

"I was bathing Arapaho—getting him ready to show," Hudlow says. "Ed Janeway, the well-known California breeder and early-day ApHC director, came over and started asking questions about the colt.

"Ed finally got around to asking me to price Arapaho. I told him I'd take $3,500. He said he'd sure take him at that price, but added that his checkbook was back in his motel room, so he couldn't pay for him until later that day.

"I went ahead and showed Arapaho to his two wins. Pretty soon, several more folks got real interested in owning him, and they started trying to get me to price the colt to them.

"I told them all that Ed Janeway had already bought him for $3,500. Well, that wasn't good enough for one of them. He offered me $5,000 for Arapaho, but I had given my word to Janeway, and that was all there was to it.

"Ed showed up shortly thereafter, paid for the colt and took him back to Santa Ynez, California, to use as a show and breeding horse."

In 1960, in need of both a top halter prospect by Navajo Britches and a junior stallion, Hudlow purchased Navajo Britches Jr. from Carl Miles. "Junior," a 1958 stallion out of Lucy Lockett R (QH), was shown by Hudlow alongside his sire for several years.

In 1963, Junior was leased, with an option to buy, to Lark Washburn of Grand Junction, Colorado. Washburn had already indicated his intention to exercise his option when the young stallion broke a leg and had to be put down.

During his brief tenure as a breeding horse, Navajo Britches Jr. managed to sire the great Nava-Patrice, a multiple-grand champion show mare and the produce-of-dam class winner at the 1968 National Show in Oklahoma City, Oklahoma.

Other well-known halter champions that Navajo Britches sired during the 1960s and 1970s included Navajo Britches Thunder, Bridgett Britches, Boomer Britches and Nava Dolly.

Navajo Britches Thunder, a 1960 stallion out of Bert's Babe, was a perennial high-point halter horse in Oklahoma in the early 1960s and the Champion Yearling Stallion at the 1961 Golden Spread Halter Futurity in Amarillo, Texas—one of the first great halter futurities ever held.

Bridgett Britches, a 1962 mare out of A's Indian Lady G, was the Reserve Grand Champion Mare and Champion Ladies Western Pleasure Horse at the 1964 National Show in Albuquerque, New Mexico.

Boomer Britches, a 1962 stallion out of

Boomer Ann, was the Champion 3-Year-Old Stallion at the 1965 National Show in Sacramento, California.

Nava Dolly, a 1967 mare out of Daddy's Doll (TB), was yet another national champion Navajo Britches daughter. She was the Champion 2-Year-Old Mare at the 1969 National Show in Baton Rouge, Louisiana, and the Champion 3-Year-Old Mare at the 1970 National Show in Huron, South Dakota.

In addition to these national champion show horses, Navajo Britches sired such regional halter and performance champions as Northern Star, Navajo Britches Hi Hand Up, Navajo Britches Rebel, Navajo Whirlaway and Thimble Britches.

In 1962, the attention of the Appaloosa world turned in part to the racetrack as the breed began to compete under pari-mutuel regulations and created its own World Wide Futurity and Derby.

The World Wide Futurity's first running took place in the fall of 1962. By the next year, reasoning that some of Navajo Britches' get would surely inherit the speed that their granddam had been blessed with, Hudlow began training a select few horses for the racetrack.

Boogie Britches, a 1961 stallion out of Ginger Girl F., was one of the first Navajo

Nava-Dolly, a 1967 mare by Navajo Britches and out of Daddy's Doll, was the Champion 2-Year-Old Mare at the 1969 Nationals in Baton Rouge, Louisiana. John Letham is seen at "Dolly's" halter, receiving the championship trophy from Kay Colvin.

Photo by Johnny Johnston, courtesy Appaloosa Museum & Heritage Center

Navajo Breeze, a 1964 stallion by Navajo Britches and out of Baker's Baby (TB), was one of the family's most durable stars. An Oklahoma Appaloosa Horse Club high-point halter champion, "Breeze" also won the Texas Futurity. Here, the blanket-hipped speedster wins a 1968 4-1/2 furlong contest over Pass Key and Amigo's Bull Lea.

Courtesy Appaloosa Museum & Heritage Center

Britches offspring to hit the track. Although an August foal, "Boogie" was put in race training in July of 1963. He promptly rewarded his owner's faith in him by winning the World Wide Futurity that fall and the World Wide Derby the following year.

Boogie Britches also made Appaloosa racing history in June of 1965 at Marble Downs racetrack in Carthage, Missouri, when he covered 300 yards in :15.82 to become the breed's first official AAA-rated racehorse.

Navajo Britches had a banner year at the 1965 World Wide. That year saw Ginger

Britches, Navajo Teardrops and Navajo Day win three of the seven time trials leading up to the finals, with Ginger Britches setting the fastest time in the trials and entering the big event as the odds-on favorite. She wound up getting nipped by a nose at the wire by Jake Snipe's big Mansfield's Comanche grandson Gold Strikes Equal, but had a tremendous showing, nonetheless.

Navajo Nick, a 1965 stallion by Navajo Britches and out of Just Barb (TB), won the World Wide Derby in 1968. After a successful racing career, he was brought home to

Shawnee and conditioned for the show ring, where he enjoyed similar success.

In September of 1972, while being readied for the Tulsa State Fair, Nick colicked and was rushed to Oklahoma State University at Stillwater. All attempts to save him failed and he passed away at the age of 7.

Just Barb, produced several full brothers and sisters to Nick, including Navajo Nixon, Navajo Agnew and Navajo Patricia. Of these three, Nixon was probably the best—winning the Fort Worth Stock Show and the Chicago International as a yearling, and becoming a winning racehorse and successful sire.

Navajo Breeze, a 1964 stallion by Navajo Britches and out of Baker's Baby (TB), turned out to be one of the family's must durable stars. "Breeze" was bred by Herman Baker of Oklahoma City and shown by him as a yearling to the Oklahoma State Halter Championship. As a 2-year-old, Breeze won the Texas Futurity, and from 1966 through 1970 he raced and won at distances ranging from 250 yards to 4-1/2 furlongs.

He raced against and defeated the best horses of his generation, including Brent Lea, Double Patch, Amigo's Bull Lea, Cricket Bars, Stay Ready, Zero Hancock and Gold Strikes Equal. He also developed into a great sire of conformation and speed.

The list of halter, performance and race champions sired by Navajo Britches is an extensive one. From the time that he stood grand champion in the halter arena at his first show in the mid-1950s, right up until he passed away at the age of 25 on October 4, 1978, Navajo Britches was an industry leader.

He and his descendants could halter, perform and run. But even more than this, they were a family of Appaloosas who bred true to type and contributed greatly to the breed's development.

In recognition of his contributions to the Appaloosa racing industry, Navajo Britches was inducted into the ApHC Racing Hall of Fame in 2002.

A consistent sire of conformation and color, Navajo Britches frequently went to the winner's circle in the get of sire class. Represented by Navajo Britches Jr., Navajo Britches' Thunder and Bridgett Britches, Navajo won the get of sire class at the 1961 Muskogee Free Fair in Muskogee, Oklahoma.

Courtesy Western Horseman

Chapter 12

HIGH SPOT
F-3559

High Spot was one of the most colorful and accomplished members of the Mansfield's Comanche clan.
Courtesy Appaloosa Museum & Heritage Center

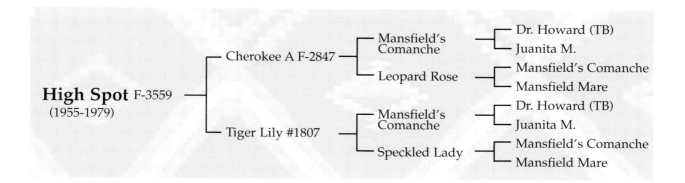

High Spot F-3559
(1955-1979)

— Cherokee A F-2847 —
— Mansfield's Comanche — Dr. Howard (TB)
— Juanita M.
— Leopard Rose — Mansfield's Comanche
— Mansfield Mare

— Tiger Lily #1807 —
— Mansfield's Comanche — Dr. Howard (TB)
— Juanita M.
— Speckled Lady — Mansfield's Comanche
— Mansfield Mare

High Spot, a 1955 stallion by Cherokee A and out of Tiger Lilly, was foaled on the vast grasslands of Jack Mansfield's Almosta Ranch in the Texas Panhandle.

As a member of the potent Mansfield's Comanche family of horses, High Spot possessed the superior breeding, color and conformation that had made the line one of the most sought-after of the day.

Even by "Comanche" standards, though, High Spot stood out.

To begin with, he was especially loud-colored. Chestnut in color, his face and jaw were white and full of small spots. His neck and chest were basically solid, but from that point back and down he was covered with spots.

High Spot was also one of the most intensely line-bred members of the Comanche clan.

Cherokee A—his sire—was a 1946 stallion by Mansfield's Comanche and out of Leopard Rose by Mansfield's Comanche.

Cherokee A spent most of his life in relative obscurity as a range stallion on the Mansfield Ranch. Sold as an aged horse to Dr. Robert Adams of Oklahoma City, Oklahoma, he went on to sire such horses as She'll Do, who once reportedly sold for $10,000; Chief of Swan Lake, a great Louisiana halter and performance champion; and He'll Do, winner of his trial heat at the 1962 World Wide Futurity.

Tiger Lilly—High Spot's dam—was a 1950 daughter of Mansfield's

Comanche and out of Speckled Lady by Mansfield's Comanche.

In the fall of 1956, pioneer Appaloosa breeder and promoter Roy G. Wood of Chelsea, Oklahoma, made a trip to the Mansfield Ranch in search of show and breeding stock. He came away with a truckload of horses, including one particularly loud-colored yearling stallion. Back in Chelsea, Wood used the Mansfield horses to highlight one of his early Appaloosa sales.

Ace Hooper, pioneer Appaloosa breeder from Plainview, Texas, was a participant at that sale and recalls some of the events surrounding it.

High Spot was born on the Mansfield Ranch of Vega, Texas, and sold to Roy G. Wood of Chelsea, Oklahoma, as a yearling.

ApHC registration file photo

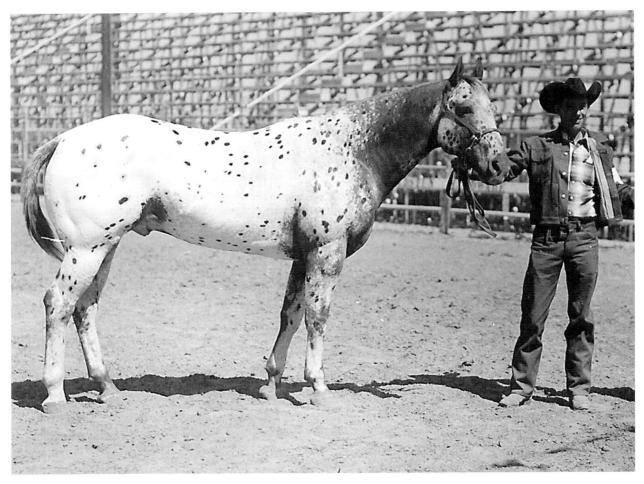

High Spot was shown by Ralph May Jr. to Champion Stallion honors at the 1960 Baird, Texas, show.

Courtesy Western Horseman

"Roy Wood was a friend of mine," he says. "We had done business for a number of years, and he called and asked if I'd come up to Chelsea and help him with a sale. I said I would and got up there a day early to look the horses over.

"Now, one of the yearling stallions that Roy had brought back from the Mansfield Ranch sure caught my eye. He was wilder than a March hare but he sure was good-looking. Roy told me that he had a sealed bid on the colt for $300; I told him I'd go $325. He took me up on it and I bought that colt then and there. We never did run him through the sale. That colt was High Spot.

"Tiger Lilly, his mama, sold to Francis Johnson of Hutchinson, Kansas, at that sale. As I recall, she was a big, upstanding mare—probably stood 15-1 or 15-2. She was loud-colored, and one of the things I remember most about her was her long, slim neck.

"I trailered High Spot back to Plainview and sold him to Dr. J. V. Miller and my brother, L. G. Hooper. They partnered on him for several years, and then "Doc" bought out L. G.'s half."

After registering their new acquisition with ApHC as High Spot T-1110 (later F-3559), the new partners readied him for the show ring.

One of the stallion's first winning appearances at halter was on June 9, 1957, in Abilene, Texas. He was named the Grand Champion Stallion at the show, with Reserve honors going to Elvin Blevin's top yearling stallion, Quavo B (also a Comanche descendant).

For the next several years, High Spot was shown throughout the Lone Star State against the greatest stallions of the day, including Rustler Bill, Top Hat H., Little Britches K, Navajo Britches, Quanah and a host of others. He was hard to beat.

High Spot's first full foal crop hit the ground in 1958. From that point on, it was apparent that his greatest value to the breed would be as a sire.

High Stake, a 1958 stallion by High Spot and out of Nell H (QH), was his sire's first show-ring superstar.

Bred, owned and shown by Ace Hooper, High Stake was the Grand Champion Stallion at the 1961 National Show in Fort Worth, Texas, and the 1962 National Show in Springfield, Illinois. In a whirlwind career that lasted only a few short years, he earned more than 80 grands, reserves and firsts at halter.

Retired from halter after the 1962 National Show, the popular young stallion died of a twisted intestine the following fall.

Ace-O-Diamonds, a 1959 gelding out of Sugar Foot Strole, was another early High Spot star. Good enough to be a high-point halter stallion, he was subsequently gelded and developed into a great all-around halter, performance and race gelding.

Among the other early-day High Spot get to represent their sire in the show arena were Hi Lacy Lady, High Time and High Lisa.

Hi Lacy Lady, a 1961 mare out of Bitsy (TB), was a high point halter mare and winner of the yearling filly division of the Golden Spread Appaloosa Horse Club's prestigious halter futurity.

High Time, a 1961 stallion out of Dallas K. S., was sold to R.L. Chastain of Indiantown, Florida. With Jack Hennig in the saddle, High Time was the Champion Stock Horse at the 1964 World Champion Playoffs in Sedalia, Missouri (Hennig's first world championship).

Hi Lisa, a 1962 mare out of Patched Hose (QH), was colored almost identically to her sire. Like "Lacy," she, too, was a high-point halter mare and halter futurity winner.

By this time, High Spot's popularity as a

This is a rare shot of three early-day Appaloosa stallions in action. Go Boy, a 1957 stallion by Big Boss and out of Molly, does the cutting, while High Spot (foreground) and Rustler Bill (right) fill in as turnback horses.

***Courtesy* Western Horseman**

Ace-O-Diamonds, a 1959 gelding out of Sugar Foot Strole, was a high-point halter stallion. Subsequently gelded, he turned into an all-around halter, performance and race gelding.

Courtesy Appaloosa Museum & Heritage Center

sire was secure and, as it continued to grow, he attracted countless new admirers to the Appaloosa breed.

One of these was the well-known and highly respected Texas horse-woman, Rebecca Tyler. Most widely known as the founder of the Paint Horse registry, Tyler's sights were set on a slightly different color pattern when she bred Sugar Bars Gal (QH), an own daughter of Sugar Bars, to High Spot in 1961.

The result of this cross was the great Sugar Hi Spot, the Grand Champion Mare at the 1964 National Show in Albuquerque, New Mexico, and the 1968 National Show in Oklahoma City, Oklahoma.

High Stake, a 1958 stallion by High Spot and out of Nell H (QH), was bred by Ace Hooper of Plainview, Texas. Conditioned and shown by Hooper, the colorful stallion earned Grand Champion Stallion honors at both the 1961 National Show in Fort Worth, Texas, and the 1962 National in Springfield, Illinois.

Courtesy Ed Roberts

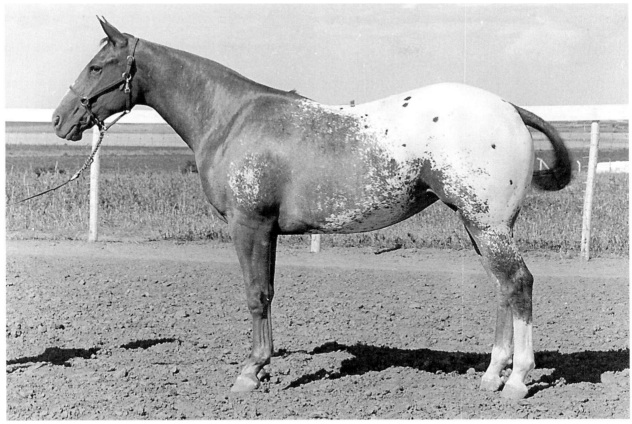

Hi Lacy Lady, a 1961 mare by High Spot and out of Bitsy (TB), was a high-point halter mare and halter futurity winner. **Courtesy Dr. J. V. Miller**

The High Spot–Sugar Bars Gal cross was repeated in 1967. Sugar Hi Bar, a 1968 mare, was the result. Sold to the Saddle & Scalpel Ranch of Keller, Texas, she was named the Champion Yearling Filly and Junior Champion Mare at the 1969 National Show in Baton Rouge, Louisiana.

Among the other champions sired by High Spot during the J. V. Miller era of his life were High Spot's Pride, Waldon's Spot Cash, High Spot Jr., Pay Sand, Miss Lohi, Sugar Hi Man, High Spot's Image, Doc's High Again, F's High Candy, Spanish Hy Tone and Whiskey Rivers.

In addition to these great champions and many more just like them, High Spot became known as a sire of broodmares. His daughters were sought after as welcome additions to

Hi Lisa, a 1962 mare by High Spot and out of Patched Hose (QH), was also a halter futurity winner.

Courtesy Dr. J. V. Miller

Sugar Hi Spot, a 1962 mare by High Spot and out of Sugar Bars Gal (QH), was named the Grand Champion Mare at the 1964 National Show in Albuquerque, New Mexico, and the 1968 National Show in Oklahoma City, Oklahoma.
Courtesy Appaloosa Museum & Heritage Center

Sugar Hi Bar, a 1968 full sister to Sugar Hi Spot, was the Champion Yearling Filly and Junior Champion Mare at the 1969 National Show in Baton Rouge, Louisiana.
Photo by Johnny Johnston, courtesy Appaloosa Museum & Heritage Center

breeding programs from coast to coast.

Among High Spot's top maternal grandget were such champions as Monte's High Regards, the Champion Yearling Filly and Junior Champion Mare at the 1972 National Show in Columbus, Ohio, and High Bar, a top California halter horse and sire.

In April of 1976, High Spot—then 21 years old—was sold to Paul and Beverly Hope of Senoia, Georgia. The Hopes assembled a select band of mares to cross on High Spot, with a definite emphasis on cutting bloodlines.

High Spot resided at the Hope Ranch for three years. ApHC records reveal that he sired four foals in 1977, nine in 1978, one in 1979 and

Whiskey Rivers, a 1972 stallion by High Spot and out of Soft Slippers (QH), was sold to Blaine and Laura Sordahl of Rapid City, South Dakota. "Whiskey" developed into a top "North Country" show horse and sire. Laura is seen at the halter.

Courtesy Laura Brest

one in 1980.

The stallion died in 1979, at the age of 24, apparently of natural causes.

In general, the High Spots were known to be quiet-dispositioned, highly colored, willing athletes. High Sign, a 1972 stallion by High Time and out of Little Naz (QH), remains a classic example of the family.

The earner more than 55 world and national championships in reining, heading, heeling, calf roping, and working cow horse, High Sign won the open calf roping at the 1979 AQHA All-American Quarter Horse Congress over 123 horses, and took home National Reining Horse Association (NRHA)

bronze trophies in 1988 and 1989.

He also did his part to see that the family name was perpetuated by siring the earners of one performance superior, two versatility championships and 13 bronze medallions.

From the plains of West Texas, through show arenas and breeding farms throughout the country, High Spot and his descendants plowed new ground and had a positive impact on the popularity of the breed as it grew and prospered from the 1950s to the 1980s.

From High Stake to High Sign and beyond, the quality was constant and the achievements profound.

Chapter 13

TOP HAT H.
#4164

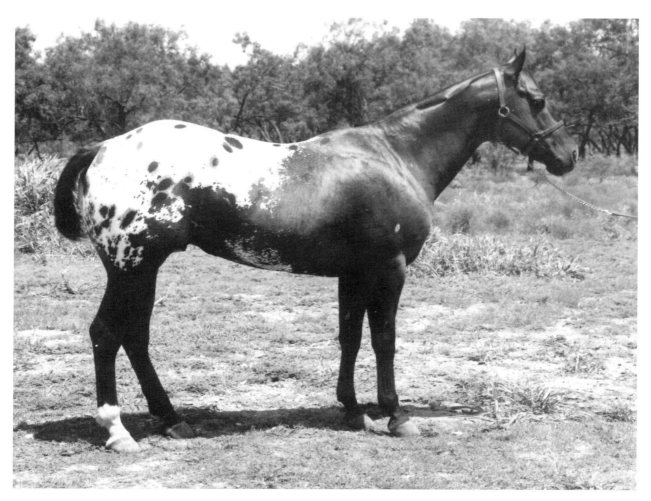

Top Hat H. was a rare blend of the Roan Hancock (QH) and Mansfield's Comanche lines. He founded his own great family of halter, performance and race horses.

Courtesy Appaloosa Museum & Heritage Center

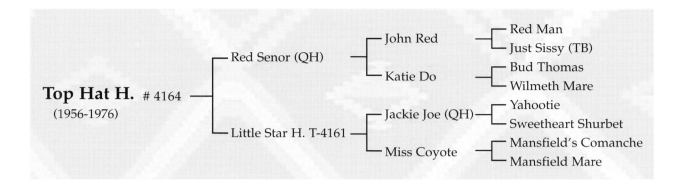

Top Hat H. #4164
(1956-1976)

Red Senor (QH)
— John Red
— — Red Man
— — Just Sissy (TB)
— Katie Do
— — Bud Thomas
— — Wilmeth Mare

Little Star H. T-4161
— Jackie Joe (QH)
— — Yahootie
— — Sweetheart Shurbet
— Miss Coyote
— — Mansfield's Comanche
— — Mansfield Mare

Top Hat H. was foaled on June 9, 1956, on the Plainview, Texas, ranch of Ace Hooper.

Ace, a well-known West Texas horseman, had become acquainted with Jack Mansfield and his "Comanche" line of horses several years earlier. In 1951, Ace loaned Mansfield an unregistered Quarter Horse stallion named Jackie Joe specifically to use on a band of 16 Comanche-bred mares. The two men agreed to split the resulting foals.

Twelve live foals were produced – six colts and six fillies. In keeping with the common practice of the day, the Mansfield cowboys did not ride mares, so the ranch kept the colts and Hooper took the fillies,

One of the most colorful fillies in the bunch was Little Star H.

" 'Little Star' was an excellent mare," Hooper recalls. "She was jet black, with a big, spotted blanket, stood an even 15 hands and weighed 1,100 pounds. She broke out so well that we used her for everything. We roped off her, ponied race colts off her, and she was one of my daughter Kay Lynn's favorite riding horses.

"But we were so busy with racehorses back then that we never showed the mare. I think she would have done well if we'd given her half a chance."

In 1955, Hooper bred Little Star to an appendix-registered Quarter Horse stallion named Red Senor. Top Hat H. was the result.

" 'Top Hat' was Little Star's only foal," Hooper says. "Several years after he was born, I re-bred her to a running Quarter Horse I owned. Eleven months later, she gave birth to twin spotted fillies. I was away when she had them, and I lost her and both foals."

Top Hat's sire, Red Senor, was a red roan son of John Red. Hooper owned both stallions and remembers each as big, athletic horses with more than their fair share of speed.

Top Hat H.'s early life was rather uneventful.

"Top Hat was a laid-back kind of colt," Hooper says. "He was easy to teach and easy to break. Pete Phelps, who was training race-horses for me at the time, broke Top Hat when he was 2. Then we started showing him at halter, and he was tough to beat. We stood grand with him at the San Antonio Livestock Exposition, won the Tri-State Fair at Amarillo three or four times, and also won at a bunch of smaller shows.

"Top Hat was hard to fault as a conformation horse. He had the greatest neck and throatlatch in the world; a good, strong back and loin; heavy gaskins and a big old hip."

Even before he was retired from his career as a show horse, Top Hat was started on his way as a breeding horse. From 1959 through 1961, 25 of his get were born.

The most notable of these was Pan Zareta, a 1961 mare out of More Flame (QH). Sold to Bill Blackmon of Odessa, Texas, she was the 1964 World Champion Junior Cutting Horse and the 1965 National Champion Junior Cutting Horse.

By the early 1960s, Top Hat H. had established himself as one of the breed's most promising young show horses and sires. And so it came as quite a surprise to many when Ace Hooper decided to sell him.

"In 1961," Hooper says, "I had both Top Hat H. and a 3-year-old colt named High Stake in my barn. Both horses were highly colored, both were tough halter horses and

Pan Zareta, a 1961 mare by Top Hat H. and out of More Flame (QH), was a National and World Champion Junior Cutting Horse.

Photo by Johnny Johnston, courtesy Appaloosa Museum & Heritage Center

both had a lot of athletic ability. I didn't feel that I needed two studs of their caliber at the same time, and with the National Show and Sale coming to Fort Worth that year, I decided to show High Stake at halter and consign Top Hat to the sale.

"And, for once, everything went according to plan. High Stakes was named the Grand Champion Stallion and Top Hat H. topped the sale."

Cecil Dobbin of Colorado Springs, Colorado, was the auctioneer of the 1961 National Sale. Among the spectators at that prestigious event were Fort Worth business-man W. F. "Bud" Hicks and his wife, Delores. The Hickses were long-time acquaintances of Dobbin, but did not own any horses and had

not come to the sale to buy any.

Whether it was Dobbin's enthusiasm over the horse, the excitement of the auction, or some gut instinct on the part of a successful businessman that prompted Hicks to pur-chase Top Hat H. at that sale remains unknown. It was probably a combination of all three factors.

In any event, for $9,000 the Hickses found themselves the new owners of a very popular grand champion 5-year-old Appaloosa stal-lion. The only problem was that they were not sure what to do with him.

"After the sale, I hunted up Cecil," Bud Hicks says, "And I said, 'Well, 'Cec,' now that I own an Appaloosa stallion, what am I going to do with him?' "

A hasty conference ensued, with the result being that Dobbin took possession of Top Hat and hauled him back to Colorado to be shown by his ranch manager, Harry Reed

In the fall of 1961, Reed took Top Hat to the Colorado State Fair in Pueblo, where he was named Grand Champion Stallion. Reed and Cecil then located and purchased several Quarter Horse mares for the Hickses, to be bred to Top Hat that fall.

Back in the Lone Star State, the Hickses had began to formulate plans for a full-fledged Appaloosa breeding program to be centered on Top Hat H. and headquartered in Texas. In the spring of 1962, Reed returned Top Hat to the Hickses and stayed on to manage their newly acquired

ApHC Hall of Fame horseman, Harry Reed not only showed Top Hat H. at halter, but managed to put a good handle on him as well.

Courtesy Harry Reed

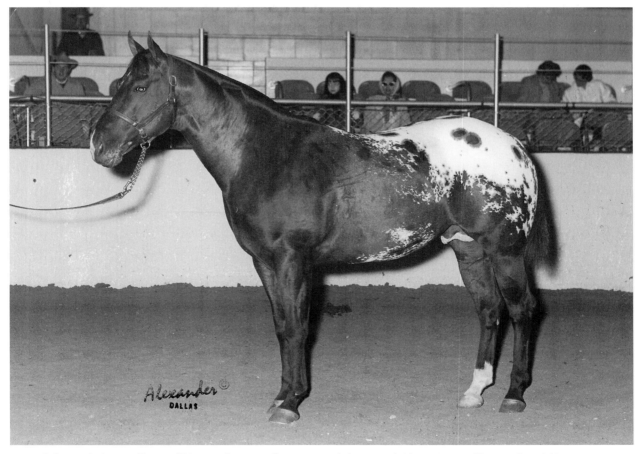

One of the top halter stallions of his era, "Top Hat" was named the Grand Champion Stallion at the 1963 Southwestern Exposition and Fat Stock Show in Fort Worth, Texas.

Courtesy Western Horseman

"TOP ETTA"

ALBUQUERQUE, N.M.   SEP. 12, 1965   L.J.BURR, UP
NAVAJO DAY (2nd)   350 Yds 19:36   PEPPY HAND (3)
J.E.BAKER, OWNER   C.L.BURR, TRAINER

Top Etta, a 1963 mare by Top Hat H. and out of Jane Star (QH), was an early-day race star and a top producer, as well. She is seen here as a 2-year-old, defeating Nava Day and Peppy Hand in a 350-yard sprint.

Courtesy Appaloosa Museum & Heritage Center

"TOP SCAT"

SUNLAND PARK, N.M.   APR. 27, 1968   L. BYERS, UP
HAYES ROMAN CLOUD (2nd)   440 Yds 23.13   ZERO HANCOCK (3)
          L. RUTHERFORD, OWNER & TRAINER

Top Scat, a 1964 stallion by Top Hat H. and out of Maxine B, was yet another top racehorse. In this 440-yard contest, held in 1968 at Sunland Park, New Mexico, he emerges victorious over celebrated runners Hayes Roman Cloud and Zero Hancock.

Courtesy Appaloosa Museum & Heritage Center

Top Star H, a 1964 full brother to Top Etta, was a legitimate two-way threat. A stakes-winning racehorse, he is seen here in racing shape earning Grand Champion Stallion honors at the 1967 New Mexico State Fair in Albuquerque.

Photo by Far West Photography, courtesy Western Horseman

Triangle H Ranch in Euless.

"We felt that we wanted to place our emphasis on speed and conformation," Reed says, "and we felt the quickest way to do that would be to assemble the best group of Quarter Horse mares that we could find and breed them to Top Hat H."

In a remarkably short period of time, the Hickses, under Reed's guidance, did just that. Official AAA-rated race mares, AQHA champion producers, and daughters of such famous sires as Bert, Joak, Bartender, Dexter, Osage Star, Little Wimpy and Hired Hand were acquired.

Almost overnight, a breeding program was assembled that would take the Texas show and race scene by storm for the next three years.

The first foal sired by Top Hat H. for the Hickses was Top Hank. Out of Debbie Hank (QH) and foaled in July of 1962, he was the

National Champion 2-Year-Old Stallion at the 1964 National Show in Albuquerque, New Mexico, and the Grand Champion Stallion at the Southwestern Exposition and Fat Stock Show in Fort Worth, Texas; the San Antonio Livestock Exposition in San Antonio, Texas; and the Houston Livestock Show & Rodeo in Houston, Texas.

Top Etta, Top Star H. and Top Pat—full siblings by Top Hat H. and out of Jane Star (QH)—were three more early Hicks-bred champions.

Top Etta, a 1963 mare, was a world-record-holding race mare and a top producer of such horses as Roman Jet and Top Chick (the Appaloosa). Top Star H, a 1964 stallion, was a top halter horse and racehorse, and a world champion sire. Top Pat wound up in Colorado and became one of that region's great all-around halter and performance horses.

Top Debbie, a 1963 full sister to Top Hank, went on to claim national champion produce of dam honors. Top Bert, a 1963 stallion out of Maxine B (QH), became a record-holding racehorse. Top Baby, a 1965 mare out of Bonnie Dexter, was the Champion 3-Year-Old Mare at the 1968 National Show in Oklahoma City, Oklahoma, and the Champion Aged Mare at the 1969 Nationals in Baton Rouge, Louisiana.

On Top N, a 1965 gelding, won four national titles, including Grand Champion Gelding at the 1970 National Show in Huron, South Dakota, and the 1971 Nationals in Las Vegas, Nevada.

Among the other race, halter and performance champions produced by Top Hat H. and the Triangle H Ranch between 1963 and 1965 were such horses as Top Valley, Top Scat, Top Bonnie and Top Time Bob.

By 1965, however, the pressures of Bud Hicks' business commitments dictated a change in his Appaloosa program. After much deliberation, the Hickses decided to have a complete dispersal, to be held at the Texas State Fairgounds sale barn in Dallas on May 22, 1965.

Top Hat H., as expected, topped the sale, going to Thayer and Elizabeth Hobson's famous Deer Ledge Ranch in Comfort, Texas.

The rest of the Triangle H/Top Hat H. family was dispersed to the four corners of the country, where their impact as show, race and breeding horses was positive and permanent.

Top Baby, a 1965 mare by Top Hat H. and out of Bonnie Dexter, was owned by Ken and Helen Kebler of Colorado Springs, Colorado. She was the Champion 3-Year-Old Mare at the 1968 National Show in Oklahoma City, Oklahoma, and the Champion Aged Mare at the 1969 Nationals in Baton Rouge, Louisiana.

***Photo by Johnny Johnston, courtesy* Western Horseman**

After relocating to his new home in Deer Ledge, Top Hat H. made one of his most significant contributions to the Appaloosa world in the form of a black, blanket-hipped colt by the name of Top Quest.

Top Quest was sold in utero to none other than Bud Hicks.

"Bud had tried to buy the great Ledge Deck before he was born," Harry Reed says, "but Elizabeth wouldn't agree to it because they had had to work so hard to talk the owner of Top Deck (TB) into accepting an Appaloosa mare for breeding. Of course, Ledge Deck went on to be one of the all-time great racehorses.

"The next year, Bud tried the same pitch on Elizabeth for the Top Hat H. foal that Gimpy's Wimpy was carrying, and this time Elizabeth agreed. That was how Bud wound up with Top Quest."

As a 2-year-old, Top Quest was sold to L. G, Mosley of Lancaster, Texas, and Sam Nelson of Dallas, Texas. In time, Nelson became the sole owner of the horse and developed him into one of the premier sires of the breed. Among his champion get were Sun Down Q., Misty Quest, Tuff Quest, Laura Quest, Moola Quest, The T.Q. Dude and Questionairo II.

Top San, a 1970 stallion out of Georgette

Siemon (QH), was yet another noteworthy son of Top Hat to be born during the Hobson era.

Top San was bred by Dr. Martin Kralicke's Saddle and Scalpel Ranch of Muenster, Texas. Kralicke and his daughter, Margaret Cotter, were long-time Appaloosa fanciers and had owned and showed top national champions such as Sugar Hi Spot and Miss Double Deck.

To them, Top San represented the ultimate in a show horse and sire.

"He was such a unique individual," Margaret Cotter says. "He had that super disposition, lots of smarts, lots of heart and tons of ability."

Turned over to Bob Smith to be shown, Top San was the National Champion Yearling Stallion and National Grand Champion Junior Stallion at the 1971 Las Vegas, Nevada, National Show.

Retired to stud, he sired such great show horses as Dandy San and the three full sisters Flying Bar San, Flying San and Fly To Paradise.

Top Hat H. was at Deer Ledge for only two years. Shortly after entering the Appaloosa business, Thayer Hobson passed away and most of the Deer Ledge horses, including Top Hat, were sold at a near-dispersal held at the ranch in August of 1967. Top Hat H. once again topped the sale—selling for $11,000.

His purchaser, for what he later admitted was a purely sentimental reason, was Bud Hicks. This was, however, to be the last time the great stallion would change hands.

Hicks' situation as far as the horse business went was really no different than it was eight years earlier when he had bought Top Hat. He had no place to keep him and no mares to breed to him. But he did know Bob Smith in Keller, Texas.

"Bud called me the day after the Deer Ledge sale," Smith recalls. "He said, 'Bob, I need you to go down to Comfort, Texas, and pick up a horse I bought there yesterday.'

This is a circa 1970 or 1971 shot of Top Hat H. at the Bob Smith Ranch in Azle, Texas.

Courtesy Bob Smith

On Top N, a 1965 gelding by Top Hat H. and out of Sister Taylor was a mutiple National Champion halter gelding. That's young Travis Cole hanging on to the lead shank.

Courtesy Ed Roberts

"I remember asking Bud what horse he'd bought, and he said, 'Well, you're not going to believe it, but I've bought old Top Hat back. I don't really have a place for him, so why don't you just bring him up to your place and stand him to outside mares for me?'

"I agreed, and the old horse stayed here until he died."

The stallion's twilight years were ones of quiet accomplishment and good care.

"When Elizabeth Hobson bought Top Hat from Bud," Smith says, "she took him down to Comfort, pulled his shoes and turned him out with a bunch of mares on that rocky old ground they have down there.

"Top Hat came up lame, and someone convinced her that the only thing to do would be to fire his legs. They wound up crippling the old horse, but he still managed to get around and breed those mares after I got him up here.

"Top Hat was a horse with a great personality. One of the funniest things about him was the way he snored when he slept.

"One year I had him at the Fort Worth Stock Show, just as an exhibit. When I arrived at his stall one morning to feed him, a guy walked up to me and told me that Top Hat had colicked overnight and he couldn't get ahold of anyone, so he just walked him all night.

"I asked him how he knew the horse was sick and he described the horrible groaning noise Top Hat was making as he lay in his stall. Turned out the old horse was just sawing logs, and by the time I got there the next morning, both he and the guy were so tired they couldn't see straight."

On May 19, 1976, the Smiths found Top Hat dead in his stall.

"There was no sign of a struggle," Smith says. "I firmly believe old Top Hat just went to sleep and never woke up. He was in good health and had covered two mares the day before; both had foals the next year."

Top Hat H. lies buried on the Bob Smith Ranch, with a small tombstone marking his final resting-place.

In recognition of his many contributions to the breed as both a show horse and sire, he was inducted into the ApHC Hall of Fame in 1988.

Chapter 14

RUSTLER BILL
F-3372

Rustler Bill was born on the Northern Plains, but went on to become one of the best-known show horses and sires in Texas.

Courtesy Appaloosa Museum & Heritage Center

Rustler Bill F-3372
(1954-1984)

- Matador Dun
  - Unknown
    - Unknown
    - Unknown
  - Unknown
    - Unknown
    - Unknown
- Cheyene Gold F-2671
  - Unknown
    - Unknown
    - Unknown
  - Unknown
    - Unknown
    - Unknown

If any one time in the history of the Appaloosa show horse could be designated as the "Coming of Age" era, it would be the mid-1950s through the mid-1960s. If any one place could claim embracing that era, it would be the state of Texas.

While the breed as a whole experienced unparalleled growth and prosperity during this time, nowhere was it more evident—nowhere were the numbers any greater or the quality any deeper—than in the show rings of Texas.

On any given show day in Texas during those years, the likes of Little Britches K, Chief of Fourmile, Quanah, High Spot, Carey's Little Chief, Quavo B., Tejas Punto, Chief of Swan Lake, Navajo Britches, High Hand, Top Hat H., Joker B. and Bright Eyes Brother might be competing against each other in halter and performance.

Throughout the period, however, any horse on the pathway to success in the Lone Star State had to negotiate around Rustler Bill.

Riley Miller of Justiceburg, Texas—the man who broke Rustler Bill to ride—owned several of the famous stallion's full brothers, including Johnny Iron Lightning (whose name was later changed to Cheyenne D. Bill).

Courtesy Riley Miller

127

In December of 1958, Fred Wimberly of Fort Worth, Texas, purchased Rustler Bill for his 15-year-old son, David, to show. At the 1960 Houston Livestock Exposition in Houston, Texas, "Rustler" was named as the Grand Champion Stallion over a field of such early-day greats as Tejas Punto, Cooterville Echohawk, Chief of Swan Lake and Joker Boy.
***Courtesy* Western Horseman**

Rustler Bill was not a native Texan. Appaloosa Horse Club records show him to be a 1954 bay stallion by Matador Dun and out of Cheyene Gold. His breeder is listed as Kenneth West of Eagle Butte, South Dakota.

Official records notwithstanding, there has always been a certain amount of uncertainty surrounding Rustler Bill's pedigree.

On his original registration application, his sire was listed as a bay Quarter Horse stallion and his dam as a sorrel Appaloosa mare. At a later date, the stallion was identified as Matador Dun—by a Matador Horse and out of a Matador Mare—and the Appaloosa mare was registered as Cheyene Gold F-2671.

But is the pedigree a valid one?

Arthur Reeves, pioneer South Dakota Quarter Horse breeder and 2001 South Dakota Horseman of the Year, thinks not.

"Bud Annis, a part-Sioux Indian, lived on the Cheyenne River Reservation," Reeves says. "He lived on the southern edge of the reservation, on land that bordered the Cheyenne River. Bud's brother-in-law, Kenneth West, lived 10 or 12 miles from him. I knew both men personally. In fact, Gene, my youngest son, is married to one of Bud's daughters.

"In the late 1940s and early 1950s, two huge Southern cattle outfits had most of the Cheyenne River Reservation's pasture lands leased. The Matador Ranch of Channing, Texas, had the northern portion leased, and the Diamond A Ranch of Thatcher, Colorado, and Wagon Mound, New Mexico, had the southern portion tied up. Both leases involved more than a million acres.

"The Matador shipped a bunch of ranch horses up to South Dakota, but no breeding animals," Reeves continues. "The Diamond A, on the other hand, shipped a full compliment of ranch horses, several red dun stal-

One of the Lone Star State's most-accomplished show ring teams, "Rustler" and David competed in halter and a wide variety of performance events.

Photo by R. Glenn Keylon, courtesy Appaloosa Museum & Heritage Center

In addition to being a top halter horse, Rustler Bill was also a talented performer. Here he is competing in cutting at a circa late 1950s Texas Appaloosa show.

Photo by Alexander, courtesy Appaloosa Museum & Heritage Center

lions, and a boxcar load of red dun and grullo broodmares.

"In the mid-1950s, the Diamond A relinquished their lease. Instead of hauling their horses back to New Mexico, they branded them and turned them loose on Bud Annis's place.

"Later, the ranch came back up and dispersed all of the horses. By way of payment, they gave Bud the two red dun studs and several mares. Later, Bud gave one of the studs to Kenneth.

"I saw Kenneth's red dun stud on more than one occasion. I remember him as a nice-headed horse that stood right at 14-2 hands high. He was a 'thick-made' horse with good conformation all over. And he was, without a doubt, the real sire of Rustler Bill."

In addition to having first-hand knowledge of the top side of Rustler Bill's pedigree,

Reeves is also privy to some information concerning the bottom.

"I also knew Cheyene Gold, before she was named and registered," he says. "She was a little sorrel mare, with some white spread over the top of her hips. I can't finger her exact breeding, but I always suspected that it had something to do with Joe Hiatt's horses.

"Joe was another part-Sioux Indian who lived on the reservation. When I came up to this country from Southern Colorado in 1949, Joe bragged that he had more than 600 horses. And most of those were Appaloosas.

"Scope Yellow Head, Kenneth West's nephew, told me that Cheyene Gold was sired by an Appaloosa stallion owned by a white man who lived just south of the reservation.

"Scope said the stud was nice—so nice that he and a couple of other guys would sneak mares across the river after dark and get 'em bred. That white man's stud sure could have come from Joe Hiatt's breeding. Everything about the location and time period makes sense."

However the red dun stud and Cheyene Gold were bred, one thing is for certain: their combined blood was good enough to produce four high-quality, loud-colored sons.

Bred to the red dun stud as a 2-year-old in 1953, Cheyene Gold produced Rustler Bill the following spring. Bred back the same way, she produced Chancie Mandan in 1955, Johnny Iron Lightning in 1958 and Wrangler Bill in 1959.

Chancie Mandan, Johnny Iron Lightning (whose name was changed to Cheyenne D. Bill) and Wrangler Bill all went on to become moderately successful show horses and sires. None of the three, however, came even close to matching the accomplishments of their famous older brother.

Kenneth West sold Rustler Bill to Ernest Hemrick of Mobridge, South Dakota, as a 2-year-old. Hemrick, a horse-trader, hauled the colorful colt south and sold him to Claude Barrington of Lubbock, Texas.

Barrington, who was also a horse trader, then sold "Rustler" to Lee Tom Alls of Aspermont, Texas. Alls registered him with ApHC as Rustler Bill T-1546 (later F-3372) and took him to Riley Miller of Justiceburg, Texas, to be broke to ride. Miller, who still owns and operates the 32,000-acre ranch that was homesteaded by his grandfather, has fond memories of the experience.

"Tom brought Rustler to me when he was a 2-year-old," Miller says. "He was just the best kind of horse to get along with. He wanted to try to do everything right. I first broke him to ride and then put some advanced training on him on two other occasions.

"To start with, I'd just ride Rustler around the pen. If he'd do what I asked him to, I'd get off and put him up. Then I'd go back later in the day and ride him a little more.

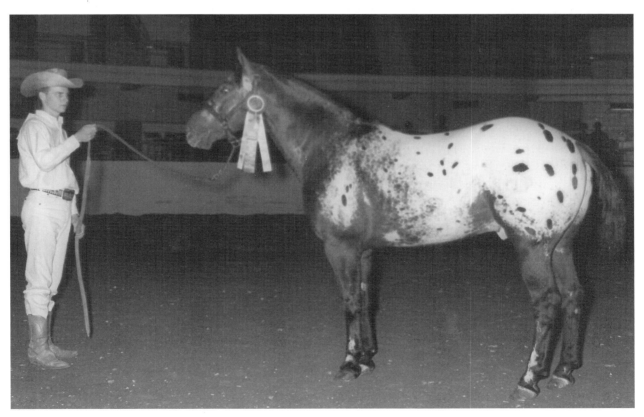

Shown at the 1961 National Show in Fort Worth, Texas, Rustler Bill placed second in a class of 79 aged stallions.
Courtesy Western Horseman

Sometimes, I'd ride him six or seven times. But the sessions were short; I never did raise a thimbleful of sweat off him."

Alls began showing Rustler Bill as a 4-year-old in 1958. In a show held June 7, 1958, in Plainview, Texas, the loud-colored stallion was named Grand Champion Stallion over Carey's Little Chief and Top Hat H. By the end of the year, Rustler had attracted enough attention to elicit a purchase offer that was too good to refuse.

In December of 1958, Fred Wimberly of Fort Worth, Texas, purchased the then-4-year-old stallion for his 15-year-old son, David, to show. Age notwithstanding, the team of David Wimberly and Rustler Bill proceeded to take the Texas show circuit by storm.

The pair's first show together was the 1959 San Antonio Livestock Exposition in San Antonio, Texas. There, Rustler Bill placed second in aged stallions—sandwiched between Bright Eyes Brother and Joker B. Fifth place in the class went to Navajo Britches. At the 1960 and 1961 Houston Fat Stock Shows, he was named the Grand Champion Stallion.

At the 1961 Southwestern Exposition and Fat Stock Show in Forth Worth, the pair encountered a class of what could have been the greatest collection of foundation Appaloosa stallions ever seen together.

First Place Aged Stallion and Grand Champion honors at the show went to High Spot; second place and Reserve went to Rustler Bill. They were followed by High Hand, who placed third; Little Britches K, who placed fourth; and Top Hat H., who placed fifth.

At the same show, Billy Tom, a 1959 stallion by Rustler Bill and out of Blue's Melody (QH), won first place in the 2-year-old stallion class.

Halter was not the only event at which Rustler Bill and David Wimberly excelled. In a 22-month period extending roughly from the stallion's purchase in 1958 through the end of September 1960—with travel severely restricted during the school year—Rustler Bill and his youthful partner won more than 100 performance trophies.

Indicative of the kind of show that they could be counted on to have was the 1960 Meridan, Texas, event. At this show, competing against the best that Texas had to offer, Rustler Bill was first in aged stallions, first in senior reining, first in the reining championship, second in senior cutting, third in the rope race, fourth in trail and sixth in the barrel race. All with a teenage trainer and rider.

During the highly competitive 1960 Texas show season, which encompassed 28 shows throughout the state, Rustler Bill finished second to Tejas Punto in aged stallions and sixth overall at halter. In addition, he placed third to Mackey's Pride and Double Five Domino in cutting and third to Pancho A and Chief of Swan Lake in the race for high point performance honors.

At the huge 1961 National Show in Fort Worth, Rustler Bill took part in a family affair. He placed second to Cooterville Echohawk in a class of 79 aged stallions; Cheyene Gold won the produce-of-dam class; Wrangler Bill won the children's Western pleasure with David's cousin Cheryl Thompson aboard; and Rustler Rusty, a 1960 stallion by Rustler Bill and out of Sadie Ann, stood first in a class of 61 yearling stallions.

Rustler Bill and David Wimberly continued to hit the show circuit to a lesser extent for the next two years. All in all, they took home 31 grand championships at halter and more than 200 trophies in halter and performance.

It was around this time that Rustler Bill's get were beginning to make their mark in the show ring. In addition to the already-mentioned Billy Tom and Rustler Rusty, Strawberry Bill, Rustler Star M and Rustler's Queen were also grand champion halter horses.

At about the same time, Rustler Zip TW, a 1961 stallion out of Baby Doll Dex (QH), embarked on his sterling show career. In 1962, "Zip" won the yearling stallion class at the Fort Worth Stock Show. Later that summer, he was named the National Champion Yearling Stallion at the National Show in Springfield, Illinois.

In the fall of 1962, David Elkins, another

Rustler Zip TW, a 1961 stallion by Rustler Bill and out of Baby Doll Dex (QH), was a three-time National Champion halter horse. **Photo by Alexander, courtesy Appaloosa Museum & Heritage Center**

Rustler Sugar TW, a 1962 mare by Rustler Bill and out of Sugar Bubbles, was the Champion 3-Year-Old Mare at the 1965 National Show in Sacramento, California.
Photos by Johnny Johnston, courtesy Appaloosa Museum & Heritage Center

Rustler Badger, a 1964 stallion by Rustler Bill and out of Miss Marva (QH), was the Champion Yearling Stallion at the 1965 National Show.

Photos by Johnny Johnston, courtesy Appaloosa Museum & Heritage Center

young Texan, began showing Appaloosa horses. Among the first horses he showed was Midnight Billie D.E., a 1961 filly by Rustler Bill and out of Dixie. With David at the lead shank, she placed first in the 2-year-old filly class at the 1963 Houston Livestock Show.

At this point, David Elkins and his father, T. J. Elkins, decided to get into the Appaloosa business on a full-time basis.

They decided that they liked the Rustler Bill horses so well that they purchased him, Rustler Zip and Rustler Sugar TW, a 1962 mare out of Sugar Bubbles. In support of their long-range breeding goals, they also assembled a top set of King P-234, Poco Bueno, Jessie James and King Ranch-bred mares.

With this set of powerful genetics in place,

the Elkins's Zip Appaloosa Ranch immediately began to make its presence felt.

The first big-time show for the Saginaw, Texas-based operation was the 1963 National Show in Boise, Idaho. There, Rustler Zip won the 2-year-old stallion class and was named the Reserve Grand Champion Stallion. "Sugar" won the yearling filly class and Rustler Bill won the get-of-sire award.

The Zip Appaloosas were not shown at the 1964 Nationals, but at the 1965 National Show in Sacramento, California, they took up right where they had left off. Rustler Badger, a 1964 stallion out of Miss Marva (QH), was the National Champion Yearling Stallion. Rustler Sugar was named champion of the 3-year-old mare class, and Rustler Zip was the champion aged stud.

In addition, "Zip" earned honors as the Grand Champion Stallion, and Sugar was the Reserve Champion Mare. In performance, Zip placed second in men's Western pleasure and Sugar placed second in junior reining.

Whimpy's Sugar, a 1964 filly by Strawberry Bill and out of Sugar Bubbles, also won the yearling filly class, and Rustler Bill earned his second National Champion Get-of-Sire award.

In 1964, the Texas Appaloosa Horse Club (TApHC) implemented a point system to award registers of merit and TApHC championships. That same year, Rustler Bill was brought out of retirement at age 10 to earn a championship alongside Zip and Sugar. In addition, Sugar was the Texas overall high-point halter horse, while Zip was the state's high-point halter stallion.

In November of 1966, citing a variety of reasons, the Zip Appaloosa ranch held a dispersal sale. At this hallmark event, in addition to the obvious headliners—Rustler Bill, Rustler Zip, Rustler Sugar and Rustler Badger—two weanling 7/8th brothers who would go on to make monumental contributions to the breed passed under the auctioneer's gavel.

Rustler Charger, a 1965 stallion by Rustler Bill and out of Miss Bueno Sue (QH), eventually was a 12-time national and world champion in reining and roping, and was the founder of a separate and enduring family of halter and performance horses.

Rustler's Risk, a 1965 stallion by Rustler Bill and out of Blue Mond Jessie (QH), went on to become the 1969 National and World Champion Junior Cutting Horse, and the first

Rustler's Risk, a 1965 stallion by Rustler Bill and out of Blue Mond Jessie (QH), was the Champion Junior Cutting Horse at the 1969 National Show in Baton Rouge, Louisiana, and the 1969 World Performance Playoffs in Lincoln, Nebraska. Shown in National Cutting Horse Association (NCHA) competition by Sam Wilson, the loud-colored stallion was one of the first Appaloosas to crack the NCHA top 10.

Photo by J. Garrett, courtesy Appaloosa Museum & Heritage Center

Appaloosa cutting horse to crack the NCHA top ten.

As for Rustler Bill, his saga continued. Both he and Rustler Badger were sold in the Zip dispersal to Ralph Henley of Wagoner, Oklahoma. Henley stood Rustler to a full book of mares in 1967 and then sold him in June of that year to Frank and Nancy Pritchard of Seekonk, Massachusetts.

Like Henley, the Pritchards utilized Rustler for just one breeding season. In April of 1969, they sold him to Dean Fitzwater of Portland, Oregon. Fitzwater owned Rustler for 15 years. In August of 1984, he transferred the then-30-year-old stallion to James and Carol

Underwood of Kamrose, Alberta, Canada. ApHC records indicate the foundation sire died shortly thereafter.

The Rustler Bill story is one of many twists and turns.

Born on the Northern Plains of South Dakota, he achieved prominence on the Southern Plains of Texas. Owned during his lifetime by no fewer than 10 people and shunted from coast to coast, he still managed to make an indelible mark on the breed as a show horse and sire.

In recognition of that fact, Rustler Bill was inducted into the Appaloosa Horse Club Hall of Fame in 1996.

Rustler Charger, a 1965 stallion by Rustler Bill and out of Miss Bueno Sue (QH), was the Champion Calf Roping Horse at the 1969 Nationals. Richard Fry is up on "Charger" in this shot.

Photo by Johnny Johnston, courtesy Western Horseman

Toby I F-203—1936 stallion by Old Blue and out of Trixie—with Ardith Racicot.

Red Eagle F-209—1946 stallion by Ferras (AHC) and out of Painter's Marvel F-47—with Thomas Clay and Claude Thompson.

Apache F-730—
1942 stallion by
Better Still (TB)
and out of Queen—
with Orvil Sears.

Chief of Fourmile F-2219—1952 stallion by Piccolo (TB) and out of Kamiak Trixie F-3255—with Kate Bearden

138

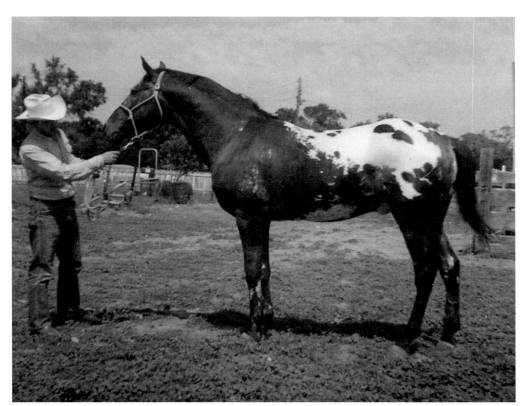

Patchy F-416—1939 stallion by Patches and out of Miss Rosalia (TB)—with Don Imboden

Patchy Jr. F-1380—1952 stallion by Patchy F-416 and out of Leopard Lady F-167.

Sundance F-500—1932 stallion by Daylight and out of Cheeco—with P.S. "Doc" Edwards.

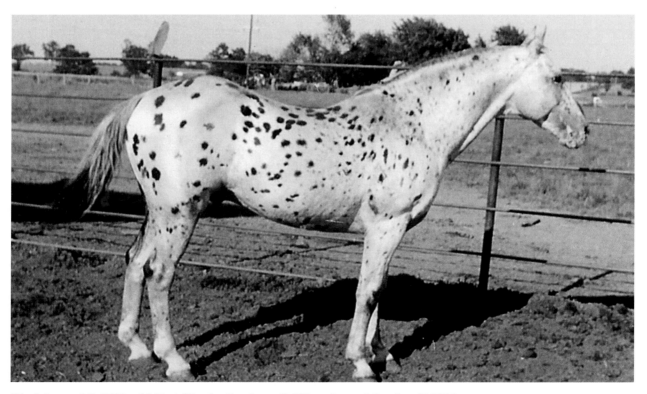

Black Leopard F-1569—1947 stallion by Sundance F-500 and out of Sundust F-1335.

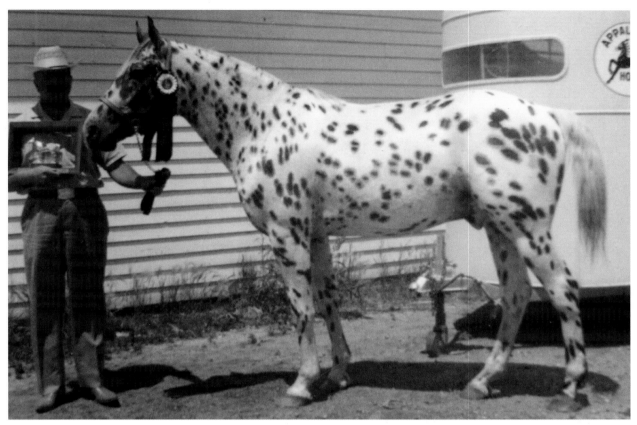

Bambi E. F-2497—1954 stallion by Woodrow Shiek F-502 and out of P.V.F. Butterfly F-3486—with Lee Warne.

Patchy Yamini's Mi Thega F-2908— 1960 mare by Patchy Yamini F-1907 out of Mi Wacon F-1892—with Mary Ann Fox.

Mansfield's Comanche F-3096—1933 stallion by Dr. Howard (TB) and out of Juanita M. T-21,700.

High Spot F-3559—1955 stallion by Cherokee A. F-2847 and out of Tiger Lily # 1807.

Juanita M. T-21,700—1930 or 1931 mare by Cortez and out of Senorita. The dam of Mansfield's Comanche.

Rustler Bill F-3372—1954 stallion by Matador Dun (QH) and out of Cheyene Gold F-2671.

Boogie Britches # 15,649—1961 stallion by Navajo Britches F-2709 and out of Ginger Girl F—with Bill and Phyllis Hudlow.

Navajo Nick # T-62,236—1965 stallion by Navajo Britches F-2709 and out of Just Barb (TB)—with Bill Hudlow.

Peavy Bimbo F-4557—1951 stallion by Little Joe Jr. (QH) and out of Chipeta.

Wapiti # 5445—1955 stallion by Gold Heels (QH) and out of Cuadroon.

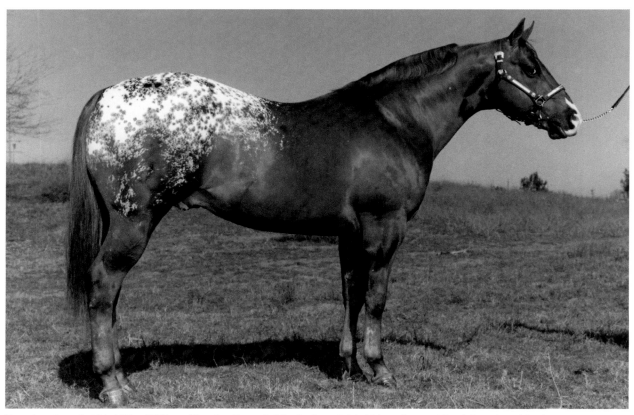

Rancher Sam # 184,695—1972 stallion by Peavy's Uncle Sam # 39,456 and out of Dude's Misty (QH).

Quadroon # 148,818—1969 stallion by Mr. Quadroon # 143,724 and out of Peavy's D'Athena (QH).

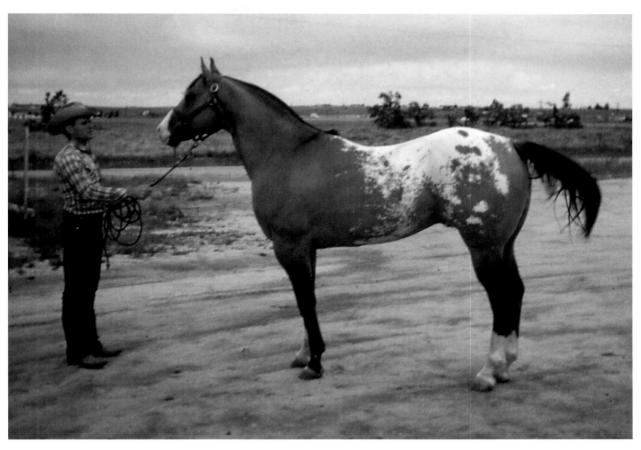

Bright Eyes Brother F-3047—1950 stallion by Billy Maddon (QH) and out of Plaudette—with Harry Reed.

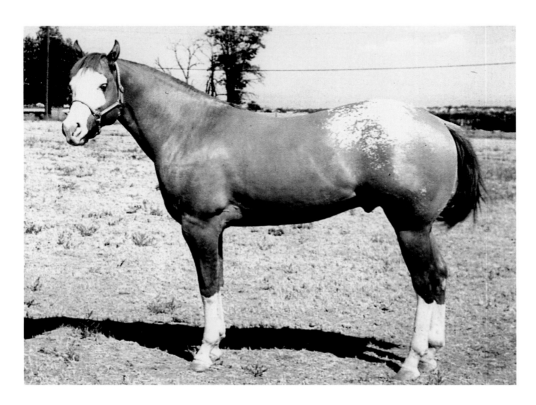

Mighty Bright # 9760—1960 stallion by Bright Eyes Brother F-3047 and out of Peggy's Delight # 6163.

Hands Up F-2217—1947 stallion by Vinita London (TB) and out of Lucy Palousy F-2520.

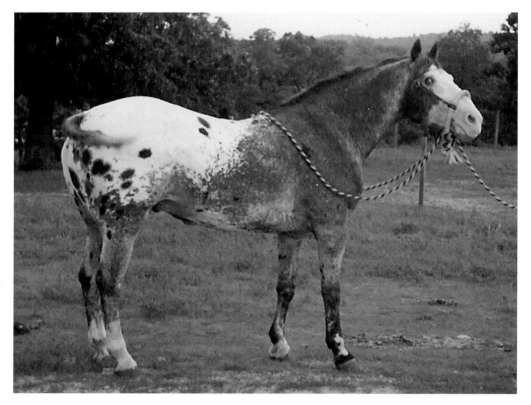

Mr. Duplicate Hand T-279,172—1978 stallion by Mr. Duplicate (QH) and out of Feather Up T-206,235—with Dennis O'Leary.

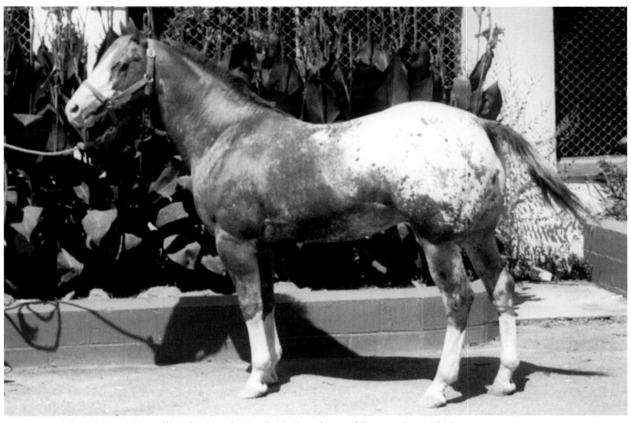

High Hand F-3366—1952 stallion by Hands Up F-2217 and out of Deacon Bess (QH).

Doctor Judge #12,545—1960 stallion by High Hand F-3366 and out of Pinkey (QH).

Absarokee Sunset # 7322—1958 stallion by Flamingo of AA F-3982 and out of Powdered Sugar T-1266.

Absarokee Sun #27,034—1961 stallion by Absarokee Sunset # 7322 and out of Senator Louise (QH).

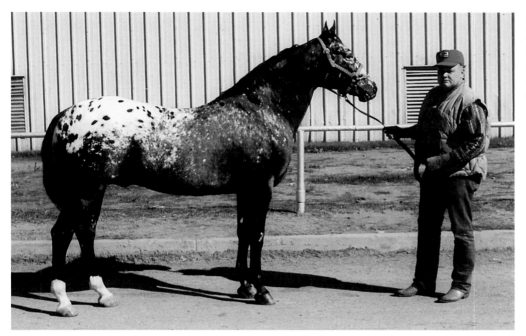

*Colida # 7681—
1957 stallion by
unknown and out of
Lady Chesty
(QH)—with Bill
Cass.*

*Flying Star #
50,237—1963 stal-
lion by Colida #
7681 and out of
Patsy Hull (QH)*

Chapter 10

JOKER B.
F-678

Joker B. F-678—1941 stallion by Red Dog (QH) and out of Blue Vitriol.

Photo by Darol Dickinson

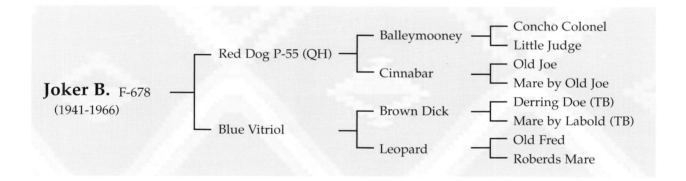

Joker B. F-678
(1941-1966)
— Red Dog P-55 (QH) — Balleymooney — Concho Colonel / Little Judge
— Cinnabar — Old Joe / Mare by Old Joe
— Blue Vitriol — Brown Dick — Derring Doe (TB) / Mare by Labold (TB)
— Leopard — Old Fred / Roberds Mare

One of the most influential sires in the history of the Appaloosa breed was supposed to be a Quarter Horse.

Joker B. was bred by Jack Casement of northwestern Colorado, and was foaled July 21, 1941, on the horseman's ranch 10 miles north of Steamboat Springs. Casement was not only a Quarter Horse breeder; he was also one of the founding fathers of the American Quarter Horse Association (AQHA). So, when he bred his great sire Red Dog P-55 to a blue roan mare named Blue Vitriol, he was hoping to get a good, solid-colored Quarter Horse foal.

What he got was a bay colt with a big white blanket over his loin and hips—good but definitely not solid-colored.

Where did all this color come from?

Not from Red Dog. That home-bred sorrel stallion was steeped in the blood of some of the greatest foundation Quarter Horse families of the time—Concho Colonel, Little Steve, Harmon Baker and Peter McCue among them. There was no spotted blood to be found there. It had to come from the colt's mother.

Blue Vitriol was bred by AQHA Hall of Fame inductee Coke Roberds of Hayden, Colorado. She was sired by the seven-eighths Thoroughbred Brown Dick, making her a half-sister to the great Marshall Peavy sire Ding Bob P-269. No Appaloosa blood here, either. But Blue Vitriol's dam was a mare called Leopard, who was an own daughter of

In this circa early 1940s shot taken on the Jack Casement Ranch near Whitewater, Colorado, Red Dog P-55—Joker B.'s sire—is shown at the far left. Immediately in front of the foundation Quarter Horse stallion is Blue Vitriol—Joker B.'s dam.
Courtesy Mel & Aggie Marvin

Although sometimes characterized as being a leopard-patterned Appaloosa, Joker B. was in reality a blue roan, blanket-hipped horse.
Photo by Chuck Bearden

the legendary Roberds stallion Old Fred.

Leopard's dam was a Roberds mare sired by Primero (TB) and her dam was a Roberds mare sired by Coke's first herd sire, Arab, a spotted stallion. Roberds had produced this horse before the turn of the century by breeding a running mare to a stallion owned by a circus that was headquartered in Denver, Colorado.

Behind Blue Vitriol, then, was an unbroken line of Appaloosa color.

Understanding where the color came from did not solve the dilemma that Jack Casement faced back in 1941—what to do with a spotted colt? The problem was solved the following summer when a neighbor

named Jack Blasingame took a shine to the colt and offered to buy him.

In an early 1990s interview with *Western Horseman* publisher Dick Spencer III, Blasingame recalls the circumstances surrounding the incident.

"We were trailing the yearling steers to Steamboat Springs, Colorado," he says. "It was a two-day drive ... and we stayed all night with them at Casement's the first night and got through a little early. Jack suggested we look at his yearling colts close by in a pasture."

Earlier accounts of what transpired next indicate that the Casement Appaloosa was, in effect, sold to finance the purchase of a vacuum cleaner. Not true, according to Blasingame.

"I asked about the Appaloosa colt, and Jack said he didn't own the son-of-a-gun—that he had given him to his wife and he was going to get him off the ranch. I asked what she would likely want for him, and he said about $250, as she wanted one of those Servell refrigerators that you filled with kerosene, and that's what they cost.

"So we went to the house and Xenia was really happy to know she owned the Appaloosa colt, and the refrigerator idea pleased her very much. So I just paid her for him and said I'd be back to get him as soon as I got through riding the high country to keep cattle from getting snowed in.

"Bear in mind that $250 was a half-year's wages in 1942, so I had quite an investment....

"In about two weeks, Bob Cantrell of Reno, Nevada, came by Casement's and he was very interested in my new colt. Before he left the next morning, he made me put a price on him. I priced him at $750, and he said if he bought him he would load him and send me a check. So he looked again and bought him and took him to Reno."

The price that Cantrell gave Blasingame for the colt was a tidy sum for any horse in the early 1940s.

Cantrell kept the Appaloosa for only a short while before selling him to Tommy Young of Las Vegas, Nevada, for $400. By the time Young got him, the colt was called Domino. But Young had once ridden a horse named Domino who he didn't like, so he started calling the youngster "Joker."

As he shed out as a yearling, Joker changed color somewhat. His bay foreparts roaned to an attractive dark blue and his face acquired the distinctive "varnish mark" that would make him so easily identifiable in the years to come.

Young broke Joker to ride as a 2-year-old and began using him for general ranch work. As the young stallion matured, Young and several other cowboys used him as a rodeo calf roping and bulldogging mount. No emphasis was put on breeding the colt while Young owned him. If a friend or neighbor wanted a mare bred, it was usually done for free.

In 1946, Joker changed hands again. Lee Berry of Barstow, California, took a mare to breed to the now-5-year-old stallion and fell

Sold to Bill Benoist in early 1953, Joker B. was promoted as both a show horse and sire.
Courtesy Appaloosa Museum & Heritage Center

Joker B. and Bill competed in the trail class at the 1956 National Show in Elko, Nevada. If "Joker" seems a little concerned, it's because the cage he's eyeing contains a live mountain lion.

Courtesy **Western Horseman**

in love with him. For $1,500 he became Joker's fifth owner. Berry registered him with the Appaloosa Horse Club. The name Joker was already on file, so he added the letter "B." (as in Berry) to distinguish his horse.

Joker B.'s role under his new owner was still basically that of a using horse.

Contrary to some published accounts, the colorful stallion was never accepted for registration by the American Quarter Horse Association (AQHA). In November of 1949, he was accepted for registration in the American Quarter Racing Association (AQRA)—a Tucson, Arizona-based association that identified horses for racing purposes only.

By the early 1950s, Joker B. had begun to acquire a bit of a reputation as a sire, with a number of his mostly-unregistered sons and daughters turning up in show rings and rodeos throughout the Far West.

In November of 1951, Bill Benoist of Long Beach, California, purchased an Appaloosa mare named Sherman's Cheetah, who was in foal to Joker B. In March of 1952, she foaled a stud colt named Jato.

In January of 1953, Benoist decided to hunt up the colt's sire because he wanted to breed his mare back. After locating Berry and getting his first look at Joker B., he negotiated a purchase and became the stallion's sixth owner. Benoist became the first person to

One of the most versatile performance horses of his era, Joker B. is seen here competing in open barrel racing with an unknown rider aboard.

Courtesy Appaloosa Museum & Heritage Center

campaign Joker B. at Appaloosa shows, the first to build a breeding program around him and the first to actively solicit outside mares.

While under the California horseman's ownership, Joker B. competed in halter, roping, reining, cutting, heading and heeling, bulldogging, barrel racing and pole bending. Vivian Dorr, one of the better-known trick riders on the West Coast, even did a little trick riding on him.

Benoist also raced Joker B. At the age of 13, the stallion reportedly won six of eight starts, including two match races against Quarter Horses at Los Alamitos Race Course near Los Angeles.

Joker competed at the 1953 National

Appaloosa Show in Quincy, California; the 1954 National Show in Deer Lodge, Montana; and the 1956 Nationals in Elko, Nevada. At the Quincy show, he became a National Champion by virtue of his first-place finish in the 1/8-mile race.

During this portion of his life, Joker B.'s reputation as a sire began to solidify.

Among the first Benoist-bred Joker B horses to make a splash on the show circuit were Joker Boy, a 1955 stallion out of Miss Ritz, and Jessie-Joke, a 1957 mare out of Sorrel Jessika (QH).

Sold to Chester Pickle of Alice, Texas, Joker Boy went on to become a champion halter and performance horse. Jessie-Joke, who was

Joker's Flying Star, a 1955 gelding out of Midge Carr (QH), won the junior reining at the 1959 International Appaloosa Show in San Antonio, Texas, with owner/trainer Phil Wright of Riverside, California, in the saddle.

Photo by Mitchell Photography, courtesy Western Horseman

also sold to Pickle, went on to gain instant fame by being named the Grand Champion Mare and Champion Yearling Filly at the 1958 National Appaloosa Show in Hutchinson, Kansas.

Sold to Jim Wild of Sarcoxie, Missouri, in February of 1959 for a record price of $7,500, "Jessie" went on to be named the 1959 National Champion 2-Year-Old Mare. Retired to the broodmare band and bred to such legendary stallions as Bright Eyes Brother, Wapiti and Coke Roberds (the horse), she would also become a superior producer.

Among the other Benoist-bred Joker B horses to attain national prominence in the show

ring were Joker's Flying Star, a 1955 stallion out of Midge Carr (QH), M. J. B., a 1957 stallion out of Norell's Myrtle B., and Joker's Flippant Miss, a 1957 mare out of Punkinlight.

At the 1959 National Show, M. J. B. earned dual honors as the Grand Champion Stallion and the Champion 2-Year-Old Stallion, and Joker's Flying Star was the winner of the Children's Western pleasure class. Then, at the huge 1961 National Show in Fort Worth, Texas, Joker's Flippant Miss took home the coveted high-point performance horse trophy and was also named the National Champion English Pleasure Horse.

Finally, the Benoist-bred Arda-Joke B, a 1956 mare out of Bayarda-B, and Moka B., a 1959 mare out of Norell's Myrtle B., were regional halter champions, as well.

Up to this point, Joker B. had accomplished enough to ensure himself a spot in the annals of Appaloosa history as one of its leading foundation show horses and sires. But in 1959, at the age of 18, he changed hands once more. This time he went to the man who would make him the best-known Appaloosa in the world.

Carl Miles was an Abilene, Texas, oilman who had been involved with Appaloosas for several years when he purchased Joker B. in February of 1959 from Benoist for $10,000. He moved the colorful stallion to his Cee Bar Appaloosa Ranch near Celina, Texas. Miles was an energetic Appaloosa enthusiast, and in Joker B. he had the perfect vehicle to promote the breed.

Although he continued to show Joker B. on a limited basis, Miles expanded the colorful stallion's duties. Joker B. was ridden in parades by notables such as Texas Governor John Connally, he carried Miss Texas Linda Loftis as she sang the National Anthem during the grand entry at the Fort Worth Stock Show, and he and the Cee Bar Ranch were featured in a one-half hour segment of NBC's

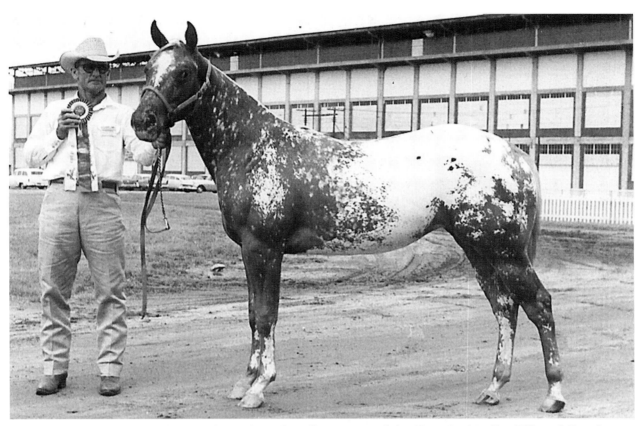

Jessie-Joke, a 1957 mare by Joker B. and out of Sorrel Jessika, was named the Champion Yearling Filly and Grand Champion Mare at the 1958 National Show in Hutchinson, Kansas. **Courtesy Western Horseman**

M.J.B., a 1957 stallion by Joker B. and out of Norell's Myrtle B., was the Champion 2-Year-Old Stallion and Grand Champion Stallion at the 1959 National Show in Santa Barbara, California.
Photo by Miehle Studios, courtesy Appaloosa Museum & Heritage Center

In February of 1959, Joker B. was purchased for $10,000 by Carl Miles of Abilene, Texas. A tireless promoter of the breed, Miles is shown here in a 1962 publicity shot with Joker and Miss Texas Linda Loftis.

Courtesy Appaloosa Museum & Heritage Center

Today television show that aired on June 27, 1962.

Miles built up a tremendous advertising campaign around Joker B. and his get, with full-page ads becoming fixtures in *Western Horseman* magazine, and framed reproductions of Darol Dickinson's oil portrait of the stallion appearing in hotels and restaurants in every part of the country.

Joker B.'s first foal crop for Miles came in 1960 and numbered only 16 head. Of these, eight became winning show horses. Included among them were such superstars as Joker's Miss Reed, Joker's Star B., Joker's Sundance, Joker Jack, Joker's Cindy Cee, Joker's Humdinger and Joker's Sleepy.

With a host of California- and Texas-bred champions now representing him in the show ring, Joker B. was on the verge of becoming a super-sire.

At the 1962 Appaloosa National Show in Springfield, Illinois, Joker's Queen Ann,

Joker's Humdinger and Moka B. won the National Championship in the get of sire class for their daddy. At the 1963 National Show in Boise, Idaho, Joker's Flying Star was the champion calf-roping and ladies western pleasure horse.

At the 1966 Nationals in Syracuse, New York, Joker's Tip Cee, a 1962 mare out of Tipsy Cee, was named Grand Champion Mare, and Joker's Monte, a 1962 stallion out of Moose Milk, was the Champion Junior Reining Horse.

At the 1967 National Show in Walla Walla, Washington, Joker's Bluff, a 1964 mare out of Buffalo Girlie (QH), won three classes: 3-year-old mares, junior reining and youth reining. This great mare then went on to become a multiple National Champion producer and one of the breed's premier matrons.

Joker's Flippant Miss was a 1957 mare by Joker B. and out of Punkinlight, was the Champion Performance Horse at the 1961 National Show in Fort Worth, Texas.
Courtesy Appaloosa Museum & Heritage Center

Joker's Miss Reed, a 1960 mare by Joker B. and out of Flax Reed (QH), was a top halter mare and a national champion producer. She is seen here with owner Jim Wild of Sarcoxie, Missouri, after being named the Grand Champion Mare at the 1963 Houston Livestock Show.

Photo by Jim Keeland, courtesy Jim Wild

Joker's Bluff, a 1964 mare by Joker B. and out of Buffalo Girlie, was one of the best. A three-time champion at the 1967 National Show in Walla Walla, Washington, she went on to become a multiple national and world champion producer.
Photo by Johnny Johnston, courtesy Appaloosa Museum & Heritage Center

In early-day National- and World Champion Playoff cutting competition, the Joker B.s fared especially well. In 1966, Joker's Tip Cee was both the National- and the World Champion Junior Cutting Horse. In 1967 and 1969, Joker's Star B., a 1960 stallion out of Lucky Lockett R. (QH), earned honors as the World Champion Senior Cutting Horse. In 1973, Joker B. Fleet, a 1962 gelding out of Tinkle, was the National Champion Senior Cutting Horse.

Like their sire, the Joker B. foals were versatile show horses. When the year-end awards were tabulated for the Texas Appaloosa

Horse Club in 1963, 16 Joker B. get occupied spots in the top 10 in halter, reining, roping, cutting, pleasure and stake racing.

Throughout the 1960s, the Joker B.s remained at or near the top of the Texas show horse scene. Among their number were such durable regional performers as Joker's Dude, Joker's Cee Bar, Joker's Queen Ann, Joker B. Peavy, Joker's Mindy Fe, Joker's Traveler, Joker's Wild, Joker's Carmen, Joker's Dun Spot, Joker's Leader, Joker's Scorpion and Cedar Hill Joker.

Due to his offsprings' accomplishments, Joker B. was awarded the Premier Sire Award

No. 1 by the Texas Appaloosa Horse Club in 1965.

Also like their sire, the Joker B.s could run a little. Joker's Moneca, a 1961 mare out of Cutie Pie, won 10 of 14 starts as a 2-year-old and set several world and track records. Sold to Thayer and Elizabeth Hobson, she was the only Appaloosa mare ever bred to the great Top Deck (TB). That mating resulted in Ledge Deck, the winner of the 1969 World Wide Futurity and the 1970 World Wide Derby.

"Moneca's" full sister Joker's Cupie, a 1962 mare, and full brother No Joke, a 1966 stallion, were also winning racehorses. And Gimpy's Wimpy, a 1962 Joker B. granddaughter, won the 1964 World Wide Futurity and the 1965 Oklahoma and Texas Derbies.

Getting back to Joker B. himself, by 1965 the now-24-year-old stallion's name was virtually a household word. Few achievements were left for the stallion, but Miles, the tireless promoter, saw one more feather to add to

the old horse's cap. In November of that year he sold the popular stallion at public auction to a four-man syndicate of which he was a member. The other three participants were Frank Horlock, Jr. and John Lyle of Houston, and Jack Ryan of Corpus Christi, Texas.

In 1966, his final season at stud, Joker B. continued to breed sound, settling more than a dozen mares. The future looked bright, but then, at around 8 p.m. on July 13, 1966, the 25-year-old stallion died. His death was attributed to a heart attack and he was reportedly buried at Cedar Hill Farms near Willis, Texas.

Although Joker B. spent the first half of his life in relative obscurity, making his living as a stock horse, he earned a place in Appaloosa history as one of the breed's most talented foundation performance horses and sires.

In recognition of his accomplishments in both areas, he was elected to the Appaloosa Hall of Fame in 1988.

Joker's Tip Cee, a 1962 mare by Joker B. and out of Tipsy Cee, earned multiple honors as the Champion Aged Mare, Grand Champion Mare and Champion Junior Cutting Horse at the 1966 National Show in Syracuse, New York.
Courtesy Appaloosa Museum & Heritage Center

Chapter 16

OLD BLUE MARE

The Old Blue Mare (left)—one of the most influential mares in the history of the breed.

Courtesy Peavy Estate

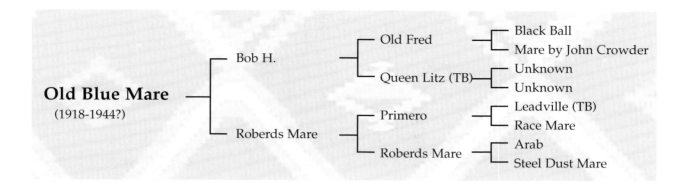

Old Blue Mare (1918-1944?)	Bob H.	Old Fred	Black Ball
			Mare by John Crowder
		Queen Litz (TB)	Unknown
			Unknown
	Roberds Mare	Primero	Leadville (TB)
			Race Mare
		Roberds Mare	Arab
			Steel Dust Mare

She was foaled in the early 1900s on the western slope of the Colorado Rockies and lived out her entire life in relative obscurity. She was never registered, never shown and wasn't even broke to ride. For all of this she remains the single most influential mare in the history of the Appaloosa breed.

She was known as the "Old Blue Mare."

To fully understand this cornerstone producer, it is necessary to take a closer look at the Appaloosa (ApHC) and Quarter Horse (AQHA) registries.

Both registries were incorporated at approximately the same time—ApHC in 1938 and AQHA in 1940—and both accepted into their early stud books a number of outstanding roan mares whose roots traced to the breeding program of AQHA Hall of Fame inductee Coke Roberds of Hayden, Colorado.

It was not fully understood or accepted by AQHA until years later that some of these horses were in reality roan Appaloosas, with the final irrefutable proof being the loud-colored Appaloosa offspring they produced when bred to solid-colored horses.

These roan horses were members of one of the oldest documented Appaloosa families in existence, one that would have a far-reaching and positive impact on both the Appaloosa and Quarter Horse breeds and one that would ultimately produce the Blue Mare.

But let us start at the beginning.

Coke Roberds was born near the Brazos River in West Texas in 1870. Before he was of school age, his father, Gideon, moved the family to a ranch near Trinchera, Colorado, in the south-central portion of the state.

As a young man, Coke went to work for the Holland and Easley Ranch in West Texas. In the late 1890s—looking to breed some good ranch horses for his own use—he acquired a set of between seven and nine Steel Dust mares.

In the early 1900s, Coke changed jobs and went to work for the A-ll Ranch in the

Mavis Peavy—pioneer schoolteacher, rancher's wife and ApHC Hall of Fame inductee—is seen on Sheik P-11 in this photo taken in the mid-1920s. **Courtesy Peavy Estate**

Marshall Peavy—pioneer rancher, horse breeder and AQHA Hall of Fame inductee—is seen on Ding Bob P-269 in this photo taken in the late 1920s or early 1930s.

Courtesy Peavy Estate

Oklahoma Panhandle. Shortly thereafter, he bred a running mare—which he either owned or borrowed—to an Appaloosa stallion known as the Circus Horse.

Various accounts claimed that this stallion belonged to the Sells-Floto Circus that was headquartered in Denver, while others listed the owner as the Barnum & Bailey Circus. In any event, the result of the cross between the Circus Horse and Coke's running mare was a blanket-hipped Appaloosa stallion named Arab. This horse was the cornerstone of all the Coke Roberds Appaloosas.

Roberds used Arab as a ranch horse, buggy horse and herd sire for several years. In time, he found himself in need of a junior stallion. His search for one took him to the ranch of Senator Casimiro Borilla of Trinidad, Colorado. There, he selected a blaze-faced, stocking-legged sorrel stallion named Primero. Primero, meaning "first" in Spanish, was sired by Leadville (TB), making him a half-brother to Borilla's famous racehorse and namesake, The Senator.

Roberds crossed Primero on the older Steel Dust mares and the younger Arab daughters

for several years. In 1908, he moved from western Oklahoma to Routt County in north-central Colorado. He shipped a group of horses—including Primero and his band of mares—by rail to their new home. En route, the train wrecked and Primero was killed. (By this time, Arab had apparently been sold or given away. There is no record of his having made the trip north.)

Among the Roberds mares to survive the ill-fated trip was a roan Appaloosa daughter of Primero. This mare, along with several other Primero daughters, was eventually purchased by Roberds-employee Jack Kitchens of Hayden, Colorado.

Around 1916, Kitchens went to California to work for the famed Kellogg Arabian Farm. AQHA Hall of Fame inductee Marshall Peavy of Clark, Colorado—then all of 18 years of age—purchased the entire set of Kitchens mares and one-half of the stage was set to produce the Blue Mare.

The other half arrived in town hitched to a freight wagon.

This was, of course, Old Fred.

The story of how Coke Roberds, searching

for a replacement for Primero, found Old Fred pulling a freight wagon for a living has been repeated to the point of becoming legend.

Old Fred was a big, powerful palomino who weighed 1,400 pounds. Coke has been quoted as saying of him, "You could breed Fred to a draft mare and get the best work horse you ever hitched, and you could breed him to a race mare and get yourself a racehorse."

Si Dawson, a friend and neighbor of Roberds, bred Queen Litz (TB)—his favorite mare—to Old Fred and came up with Bob H.

Marshall Peavy, again while only 18 years old, had the foresight to purchase Bob H from Dawson in 1916 and make him his main sire. With the roan Primero daughter already in residence at the Peavy ranch, the stage was now fully set to produce the Blue Mare.

Mavis Peavy, Marshall's wife and a pioneer breeder in her own right, vividly remembers the Old Blue Mare's famous sire.

"Nobody would forget a horse as great as Bob H," she recalls. "He weighed 1,350 pounds and could run a quarter with three stopwatches on him on a circle track in :22.3 seconds."

Bob H was killed in a freak accident in 1923. He was spooked by a huge herd of sheep stampeding past his pasture and ran a tree branch into his abdomen.

Six years prior to this—in 1917—Marshall Peavy had bred Bob H to his roan mare. The result of this cross was a little grayish-blue filly known first simply as Blue, then as the Blue Mare, and finally as the Old Blue Mare.

"The Old Blue Mare was born in May of 1918, in a snow bank," Mavis says. "It was one of the worst winters Routt County had ever had. Because of the hard winter and how hard it was on her mother, she never got very big. That is probably why Marshall never broke her to ride but put her right into his broodmare band.

"Marshall was probably ahead of his time in that he believed in riding his mares before breeding them. In those days, people rode mainly studs and geldings, but Marshall believed that the mare was 60 percent or more of what her colt would be, and he wanted to know what they could do before he put them in his broodmare band."

Despite his decision to not break the Old Blue Mare and prove her through performance, Marshall had enough faith in her breeding to place her into production. Her first foal was the result of an accidental breeding.

Papoose, a 1923 mare by Bob H and out of the Old Blue Mare, was a top ranch mount, racehorse and producer.

Courtesy Peavy Estate

Baboon, a 1943 gelding by Red Dog (QH) and out of Papoose, was his famous dam's final foal. Bred by Jack Casement of Westplains, Colorado, Baboon was a winning racehorse.

Courtesy Gene Carr

Chipeta, a 1940 mare by Ding Bob (QH) and out of Papoose, was Mavis Peavy's personal ranch mount. Although registered with AQHA, the mare was in reality a marginally colored dun roan Appaloosa.

Courtesy Peavy Estate

"Bob H had been sick," remembers Mavis. "Marshall turned his 4-year-old daughter, the Blue Mare, out with him just for company. Papoose, a 1923 blanket-hipped Appaloosa mare, was the result.

"Papoose was a big mare. She weighed 1,200 pounds and could run a hole in the wind and carry you all day in the hills. Marshall raced Papoose some and it got to where people didn't want to match her.

"She was a wonderful riding horse," Mavis continues. "You know those homesteaders used to tack barbed wire everywhere and then brush would grow up all around it. When you were riding, you'd be in it before you realized it. Papoose would stand and let you untangle all four feet and lead her out of it."

In 1924, Marshall purchased a young stallion from Coke Roberds. This was Sheik, a 1918 palomino stallion by Peter McCue and out of Pet by Old Fred. (When AQHA was formed years later, Sheik would be recognized as one of its foundation sires and assigned registration #11.)

After Bob H's death, Sheik was elevated to the head of Marshall Peavy's breeding program. Bred to Sheik three times, the Old Blue Mare produced Mandy, a 1926 solid-colored mare; Flossie, a 1927 roan Appaloosa mare; and Jenny Lee, a 1928 solid-colored mare.

It is critical at this juncture of the Old Blue Mare story to more fully understand the Peavy family's philosophy regarding their foundation horses—both solid-colored and spotted.

Peavy was first and foremost a highly respected rancher and stockman. By the time AQHA was formed in 1940, he had been successfully line-breeding a family of stock horses for more than two decades.

In recognition of Marshall's accomplishments as a horse breeder, Bob Denhardt—AQHA's first secretary—made a personal trip to the Peavy Ranch to talk Marshall into registering his horses.

Peavy initially put AQHA papers on a set of six mares—Beulah P-218, Miss Coke P-219, Diana P-220, Speck P-221, Margie P-222, and Dundee P-223.

Of that watershed group, three mares—Diana, Speck and Margie—were Old Blue Mare granddaughters. Of the trio, however, Speck was the only colored Appaloosa.

Marshall knew enough about horse breeds to understand that Speck was in reality a marginally-colored roan Appaloosa. Because she was considered by him to be one of his top mares, he decided to include her in that first group of AQHA-registered horses.

Marshall and Mavis Peavy's practice of registering the best of their marginally colored Appaloosa mares with AQHA continued—with the association's tacit approval—for several decades.

To the Peavys' credit, they never registered an Appaloosa stallion with AQHA, nor did they register any loud-colored mares. Reasoning that they could dilute the color to the point of non-existence, the couple did register a number of marginally colored and solid-colored mares with Appaloosas in their pedigrees. And thus did the blood of the Blue Mare come to positively impact the Quarter Horse breed.

Mandy and Jenny Lee—the two solid-colored Old Blue Mare daughters—were registered with AQHA. Papoose and Flossie—the two loud-colored daughters—were not. Both Mandy and Jenny Lee went on to enjoy long and fruitful lives as Peavy broodmares.

Of the two, Mandy was the most prolific. Bred to Ding Bob, she produced John Henry, an unregistered 1931 black colt; and Patsy Peavy, a 1933 dun filly. (Note: While at odd with some records, the foaling dates of John Henry and Patsy Peavy as shown here are directly from Marshall Peavy's breeding book—recorded in his own hand.)

Wahoo Peavy, a 1950 gelding by Ambrose (QH) and out of Chipeta, was sold to Peavy son-in-law Wayne Bonham of Cheyenne, Wyoming. Registered with AQHA, "Wahoo" was an AQHA point-earning halter and performance horse.

Courtesy Peavy Estate

Goosie Lucy, a 1954 mare by Colorado Sorrel (QH) and out of Chipeta, was her dam's loudest-colored daughter. Owner Mary Peavy Stees—Marshall and Mavis' daughter—is seen at the halter.

Courtesy Peavy Estate

"John Henry" was sold to G. Dewey Norell of Collbran, Colorado. A top ranch horse and promising sire, he was killed in a bizarre hired hand-related incident as a young horse. (Note: This John Henry had a full brother named John Henry McCue. Foaled in 1941 and registered with AQHA, he was also sold to Dewey Norell.)

Patsy Peavy was sold to Bert Wood of Benson, Arizona. Bred to his world champion Quarter running stallion, Joe Reed II, she produced Anniversary—a leading dam of racing Register of Merit qualifiers.

Continuing on with the Blue Mare's story, as noted earlier, neither of her Appaloosa-colored daughters was ever registered. That fact did not preclude them from being fully utilized.

Papoose, who Marshall Peavy thought highly enough of to give to his young, school-teacher bride as a wedding present, entered the broodmare band late, at approximately 9 years of age. Bred to Ding Bob, she produced three famous sisters: Margie, a 1933 sorrel; Sue Peavy, a 1937 bay; and Chipeta, a 1940 dun. Margie and Sue Peavy were solid-colored, while Chipeta was marginally colored. All three were registered with AQHA.

"Papoose was supposedly mine," Mavis says, "and I did ride her until an eye injury ended her usefulness under saddle. After she was retired to the broodmare band, she was such an outstanding producer that Marshall had a hard time relinquishing control of any of her offspring.

"Margie, with her four stockings and blazed face, was the glamour girl. She just cried to be raced and was, winning 25 out of 26 and getting beat only when she was four months in foal with a catch colt that we knew nothing about.

" 'Sue' was a marvelous athlete who had plenty of speed and could turn on a dime.

"Chipeta truly was mine—mine the day she was born and mine on the day she died. I rode her for years, right up to when she got hurt in a barn aisle accident, and then I started raising foals from her."

In 1941, Marshall Peavy gave Papoose to Jack Casement. By this time, the then-18-

Flossie, a 1927 mare by Sheik P-11 and out of the Old Blue Mare, was a top Peavy producer. She is seen here with Si, a 1937 colt by Saladin.

Courtesy Peavy Estate

Peavy's Jillaroo, a 1958 mare by Colorado Sorrel (QH) and out of Chipeta, spent her entire life as a Mavis Peavy brood-mare. Seen here with the dun roan mare is VZ Silas, a 1963 colt by Due Claw (QH).

Courtesy Peavy Estate

year-old Appaloosa mare was totally blind. Despite this, Casement was able to get two foals from her. Bred to Red Dog P-55, she produced Cherokee Maiden, a 1942 sorrel mare, and Baboon, a 1943 sorrel colt.

"Cherokee" was born solid-colored and registered with AQHA. Shown at halter, this cornerstone Casement mare stood Reserve Champion Mare at the 1944 National Western Stock Show in Denver. Retired to the broodmare band, she went on to become the dam of Alfaretta and Red Wig, both AAA AQHA Champions, and the granddam of Little Chloe— the 1962 Champion Quarter Running 2-Year-Old Filly.

Baboon—Cherokee's full brother— was born with a blaze face, four stockings and a big white blanket. He was never registered but was gelded

Peavy's Uncle Sam, a 1962 colt by Due Claw (QH) and out of Papoose Peavy, spent his entire life as a Mavis Peavy herd sire. The blanket-hipped sorrel was so-named because, at birth, he was "red, white and blue."

Courtesy Peavy Estate

Bobbie N, a 1953 mare by Ranger Hancock (QH) and out of a Miller 67 mare by Ding Bob II, was one of the top halter mares of her era.
Courtesy Appaloosa Museum & Heritage Center

and raced.

As far as the Peavy-bred daughters of Papoose went, neither Margie nor Sue ever produced an Appaloosa. The same could not be said of Chipeta.

Several years before his untimely death in 1944—the result of a riding accident—Marshall Peavy was racing Margie in Tucson, Arizona. He would exercise her in the cool of the morning out on the desert. On occasion, the owner of the well-known Quarter Horse racing stallion Little Joe Jr would accompany him.

On returning home to Colorado, Marshall discussed with Mavis his interest in leasing Little Joe Jr to cross on their mares. After Marshall's death, Mavis decided to go ahead with his plans. In 1950, she leased Little Joe Jr and bred him to some of her best mares, including Margie and Chipeta. In 1951, Margie produced the AQHA-registered stallion Due Claw, and Chipeta produced the ApHC Hall of Fame stallion Peavy Bimbo (see Chapter 19).

In addition to "Bimbo," Chipeta produced a son and five daughters that would go on to make positive contributions to the Appaloosa breed (one of the five daughters—Overdue Peavy—will be discussed in a subsequent chapter.)

Bred to Ambrose, Chipeta produced Wahoo Peavy, a 1950 dun colt. Marginally-colored, he was gelded and registered with AQHA. Sold to Wayne Bonham of Cheyenne, Wyoming—Mavis' son-in-law— "Wahoo" then went on to become an AQHA point-earning halter and performance horse and, by Bonham's own admission, the "greatest horse he ever threw a leg over.'

Next bred to Gold Heels (QH), Chipeta produced Papoose Peavy, a 1952 dun mare. Bred to Colorado Sorrel (QH), she produced Goosie Lucy, a 1954 bay mare; Pita Chip, a 1957 dun mare; and Peavy's Jillaroo, a 1958 buckskin mare.

Papoose Peavy, Pita Chip, and Peavy's Jillaroo were marginally colored and registered with AQHA. Goosie Lucy was born with a big white blanket and was registered with ApHC. (Note: Both Pita Chip and Peavy's Jillaroo were eventually sold to C.L. Williams of Gallup, New Mexico, and double-registered with ApHC.)

Like her mother and grandmother before her, Papoose Peavy was used for years as a working ranch horse. Retired to the broodmare band and bred to Due Claw, she produced Peavy's Uncle Sam, a 1962 sorrel, blanket-hipped stallion.

"Uncle Sam" was first shown successfully at halter and then retired to stud. The mainstay of the Mavis Peavy Appaloosa program for his entire life, he sired such champion show and breeding horses as Rancher Sam, Peavy's Pride II, Aunt Biddy, Peavy's Ginger Lady, Cherry Sample and Pawnee Peavy GG.

The list of great Peavy-bred horses that stem from the Papoose branch of the Blue Mare family tree goes on and on—far too extensively to record here.

And, lest we forget, the tree had more than one branch. There was also the roan Appaloosa Blue Mare daughter named Flossie, who was every bit as great a producer as her half-sister.

Like Papoose, Flossie spent some time in Ding Bob's band of mares. By him she produced two full sisters—Little Buck, a 1931 buckskin mare; and Speck, a 1933 bay mare. Both were marginally colored and registered with AQHA.

Bred to Red Dog P-55, Little Buck produced "Brown Fox", a 1943 brown colt. Brown Fox was born marginally colored and registered with AQHA. As a yearling, he was shown at halter and was named Reserve Champion Stallion at the 1944 National Western Livestock Show in Denver. With age, he

developed into a classic red roan Appaloosa and he was registered with ApHC as Cooterville Norell's Little Red F-1673 (see Chapter 18).

Like Little Buck, Speck lived up to her spotted heritage. Bred to Song Hit (TB), she produced Cuadroon, a 1943 brown mare. Cuadroon was marginally colored and registered with AQHA. Bred, owned and trained for racing by Marshall and Mavis Peavy's daughter, Mary Peavy Stees of Clark, Colorado, she won the 1946 Western Slope Derby. Retired to the broodmare band and bred to Gold Heels (QH), she produced Wapiti, a 1955 bay, blanket-hipped stallion (see Chapter 20).

Bred to Exterminator (QH), Cuadroon produced Mr Quadroon, a 1963 bay, blanket-hipped stallion. Mr Quadroon was used as a

Bobbette N, a 1958 mare by Black Twist (QH) and out of Bobbie N, was the Champion Broodmare at the 1964 National Show in Albuquerque, New Mexico.

Courtesy Appaloosa Museum & Heritage Center

Miss Champagne, a 1961 mare by Star Bo and out of Miss C (QH), was a classic blend of Peavy and Roberds breeding. Bred by Dick Southern of Littleton, Colorado, the blanket-hipped palomino was the Champion 3-Year-Old Mare at the 1964 National Show.

Photo by Ralph Morgan, courtesy Dick Southern

herd sire by the Stees family for several years. His most noteworthy contribution to the Appaloosa breed was Quadroon, a 1969 bay, blanket-hipped stallion out of Peavy's D'Athena (QH).

Quadroon was shown successfully at halter. Retired to stud, he sired such great show mares as Peavy's Cajun Queen and Quadrina.

Getting back to Flossie, she still had two more outstanding contributions to make to the Appaloosa breed.

Bred to Saladin, the beautiful palomino son of Ding Bob, Flossie produced Si, a 1937 palomino colt; and Ding Bob II, a 1938 palomino, blanket-hipped colt.

Si sired only two foal crops before dying of tetanus as a 3-year-old. Among his few foals, however, was Gold Heels—Grand Champion Stallion at the 1944 National Western Livestock Show and the sire of Wapiti.

Ding Bob II—a blazed-face palomino with four high stockings and a big white blanket—was purchased as a young horse by the Miller 67 Ranch of Big Piney, Wyoming. There, he went on to found his own great family of Appaloosas. Included among them were a number of roan mares that were registered with AQHA.

The Old Blue Mare...Papoose...Flossie...

They were three un-registered Appaloosa mares who were born decades ago to a horse world that was far different from the one that exists today. Their spotted genes were never

Peavy's Cajun Queen, a 1974 mare by Quadroon and out of Margie Miss (QH), was a multiple world and national champion mare. That's owner O.J. Martens of Hutchinson, Kansas, at the halter.

Photo by Kay, courtesy O.J. and Jean Martens

intensified and yet the color and the quality bred true.

As just one indicator of the over-all producing ability of the family, a cursory inspection of *The Referee*—which lists all of the National and World Champions from 1948 through 1973—finds no less than 26 horses whose only Appaloosa blood stems from the Old Blue Mare.

The Old Blue Mare's blood continues to impact both the Appaloosa and Quarter Horse breeds. As will be discussed in the next three chapters, such noteworthy Appaloosa sires as Norell's Little Red, Peavy Bimbo, Wapiti, Coke Roberds (the horse) owe every drop of their Appaloosa heritage to her; and such notable Mighty Bright sons as

Mighty Peavy, Mighty Shiek, Mighty Marshall, Mighty Tim and Spittin' Image trace back to her as well.

In more recent years, Joe Prince—the national champion cutting horse—and Goer—the ApHC Hall of Fame show horse and sire—trace back to the Old Blue Mare; and Obvious Conclusion and Kid Clu—two of the most dominant Quarter Horse halter sires of all time—also trace back to her.

The title "most influential producer in the history of the breed" is a heavy mantle to place on any mare. By virtue of her incredible genetic potency—a potency that resulted in a long line of National and World Champion halter, race and performance horses—the Blue Mare is more than deserving of the crown.

Chapter 17

COOTERVILLE NORELL'S LITTLE RED
F-1673

Cooterville Norell's Little Red: Bred to be a Quarter Horse—destined to be a foundation Appaloosa sire.
Courtesy Western Horseman

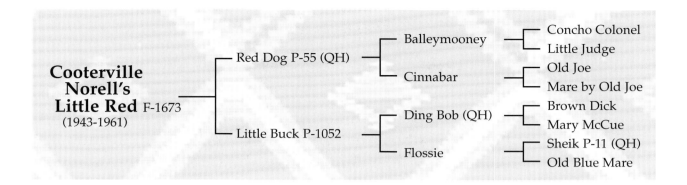

Cooterville
Norell's
Little Red F-1673
(1943-1961)

- Red Dog P-55 (QH)
  - Balleymooney
    - Concho Colonel
    - Little Judge
  - Cinnabar
    - Old Joe
    - Mare by Old Joe
- Little Buck P-1052
  - Ding Bob (QH)
    - Brown Dick
    - Mary McCue
  - Flossie
    - Sheik P-11 (QH)
    - Old Blue Mare

Cooterville Norell's Little Red, a 1943 roan stallion by Red Dog (QH) and out of Little Buck (QH), was one of the first Blue Mare descendants to impact the Appaloosa breed.

To fully understand "Little Red" and the family of horses he founded, it is first necessary to address the issue of "cropouts." To begin with, as far as the Appaloosa breed is concerned there is no such thing.

The term has most often been used to describe an Appaloosa-colored horse that is sired by an AQHA-registered stallion and out of an AQHA-registered mare. Such an Appaloosa is treated as a genetic anomaly whose coloration is a complete mystery. Nothing could be further from the truth.

Appaloosas that come from a pair of AQHA-registered parents can be explained in two ways.

The first is that a pedigree is wrong. In other words, someone—by accident or design—put a set of AQHA papers on a marginally colored Appaloosa foal that subsequently developed more color and/or produced color when crossed back on a Quarter Horse.

The second explanation is just as simple.

A number of purported cropout horses that were registered with AQHA during its formative years were actually marginally colored Appaloosa members of the Coke Roberds/Arab line of horses.

As such, they were not cropouts or genetic freaks but, rather, descendents of one of the oldest documented Appaloosa lines in existence, a line that would have a far-reaching and positive impact on both the Quarter Horse and Appaloosa breeds. It was also a

line that would ultimately produce the Blue Mare and "Little Red."

Norell's Little Red was the first "Little Red" name given this Red Dog/Little Buck offspring, reflecting the fact that he was bred by G. Dewey Norell of Collbran, Colorado.

Norell, a life-long cattle rancher and horseman, was one of the eight founding members of the Rocky Mountain Quarter Horse Association (RMQHA). As a close personal friend of Marshall Peavy's, he had relied heavily on the Peavy Quarter Horse gene pool to establish his own breeding band.

Among the Peavy-bred horses to find their way into Norell's foundation band was Little Buck, a 1931 buckskin mare by Ding Bob (QH) and out of Flossie by Sheik P-11. Flossie was, in turn, out of the Old Blue Mare.

Shortly after AQHA's formation in 1940, Norell registered a set of eight Ding Bob-bred mares with the association. Little Buck was the third of these, and she was assigned AQHA registration number P-1052. Of the set, Little Buck was the only one with a suspect background, and rightly so because she was in reality a marginally colored Appaloosa.

As the years rolled by, Little Buck's Appaloosa characteristics became more pronounced. Despite this fact, she was retained and utilized by Norell as his personal mount.

Eventually, Norell decided it was time to retire Little Buck to the broodmare band. Bred to Jack Casement's foundation Quarter Horse stallion Red Dog in 1942, she produced a marginally colored chestnut Appaloosa colt in July of 1943.

Although a registered Quarter Horse, Little Buck a was in reality a marginally colored Appaloosa and the dam of Little Red..

Courtesy Bud Norell

Originally named Brown Fox, the colt was hauled as a coming yearling to the first National Western Stock Show Quarter Horse Show in Denver. Exhibited at halter by John Martin of Whitewater, Colorado, he placed first in his class and was named the Reserve Grand Champion Stallion.

Grand Champion Stallion honors at the show went to Marshall Peavy's palomino stallion Gold Heels who, like Brown Fox, was a great-grandson of the Old Blue Mare. Among the well-known Quarter Horses that stood behind the two front-runners were Little Joe Jr, Pay Check, Frito and Tipo.

In 1946, Brown Fox was shown by Norell to Grand Champion Stallion honors at the Western Slope Quarter Horse Show in Grand Junction, Colorado. He was also broke to ride and, according to his breeder, had a "lot of cow sense and was a good rope horse."

Initially accepted into the appendix section of AQHA as a weanling, he was transferred to the permanent registry as an 8-year-old, re-named Norell's Little Red and assigned AQHA registration number 113,788.

As he aged, Brown Fox developed more Appaloosa roaning and parti-colored skin. For that reason, he was used sparingly at

stud. Norell's Bellboy (QH), a 1947 sorrel gelding out of Norell's Lucky, was his first registered foal. The following year saw two Little Red foals registered with AQHA. One of these, a mare named Norell's Blivit, was an Appaloosa.

Between 1949 and 1952, 11 Little Red offspring found their way into the AQHA registry. Of these, two were Appaloosas.

Earley Ribbon, a 1950 chestnut roan mare out of Blazella (QH), was the first one. Sold to Bill Robinson of Pleasant Grove, Utah, and bred to Hopscotch Reed (QH) in 1958, she produced ApHC Racing Hall of Fame inductee J & B's Spotted Fawn the following spring.

Both "Ribbon" and "Fawn" were then registered with ApHC, and went on to found a great family of halter, performance and race horses.

McCardo, a 1952 chestnut stallion out of Mickey (QH), was initially accepted into the appendix section of AQHA. As he developed more spots and roaning throughout his body, he, too, was re-registered with ApHC.

No Little Red foals were registered with AQHA from 1953 through 1956. In 1957, the Appaloosa stallion's last AQHA-registered get—Snow Mist—hit the ground. Out of Sunrise Webster (QH), Snow Mist developed Appaloosa color and was subsequently registered with ApHC.

By early 1956, it became apparent to Dewey Norell that he could no longer pass Little Red off as a Quarter Horse. In March of that year, he completed the necessary paperwork to register him with ApHC as Norell's Little Red T-998.

At the same time, he also registered McCardo T-995 (later F-3220) and Piance Creek T-996.

McCardo was eventually acquired by Cecil Dobbins of Colorado Springs, Colorado. A top sire of broodmares, McCardo's daughters found their way into Dobbins' early-day breeding herds as well as herds belonging to the Carey Appaloosa Ranch of Denver, and Jim Wild's Flying W Appaloosa Ranch of Sarcoxie, Missouri.

Piance Creek, a 1951 mare by Little Red out of T-Redd (QH), was sold to Ralph and Joyce Cannon of Elizabeth, Colorado. Bred to their foundation stallion, Sunspot Revel, Piance Creek produced a number of top show and breeding horses, including Red Sun.

Even prior to his being registered with ApHC, Little Red had sired several horses that made their way into the registry.

Norell's Myrtle B. T-402, a 1950 chestnut mare out of Slivers (QH), was the first of these. Born with white spots over her hips, she was sold to Bill Benoist of Long Beach, California. Bred to his stallion Joker B., she produced M.J.B., the 1959 National Grand Champion Stallion; and Moka B., a top show mare and producer.

Carey's Tommy T-4158, a 1948 chestnut gelding out of Cholla (QH), was Little Red's first legitimate show ring superstar.

Bred by John Martin, who had shown Little Red to his Denver Stock Show win years earlier, "Tommy" was sold to the Carey Appaloosa Ranch. Under their ownership, he developed into one of the breed's top halter geldings of the late 1950s and early 1960s. Among the shows that he stood grand at were the 1959 National Western Stock Show in Denver and the 1959 San Antonio Livestock Exposition in San Antonio, Texas.

Nateniyage T-856 and Carey's Streak T-857 were two more of Little Red's early-day show stars.

Nateniyage, a 1953 red roan stallion out of an unregistered Thoroughbred-type mare, was also known as Carey's Little Chief. Sold to the Carey Appaloosa Ranch, he was developed by them into one of the Rocky Mountain region's top halter stallions of the late 1950s and early 1960s.

Carey's Streak, a 1951 red roan mare out of Rags (QH), was also sold to the Carey Ranch. Under their ownership, she was named Grand Champion Mare at the San Antonio Livestock Exposition, the Colorado State Fair

Little Red is seen here in 1951—before he roaned out—being inspected for AQHA registration. Behind the stallion are (from left) breeder G. Dewey Norell, AQHA inspector Bryce Van Gundy and Wayne Smiley. Dewey's son Bud Norell holds Little Red.

Courtesy Bud Norell

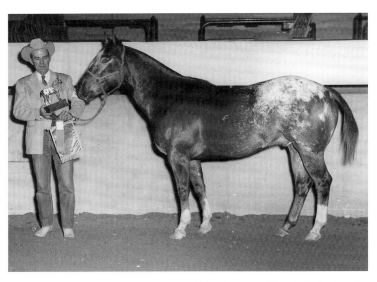

Carey's Tommy, a 1948 chestnut gelding by Norell's Little Red and out of Cholla (QH), was the Champion Aged Gelding and Grand Champion Gelding at the 1959 International Appaloosa Show in San Antonio, Texas. Johnnie Baker is seen at "Tommy's" halter.

Courtesy Western Horseman

in Pueblo, and the Mountain and Plains Appaloosa Horse Club show in Estes Park, Colorado.

In addition, she earned honors as the Champion Camas Prairie Stump Race Horse at the 1955 National Show in Colorado Springs.

The Dewey Norell era of Little Red's life produced a number of other top show and breeding horses, including Bayarda-B, Carey's Little Red No. 2 and Norell's Chi Chi.

Bayarda B, a 1952 bay mare out of Patty Cake (QH), was sold to Bill Benoist. Bred to Joker B., she produced the top show mare Arda-Joke B; and the champion show and performance gelding Mr. J. B.

Carey's Little Red No. 2, a 1954 blanket-hipped chestnut stallion out of Mabelle, was sold to the Carey Ranch. Utilized by them primarily as

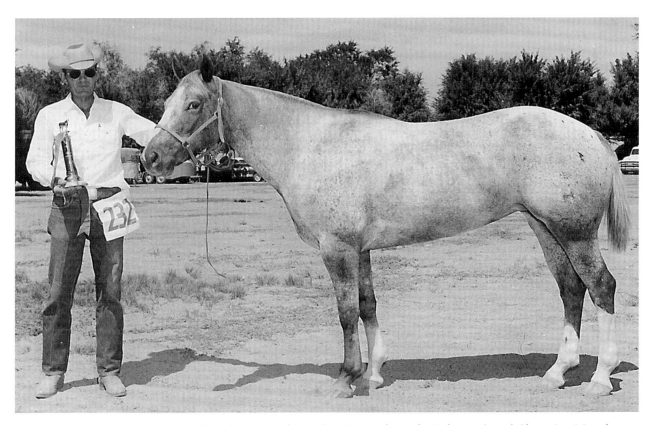

Carey's Streak, a 1951 mare by Little Red and out of Rags (QH), was shown by Baker to Grand Champion Mare honors at the 1956 Colorado State Fair in Pueblo.

Courtesy Western Horseman

Carey's Little Chief, a 1953 stallion by Little Red and out of a Thoroughbred mare, was the Grand Champion Stallion at the 1958 Wyoming State Fair in Douglas.

***Courtesy* Western Horseman**

a breeding animal, he sired Coke Roberds, a 1959 chestnut, blanket-hipped stallion out of Penny, who was acquired by Cecil Dobbins as a yearling. That same year, Coke Roberds made Appaloosa history when Dobbins sold him to the Flying W Appaloosa Ranch for an unprecedented $25,000.

Norell's Chi Chi, a 1954 mare out of Punk (QH), was initially kept by the Norells as a broodmare. Bred to Red Dog's Cowboy (QH) she produced Red Dog's Cowgirl.

"Cowgirl," a 1961 blue roan mare, was sold to Carl Miles of Abilene, Texas. Under his ownership, she was a champion race mare. Later sold to Blanche O'Connor of Bay City, Texas, she went on to earn honors as the Champion Senior Western Pleasure Horse at the 1969 World Champion Playoffs in Lincoln, Nebraska.

In the mid-1950s, Dewey Norell was visited by a pair of colorful pioneer breeders who would eventually play a major role in the Little Red story.

Hayes and Merle McDole of McDade, Louisiana, began breeding Appaloosas beginning in the late 1940s. Their search for foundation seed stock led them to the Norell Ranch where they purchased the AQHA-registered Little Red daughter Norell's Blivit.

Re-registered with ApHC as Cooterville Norell's Blivit T-502, she was among the first set of two dozen horses to be papered by the McDoles.

In the spring of 1956, the couple returned to the Norell Ranch and negotiated to purchase Little Red for a reported $500. They immediately hauled him back to Louisiana and placed him at the head of their breeding program.

Coke Roberds, a 1959 stallion by Carey's Little Red II and out of Penny, sold as a yearling for $25,000 to Jim Wild of Sarcoxie, Missouri. **Courtesy Jim Wild**

Shortly thereafter, Little Red sired the required 12 colored foals necessary for advancement to the foundation registry. At that time, his name was changed to Cooterville Norell's Little Red and he was assigned registration number F-1673.

At the head of the McDole band of highly colored Appaloosa broodmares, Little Red's breeding responsibilities increased dramatically over the course of the next four years.

From 1957 through 1960, 45 Louisiana-bred Little Reds hit the ground. Among their number were such show and breeding horses as Caddo Red Dog, Little Red Lady, Cooterville Red Bus, Myres' Tico

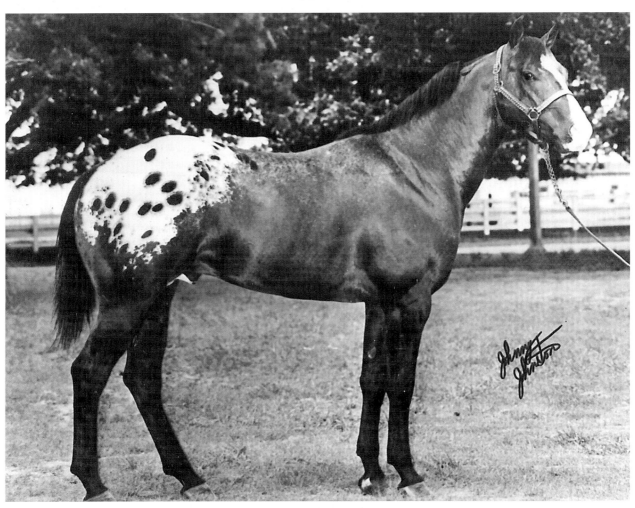

Coke's Plaudit, a 1963 stallion by Coke Roberds and out of Mary Eyes (QH), was a top show horse and sire.
Photo by Johnny Johnston, courtesy of Dave and Carol Graetz

Tico, Clark's Levee Beau and Cooterville Crawfish.

Of these, "Red Bus," "Tico Tico," and "Crawfish" stand out.

Red Bus, a 1957 stallion out of Cooterville Cee Dee, was a champion halter and performance horse. Retired to stud, he sired Royal Ripper L.—the earner of five national and world titles.

Tico Tico, a 1958 stallion out of Cooterville Pee-Wee, was the Reserve Champion 2-Year-Old Stallion at the 1960 National Show. Sold to Joe and Betty Stroube of Corsicana, Texas, he was developed by them into one of the breed's top halter horses and the sire of Tico Tornado.

"Tornado," a 1962 stallion out of Bay Bravo, was bred by the Stroubes and sold as a young horse to John Howell of Chatsworth, Illinois.

Shown primarily by ApHC Hall of Fame trainer Lloyd Donley, the blanket-hipped chestnut stallion went on to be named the Champion Performance Horse at the 1967 National Show in Walla Walla, Washington; the Reserve Champion Performance Horse at the 1967 World Champion Playoffs in Sweetwater, Texas; and the Reserve Champion Performance Horse at the 1968 National Show in Oklahoma City, Oklahoma.

In addition, he was a six-time national and world champion in Western pleasure, calf roping, Camas Prairie stump race, Nez Perce stake race and rope race.

Crawfish, a 1960 stallion out of Cooterville Cherry, was bred by the McDoles and sold as a young horse to their son, Dale, of Red Cloud, Nebraska. For the younger McDole, the snowcap-blanketed stallion founded a halter and performance dynasty.

Among Crawfish's top get were

Earley Ribbon, a 1950 mare by Norell's Little Red and out of Blazella (QH), was initially registered with AQHA. Sold to Bill Robinson of Pleasant Grove, Utah, she colored up and was re-registered with ApHC.

Courtesy Gene Carr

J & B's Spotted Fawn, a 1959 mare by Hopscotch Reed (QH) and out of Earley Ribbon, was a champion show mare and producer, and an ApHC Racing Hall of Fame inductee.

Courtesy Appaloosa Museum & Heritage Center

Myres' Tico Tico, a 1958 stallion by Norell's Little Red and out of Cooterville Pee-Wee, was the Champion Aged Stallion and Reserve Grand Champion Stallion at the 1960 Richland Hills Appaloosa Show in Fort Worth, Texas.

Courtesy Appaloosa Museum & Heritage Center

Red Dog's Ribbon, the 1968 National Champion 2-Year-Old Stallion; Kagel's Branded Man, the 1971 World Champion Trail Horse and the 1972 National Champion Men's Western Pleasure Horse; and Red Cloud's La Paloma, the 1974 World Champion 3-Year-Old Mare.

By the end of 1959, it was apparent that Cooterville Norell's Little Red's breeding career was nearing its end. The 16-year-old stallion's fertility had weakened and the decision was made to put him up for sale.

Back in Colorado, the Carey Appaloosa Ranch had built its highly successful show and breeding operation almost solely on Little Red's blood. In January of 1960, they took a measured gamble and purchased the head of the family for $10,000.

Later that year, they exhibited their top string of Little Red-bred show horses at the 13th National Show in

Tico Tornado, a 1962 stallion by "Tico Tico" and out of Bay Bravo, held six national and world performance titles. He is seen here with ApHC Hall of Fame inductee Lloyd Donley after being named the Champion Performance Horse at the 1967 National Show in Walla Walla, Washington.

Photo by Alexander, courtesy Appaloosa Museum & Heritage Center

South Sioux City, Nebraska. There, Carey's Tommy was named the Grand Champion Gelding and Champion Aged Gelding, Carey's Little Chief earned honors as Reserve Grand Champion Stallion and Champion Aged Stallion, and Myers' Tico Tico was chosen the Reserve Champion 2-Year-Old Stallion.

Represented by those three horses, Cooterville Norell's Little Red was awarded National Champion Get of Sire honors.

In many ways, that show amounted to Little Red's swan song. Appaloosa Horse Club records reveal that he sired only three registered foals after being purchased by the Carey Ranch.

Little DeBerry Bay, a 1961 mare out of Cooterville DeBerry, was solid-colored. Handprint's Little Red Finale, a 1961 stallion out of Cheri 4 Dinah (QH), and Handprints Miss Little Red, a 1961 mare out of Carey's Redwood, were both blanket-hipped.

Sold as part of a large package deal to C. E. Burmeister's Handprint Farms of Pontiac, Michigan, both "Finale" and "Miss Little Red" went on to become top show and breeding animals.

Cooterville Norell's Little Red died on April 9, 1961, at the Carey Ranch's winter training headquarters in Wichita Falls, Texas. His death was attributed to internal injuries as the result of a freak accident.

Little Red was forced to operate at a disadvantage for most of his life. Misidentified and under-appreciated, he was not heavily utilized as a breeding horse until the twilight of his life.

Despite this, his powerful Blue Mare genes stood him in good stead and he made his presence felt. Little Red was a top breeding animal, as were his sons and daughters. Together they founded a durable and versatile family of horses that contributed greatly to the advancement of the breed.

Red Dog's Cowgirl, a 1961 mare by Red Dog's Cowboy (QH) and out of Chi Chi by Norell's Little Red, was a champion halter, race and performance horse. Owned by Carl Miles of Abilene, Texas, she is seen here winning a 350-yard sprint at a 1963 Brush, Colorado, race meet. **Courtesy Western Horseman**

Chapter 18

PEAVY BIMBO
F-4557

Peavy Bimbo—a top ranch mount and potent sire, he impacted a host of top breeders' programs.
Photo by Alex Morris, courtesy Peavy Estate

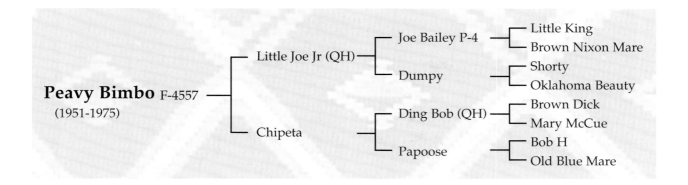

			Little King
		Joe Bailey P-4	Brown Nixon Mare
	Little Joe Jr (QH)		Shorty
		Dumpy	Oklahoma Beauty
Peavy Bimbo F-4557			Brown Dick
(1951-1975)		Ding Bob (QH)	Mary McCue
	Chipeta		Bob H
		Papoose	Old Blue Mare

As chronicled in the previous chapter, Norell's Little Red was the first noteworthy male descendant of the Blue Mare to make his way into the Appaloosa registry. Peavy Bimbo, the second prominent representative of the line, appeared on the scene shortly thereafter.

In addition to their Appaloosa heritage, "Little Red" and "Bimbo" had a number of things in common. Both were bred by Rocky Mountain Quarter Horse Association (RMQHA) founding members: Little Red by Dewey Norell of Collbran, Colorado, and Bimbo by Mavis Peavy of Westplains, Colorado. Also, both were meant to be solid-colored Quarter Horses, were initially registered with AQHA and then were later re-registered with ApHC.

"Bimbo, as we called him, was born on July 3, 1951, in the south pasture of the Westplains Ranch," Mavis Peavy says. "Ned Snader—who had just recently come to work for me—and I drove out to the pasture and found him.

"He was a loud-colored colt at birth—a dun with a big white blanket full of darker dun, haloed spots. Because of his breeding and obvious quality, I made the decision to leave him as a stallion."

Bimbo's sire was Little Joe Jr. (QH), a 1937 stallion by Joe Bailey P-4 and out of Dumpy. On the tracks, "Joe Jr." was a AA-rated racehorse when that was the highest rating obtainable. In the show ring, he was twice named

the Grand Champion Stallion of the Tucson, Arizona, Livestock Show. As a breeding horse, he was listed as late as 1973 on the AQHA Leading Maternal Grandsires of Register of Merit Qualifiers.

Bimbo's dam was Chipeta (QH), a 1940 mare by Ding Bob P-269 and out of Papoose. A line-bred Old Fred mare and a granddaughter of the Blue Mare, Chipeta was a Peavy favorite.

"Chipeta grew up to fulfill every promise

Although this photo is undated, "Bimbo's" size and coat condition indicate the shot was taken in late 1951 or early 1952.

Courtesy Peavy Estate

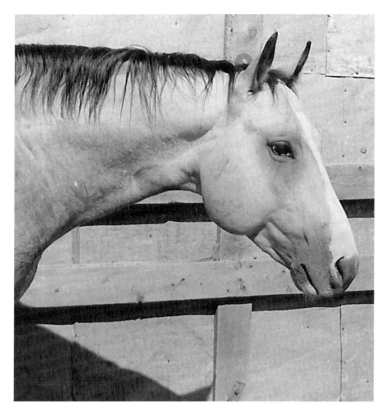

This compelling head shot of Bimbo was taken in the mid-1950s at the Peavy "Rock Ranch" near Westplains, Colorado.

Courtesy Peavy Estate

that she gave as a foal," Mavis says. "She was born a dun and shed out to be a beautiful shade of blue roan, with a few black spots. She was probably the most reliable horse I ever rode and she taught me a great deal."

Gold Heels—the hallmark Peavy show horse and sire—was foaled the same year as Chipeta. The golden palomino stallion was the winner of the first Rocky Mountain Derby, held in 1943 at the Colorado State Fair in Pueblo. Several months later, he was named the Grand Champion Stallion at the 1944 National Western Stock Show in Denver.

Chipeta was also entered in the Rocky Mountain Derby and finished a respectable third. It was not known until several months later that she had been forced to run the race under a handicap.

"Chipeta ran that race with frozen front feet," Mavis says. "At some time during the previous winter or spring, she had suffered frostbitten coronary bands. We did not realize it until they festered up and broke open after the race. Marshall began doctoring her and overcame it fairly fast."

After Chipeta's foot problems were eliminated, an incident occurred that indicated a return to the track might be in order.

"During the summer evenings," Mavis says, "it was a Peavy family affair to train the racehorses. Marshall had fashioned a racetrack on a flat piece of ground near the house.

"One time, we all went over to breeze some horses. Marshall was mounted on a daughter of Margie named Corrigan, I was on Chipeta, and the girls—Mary and "Biddy"—were on Sue Peavy and Gold Heels.

"After we warmed the horses up, we let them out. To everyone's amazement, Chipeta and I outdistanced them all.

"Coming back, we always traveled slowly enough to cool the horses out. About halfway home, Marshall looked over at me and said, 'We've been training the wrong horse. Chipeta can run.' "

Shortly after arriving at that decision, Marshall placed Chipeta with a trainer named "Doc" McClelland, to be readied for the 1943 fall race meet at Kremmling, Colorado.

"Doc McClelland was one of the few men Marshall would trust to take a horse away from home," Mavis says. "Chipeta took to the training well, so Marshall sent Doc, her, and several other horses up to Kremmling a couple of weeks ahead of the fair. He always liked to get the horses completely familiar with the new surroundings.

"One evening, Doc matched Chipeta in a race for $10. Of course she outran them all and, by the time Marshall got up there, no one was in any mood to match her again."

Shortly after the Kremmling meet, Marshall Peavy was killed in a riding accident. Mavis was left to run a large cattle ranch and horse-breeding operation with the help of two teen-aged girls and one hired man.

As noted in Chapter 17, Mavis leased Little Joe Jr. for the 1950 breeding season. Among the Peavy mares bred to him that year was Chipeta, and Bimbo was the resulting foal.

For the first two years of his life, Bimbo was allowed to grow up naturally on the Peavy Ranch. In the fall of 1953, he was started under saddle.

"Kenneth McEndeffer, who lived four miles from us, broke Bimbo," Ned Snader says. "Bimbo had a beautiful, quiet disposition and appreciated attention, more-so than most horses.

"Kenneth liked the horse so much he was practically in love with him. He was not known to pamper a horse, but he was kind to Bimbo and rode him every day. He brought

Chipeta, "Bimbo's" dam, was the epitome of the Peavy mare of the 1940s. Beautifully headed and with excellent conformation, she excelled as a ranch mount and broodmare.

Photo by John A. Stryker, courtesy Peavy Estate

Genivieve Peavy, a 1957 mare by Peavy Bimbo and out of Genivieve Girl (QH), was bred by Mavis Peavy. Sold to Lane Hudson of Denver, Colorado, the mare was shown by him to Grand Champion Mare honors at the 1962 New Mexico State Fair in Albuquerque.

Courtesy Peavy Estate

him back in the spring of his 3-year-old year, and I took over his riding."

For the next several years, Bimbo was employed full-time on the Peavy Ranch as a using horse. According to the man who rode him the most, he was an exceptional ranch mount.

"I rode Bimbo every day," Snader says. "I just started to use him for everything that needed to be done and rode nothing else for about a year.

"If you were riding with other people, he was a stud and he knew it. He was well-mannered, but you had to be sure that he was kept a little away from the other horses. He was young; he didn't know everything yet.

"He became 'cow-y' in a hurry, and got the ground well. That means he didn't stumble, because he had been ridden miles and miles

on that kind of ground. And I like that expression—'the horse getting the ground with his feet.' It's terribly important.

"In a corral, Bimbo learned to sort cattle. I tried not to use him to bring the mares in, but I had to from time to time. And I rode him in some pretty tight places when he was a 3- and 4-year-old, particularly a blizzard or two that I can remember.

"He was just absolutely super to be around, horseback or afoot."

In 1954, Bimbo was bred to several mares. Dewdrop Peavy, a 1955 mare out of Peavy's June (QH), was foaled the following spring and was his first registered get. In July of 1955, the then-4-year-old stallion was registered with ApHC as Bimbo T-1167.

In July 1956, Bimbo was entered in halter competition at the 2nd Annual Mountain and

Plains Appaloosa Horse Club Show in Estes Park, Colorado.

"That spring was miserable and wet," Mavis Peavy says. "In driving cattle and horses to the barn, the men had caved in a metal culvert. Bimbo stepped on the edge of it and cut a front foot and ankle.

"The judge at the Estes Park show fixated on that foot. He said it was a blemish and placed Bimbo near the bottom of the class. It wasn't a blemish; it was a scar. That was the first and last time we showed Bimbo."

No Bimbo foals were registered in 1956. The following year, however, saw two of his top daughters hit the ground.

Chipeta Doll, a 1957 mare out of Sow, was sold to Jim Wild of Sarcoxie, Missouri. For him, she went on to produce such top show horses as Bright Doll and Coke's Bimbo.

Genivieve Peavy, a 1957 mare out of Genivieve Girl, was sold to Lane Hudson of Denver. She went on to become one of the breed's premier halter mares, as well as the dam of Mighty Peavy and Mighty Shiek. She

Love Letter, a 1958 mare by Peavy Bimbo and out of Hugger (QH), was bred by Marshall and Mavis Peavy's daughter, Mary Peavy Stees. Sold to Cecil Dobbin of Colorado Springs, Colorado, Love Letter was named the Grand Champion Mare at the 1960 Colorado State Fair in Pueblo.

Photo by Darol Dickinson, courtesy Helen Dobbin

Miss Mavis, a 1961 mare by Peavy Bimbo and out of Ida Pearl S (QH), was bred by Mavis Peavy. Sold to Lane Hudson, she went on to become a top halter mare and producer.
Photo by Ralph Morgan, courtesy Appaloosa Museum & Heritage Center

will be discussed in a subsequent chapter.

The following year saw the birth of another top "Bimbo" daughter.

Love Letter, a 1958 mare out of Hugger (QH), was bred by Mary Peavy Stees of Steamboat Springs, Colorado—Marshall and Mavis's daughter. Sold as a 2-year-old to Cecil Dobbin of Colorado Springs, Colorado, and then re-sold to Jim Wild, Love Letter went on to become a champion show mare and the dam of Miss Love Letters, by Bright Eyes Brother; and Wapiti's Love, by Wapiti.

By the late 1950s, it became apparent to Mavis that she would have to part company with Bimbo.

"I was primarily a Quarter Horse breeder," she says. "Despite that, I held Bimbo in very high regard and desired to keep him.

"Several of my fellow Quarter Horse breeders had a problem with that. They began to question the integrity of my horses. I couldn't have that, so, much to my regret and more, I sold Bimbo to Dr. Jack Ketcham of Cheyenne, Wyoming.

"Jack was a veterinarian. Immediately after buying Bimbo from me, he turned around and sold part-interest in him to F. R. Cassell of Denver. But Jack retained the controlling interest and it was he who added the 'Peavy' to Bimbo's name."

Although she had sold Peavy Bimbo outright, Mavis reserved two breedings a year to him for the rest of his life.

Miss Mavis, a 1961 mare out of Ida Pearl, was one of results of those breedings. Sold to Lane Hudson, she, too, went on to become a top show mare and the dam of Spittin' Image and Mighty Bimbo.

Among the other noteworthy Peavy Bimbo get to be born during this era were Billy Pepper, a 1959 gelding out of Peggy (TB); Peavey's Pattern, a 1959 stallion out of Bevy Cox (QH); and Bim Bim, a 1961 stallion out of Miss Rey (TB).

Bim Bim, who was bred by Dr. Ketcham, was of particular note. One of the top Appaloosa racehorses of his era, he ran and won at distances from 220 to 870 yards.

In June of 1961, Hank Wiescamp of Alamosa, Colorado, bought out Cassell's interest in Bimbo for a reported $10,000. Wiescamp utilized the stallion in his Appaloosa breeding program for three seasons.

Among the top show and breeding offspring to be born during this stage of Bimbo's life were Chipeta Bimbo, a 1962 mare out of Spanish Lady (QH); Baboon, a 1963 stallion out of Laramie Lassie; Bimbo's Lassie, a 1964 mare out of Laramie Lassie;

Peavy's Fireball, a 1964 stallion by Peavy Bimbo and out of Little Cowgirl (QH), was bred by Hank Wiescamp of Alamosa, Colorado. Sold to E. D. Rogers of Coral Gables, Florida, Peavy's Fireball was the Champion 3-Year-Old Stallion at the 1967 National Show in Walla Walla, Washington.
Photo by Johnny Johnston, courtesy Appaloosa Museum & Heritage Center

While co-owned by C. L. Williams of Gallup, New Mexico, Peavy Bimbo won the get of sire class at the 1965 New Mexico State Fair at Albuquerque. He was represented in the class by (from left) Miss Mavis; R.M. Latigo, a 1963 gelding out of an unregistered mare; and Baboon, a 1963 stallion out of Laramie Lassie.

Photo by Darol Dickinson, courtesy Appaloosa Museum & Heritage Center

Peavy's Fireball, a 1964 stallion out of Little Cowgirl (QH); and Bimbo's Watusie, a 1964 mare out of High Kay.

Between the years of 1961 and 1964, Peavy Bimbo also contributed a key set of broodmares to the Wiescamp Appaloosa program. Eventually bred to Red Plaudit and his sons, they produced a host of top show and breeding horses.

In early 1964, the non-controlling interest in Peavy Bimbo was once again sold. This time it went to C. L. Williams of Gallup, New Mexico.

Williams was a long-time friend of the Peavy family and had been buying mares from them for years. He was also one of the few people allowed to bring outside mares to the Peavy stallions' court.

Moved by Williams to the Four Corners area of northwest New Mexico, Bimbo was again placed at the head of a well-bred broodmare band.

Among the top animals he sired during this stage of his life were Peavy's Leo, a 1966 stallion out of Leah Wright (QH), and Peggy's Fancy, a 1968 mare out of Flying Object.

And, as was the case wherever he was utilized as a sire, Peavy Bimbo also contributed a number of top breeding animals to his owner's program.

In the summer of 1968, the minority interest in Peavy Bimbo was sold for the fourth and final time. Ward Fenton of Meyers, Montana, took physical control of Bimbo and placed him at the head of his broodmare band.

Fenton and his fellow "North Country" Appaloosa breeders were quick to capitalize on the opportunity to breed to what was by this time a living legend. Bimbo's next four foal crops—born between 1969 and 1972—were among his largest ever.

From them would come such durable stars as Colonel Peavy, a 1969 stallion out of Stars Justabug; Peavy's Dandy Pants, a 1970 stallion out of Texas Sunday; Peavy Country, a 1971 gelding out of Flying Diamond's Jody; and Country Flirt, a 1972 mare out of Country Fashion.

By 1972, Peavy Bimbo's long and storied career as a foundation sire was winding down. His last three foal crops—born between 1973 and 1975—totaled just 12.

He was retired from stud at the end of the 1974 breeding season. Pensioned out by Fenton to a lush Montana meadow, he lived to the age of 24. In the spring of 1975, he passed away of natural causes.

"Bimbo bred for Ward for a few years,"

Mavis Peavy says. "Ward, thankfully and kindly, was smart enough to retire the horse from breeding at one point. Ward sent us a picture of him in a green meadow in Montana. He was in good shape and fat.

"Bimbo was a durable horse. Other than that injured ankle, I don't think he ever took an unsound step. I think that's quite a record. He did his family proud."

Mavis Peavy and Peavy Bimbo were a winning pair if ever there was one: she, a true pioneer woman of the West; he, a great foundation Appaloosa sire.

Their joint impact on the breed was positive and long-lasting. In recognition of their contributions, both were inducted into the ApHC Hall of Fame in 1988.

Chipeta Doll, a 1957 mare by Peavy Bimbo and out of Sow, was bred by Mavis Peavy. Sold to Jim Wild, the mare went on to become a top producer. In this photo, she is seen winning the produce of dam class at a 1963 Sarcoxie, Missouri, show. She is represented by (from left) Bright Doll, a 1960 mare by Bright Eyes Brother, and Coke's Bimbo, a 1963 gelding by Coke Roberds.

Courtesy Jim Wild

Chapter 19

WAPITI
#5445

Wapiti—A double-bred Old Blue Mare descendant, greatly enriched the family name.
Photo by Chuck Bearden, courtesy Jim Wild

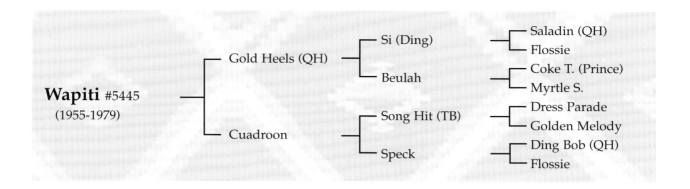

```
                                                    ┌─ Si (Ding)        ┌─ Saladin (QH)
                               ┌─ Gold Heels (QH) ──┤                   ┤
                               │                    └─ Beulah           └─ Flossie
                               │                                        ┌─ Coke T. (Prince)
Wapiti #5445 ──────────────────┤                                        ┤
(1955-1979)                    │                                        └─ Myrtle S.
                               │                    ┌─ Song Hit (TB)    ┌─ Dress Parade
                               └─ Cuadroon ─────────┤                   ┤
                                                    └─ Speck            └─ Golden Melody
                                                                        ┌─ Ding Bob (QH)
                                                                        ┤
                                                                        └─ Flossie
```

Shortly after Norell's Little Red and Peavy Bimbo arrived on the Appaloosa scene, a third classic Blue Mare descendant made his appearance.

Aptly named Wapiti—which is the Shawnee Indian word for "elk" or "animal with white on its rump"—this horse would go on to establish one of the most popular and enduring Appaloosa lines of all-time.

Wapiti, a 1955 stallion by Gold Heels (QH) and out of Cuadroon (QH), was bred by Mary Stees of Clark, Colorado. Mary—Marshall and Mavis Peavy's eldest daughter—was a top horsewoman in her own right.

As noted in Chapter 20, Gold Heels was a hallmark Peavy show and breeding stallion, and a solid-colored great grandson of the Blue Mare.

Cuadroon, a 1943 mare by Song Hit (TB) and out of Speck, came with her own set of impressive credentials. Mike Stees of Colorado Springs, Colorado—Mary's widower—remembers the Peavy-bred Appaloosa well.

"I worked for Marshall Peavy when he had the ranch at Clark, Colorado," he says. "Song Hit was a Remount horse and Marshall stood him for the U.S. government for several years.

"In 1942, Marshall bred Song Hit to Speck, one of his best mares. She was registered with AQHA but was a marginally colored Appaloosa. As a young mare, she had little more than the Appaloosa eye and a little mottled skin. Later, she developed white spots and some roaning. Cuadroon, who was also registered with AQHA, was colored just like her dam.

"In 1943," he continues, "Marshall moved from Clark to Westplains, Colorado. In the fall of 1944, he was killed in a riding accident. As I recall, Mary had purchased Cuadroon from her dad several months before his death."

After Marshall Peavy's premature passing, Mike Stees went to work for Mavis. In September of 1945, he and Mary were married. Shortly thereafter, they began preparing the then-2-year-old Cuadroon for a racing career.

Gold Heels (QH)—Wapiti's sire—was bred by Mavis Peavy of Clark, Colorado. Traded to her husband Marshall for indoor plumbing, the golden palomino earned Grand Champion Stallion honors at the 1944 National Western Stock Show in Denver, Colorado.

Courtesy Peavy Estate

The Wapiti and Jim Wild partnership remains one of the longest lasting and most influential in the history of the Appaloosa breed.

Courtesy Jim Wild

"I broke Cuadroon to ride," Mike says. "She was a little tough to break and threw me off on more than one occasion. But, eventually I made it to the point where I could stay on.

"Marshall had built a half-mile oval track up above the house, and Mary and I conditioned Cuadroon on it. She was so fast and so tough it was a chore at first to hold her in on the turns. Mary would get on Sue Peavy and crowd Cuadroon as she made it around the turns, to hold her in.

"That fall, we entered Cuadroon in the Rocky Mountain Quarter Horse Association's 2-year-old futurity—the same race Gold Heels had won in 1943. It was held at Pueblo, and we won it. The next fall, we entered Cuadroon in the Western Slope Derby at Kremmling, Colorado. She won it, too."

Shortly after the Derby, Mike and Mary leased Cuadroon to Leonard Lighthizer of Hayden, Colorado.

"Leonard was a local rancher and top racehorse man," Mike says. "He conditioned and raced Cuadroon for several seasons. He took her to race meets in Kremmling, Steamboat Springs, Hotchkiss, Craig and Hayden, Colorado, and rarely got her beat. One year, at Hayden, he entered her in a 440-yard race and won it. The next day, he put her in a half-mile race. She won it, too."

After Cuadroon was retired from the track, she was started on a second career as a ranch horse. Here again, she proved superior.

"I cowboyed a lot on Cuadroon," Mike Stees says. "She made a top ranch horse and had a world of cow sense and endurance. By this time, she had matured into quite a mare. She stood around 15-2 hands high and had a beautiful head, and a long, slender neck. She also had as much hind leg as you'd ever want on a horse. We rode her until she was 10, and then bred her."

Bred to the solid palomino-colored Gold Heels in 1954, Cuadroon produced a blood bay colt the next spring with a huge white blanket full of bay, haloed spots.

Named Wapiti, the colt was kept for the first two years of his life at Mavis Peavy's Westplains ranch. There, he was allowed to roam free and grow naturally. In 1957, he was returned to the Stees Ranch near Steamboat Springs, where he was broke to ride.

That same summer, Wapiti was sold to Ike Anderson of Steamboat Springs. Anderson put the loud-colored stallion to work as a ranch and pack horse and, in 1959, registered him with ApHC.

Between 1957 and 1959, Wapiti sired only three registered foals. One of those—Colorow A, a 1959 stallion out of Dimples—was the Mountain and Plains Appaloosa Horse Club's 1961 High-Point 2-Year-Old Halter Stallion.

In the summer of 1959, Jim Wild of Sarcoxie, Missouri, owner of the Flying W Ranch, asked Cecil Dobbin of Colorado Springs to find him a

Cuadroon—Wapiti's dam—was a top-notch race mare. She's seen here with trainer Leonard Lighthizer and an unidentified jockey after winning a mid-1940s contest in Hotchkiss, Colorado.

Courtesy Peavy Estate

Shown at the 1960 American Royal Appaloosa Show in Kansas City, Kansas, Wapiti won the aged stallion and Indian costume classes.

Courtesy Jim Wild

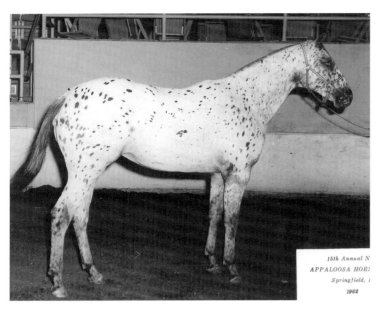

15th Annual N
APPALOOSA HORS
Springfield, I
1962

Wa-Loni, a 1961 mare by Wapiti and out of Sweet Lalana, was the Champion Yearling Filly and Best Individual Under 2 Years of Age at the 1962 National Show in Springfield, Illinois.

Courtesy Jim Wild

mature breeding stallion. Dobbin located and purchased Wapiti from Anderson, and delivered him to Wild on January 1, 1960.

Wild showed Wapiti twice at halter.

"We took 'Wap' to the 1960 National in South Sioux City, Nebraska," Wild says, "and showed him in the aged stallion class. He was not in show shape and placed sixth in a class of 51 entries. That fall, we took him to the American Royal show at Kansas City, Kansas. We entered him in the aged stallion class there and won it.

"We never showed him again at halter. We did ride him in several Indian costume classes, though, and he always performed real well in them. And I rode him quite a bit at home. He was always a pleasure to ride."

Angel Wings, a 1961 mare by Wapiti and out of Mary, was bred by Jim Wild and sold as a yearling to Delores Hicks of Fort Worth, Texas. "Angel" was named the Grand Champion Mare at the 1963 Southwestern Livestock Exposition and Fat Stock Show in Fort Worth.

Courtesy Jim Wild

Wapiti, Jr., 1961 stallion by Wapiti and out of Kadoka (QH), earned Reserve Champion Stallion honors at the same show.
Courtesy Jim Wild

Wapiti's first Flying W Ranch-bred foal crop arrived in 1961. From it came such hallmark individuals as Wa-Loni, Angel Wings and Wapiti Jr.

Wa-Loni, a 1961 mare out of Sweet Lalana, was the Champion Yearling Filly and Best of Either Sex Under 2 Years of Age at the 1962 National Show in Springfield, Illinois.

Angel Wings, a 1961 mare out of Mary, was sold to Dolores Hicks of Fort Worth, Texas, and developed by her into one of the Lone Star State's top halter mares.

Wapiti, Jr., a 1961 stallion out of Kadoka (QH), was initially kept by Wild and shown to halter championships at shows throughout the Southwest. Sold to T. J. Bryant's Boots

and Saddle Ranch of Sealy, Texas, he went on to earn honors as Champion Aged Stallion and Grand Champion Stallion at the 1966 National Show in Syracuse, New York.

From Wapiti's second Jim Wild-bred foal crop came the likes of Wapiti's Double Crown, Miss Hoop and Wapiti's Haunta.

"Double Crown," a 1962 gelding out of Houston's Pride (QH), was named the Champion Aged Gelding and the Grand Champion Gelding at the 1966 National Show.

Miss Hoop, a 1962 mare out of Component (TB), was kept by Wild and went on to be one of her era's top Appaloosa race mares.

"Haunta," a 1962 stallion out of Poca

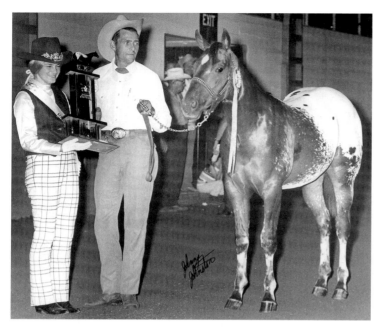

Wa-Jo-Re, a 1968 stallion by Wapiti and out of Joker's Miss Reed, was the Champion Yearling Stallion and Junior Champion Stallion at the 1969 National Show in Baton Rouge, Louisiana. ApHC Hall of Fame inductee Hadley Campbell is seen at the halter.

Photo by Johnny Johnston, courtesy Appaloosa Museum & Heritage Center

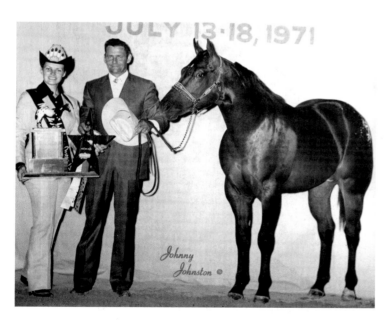

Ha-Dar-Honey, a 1969 stallion by Wapiti and out of Comanche T Bird, was the Champion Yearling Stallion at the 1969 Nationals, and the Champion 2-Year-Old Stallion at the 1970 National Show in Las Vegas, Nevada.

Photo by Johnny Johnston, courtesy Appaloosa Museum & Heritage Center

Haunta, was also a winning race-horse. Retired to stud, he sired Powder Smoke, the 1971 ApHC Champion Running Horse.

Over the course of the next half-decade, Wapiti's list of champions grew at a rapid pace.

On the show-ring side, such horses as Acorn's Wapiti Colleen, Wapiti's Third Charm, Wapiti's Love, Wa-Tusie, Wa-Lana, Miss Wagoner, Wapiti II, Wapiti's Warrior, Wapiti's Hi Regards, H.P. Miss Wapiti Roberds and Wap Deck made their mark.

On the racing scene, Wapiti's Jet and Patty Triple were proven winners.

By the late 1960s and early 1970s, Wapiti was generally recognized as one of the nation's top sires. Among the top get that bolstered that reputation were Skip Wapiti, Wa-Jo-Re, Ha-Dar-Honey, Mr. Wapiti Deck, Prince Doolin and Wapiti's Senor.

Skip Wapiti, a 1968 stallion out of Turk's Skipper Princess, was the Champion Weanling Stallion at the 1968 National Show in Oklahoma City, Oklahoma.

Wa-Jo-Re, a 1968 stallion out of Joker's Miss Reed, was the Champion Yearling Stallion and Junior Champion Stallion at the 1969 National Show in Baton Rouge, Louisiana.

Ha-Dar-Honey, a 1969 stallion out of Comanche T Bird, was the Champion Yearling Stallion at the 1970 National in Huron, South Dakota, and the Champion 2-Year-Old Stallion at the 1971 National Show in Las Vegas, Nevada.

Mr. Wapiti Deck, a 1969 stallion out of Katy Joe (QH), was a champion halter horse, and Prince Doolin, a 1968 stallion out of Alberta Mott Doolin, was a race winner.

Wapiti's Senor, a 1971 stallion out of Spanish Needles, was the Grand

Champion Stallion at the 1974 Canadian National, Ontario, and was a 2002 inductee into the Appaloosa Horse Club of Canada's Hall of Fame.

As the years rolled on, the list of Wapiti champions continued to grow.

My Precious, a 1973 mare out of Plaudy Roberds, was the Champion Yearling Filly at the 1974 World Championship Show in Oklahoma City.

Melody Of Love, a 1975 mare out of Love Affair, was the Champion Weanling Filly at the 1975 World Championship Show, and the Champion Yearling Filly at the 1976 World Championship Show in Oklahoma City.

Wapiti was also one of the few stallions to be both an American and Canadian National Champion Get of Sire winner.

Represented by Wapiti Jr., Wapiti's

Melody Of Love, a 1974 mare by Wapiti and out of Love Affair, was a two-time World Champion halter mare.
Photo by Johnny Johnston, courtesy Jim Wild

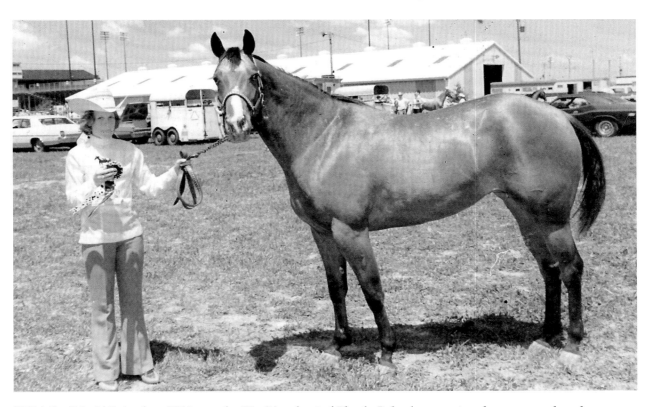

H.P. Miss Wapiti Roberds, a 1966 mare by Wapiti and out of Plaudy Roberds, was a top show mare and producer. That's owner Carol Graetz at the halter.
Courtesy Dave and Carol Graetz

Represented by (from left) Wa-Lana, Wapiti's Double Crown and Wapiti Jr., Wapiti won the get of sire class at the 1966 National Show in Syracuse, New York.

Courtesy Appaloosa Museum & Heritage Center

Double Crown and Wa-Lana, he won Get of Sire honors at the 1966 National Show in Syracuse. Represented by Wapiti Senor, Wapiti's Warrior and Wa Co Sue, he won the Get of Sire award at the 1974 Canadian National.

Wapiti was also the sire of superior breeding animals.

Wapiti II, Wap Deck, Wa-Joe-Deck, Mr. Wapiti Deck and Wapiti's Little S. all rank high as some of his better-known breeding sons.

Melody Of Love, the two-time world champion Wapiti daughter, went on to earn a bronze medallion production plaque, and My Precious and H. P. Miss Wapiti Roberds—full sisters by Wapiti and out of Plaudy Roberds—were national and world champion producers.

Little Flirt, a 1962 Wapiti daughter out of Hollywood Rocker, was a world champion producer, and Wapiti's Maid, a 1973 mare out

of Color Maid (QH), went on to produce leading sire Maid's Dream.

As well as they did in the show ring, on the racetrack and in the breeding shed, the Wapiti horses were never mass-produced. That's not to say they weren't promoted. On the contrary, Jim Wild was one of the foremost promoters of his day.

His regular advertisements for Wapiti and Coke Roberds (the horse) in *Western Horseman* magazine were classic in content and eye-appeal. The ads proved so popular and attracted so many newcomers to the breed that Jim finally requested, received and dispersed countless pieces of Appaloosa Horse Club promotional material to people who saw his ads and wanted to know more about this breed of horse.

Despite all this interest, Jim never stood Wapiti to a wide-open book. Outside mares were limited to 10 a year and the sky would fall before that number would be raised.

Miss Hoop, a 1962 mare by Wapiti and out of Component (TB), was one of the top Appaloosa racehorses of her era. In this photo, she is seen winning the 1964 Texas Appaloosa Horse Club Futurity over Nava Star and Ghost of Comanche.

Courtesy Jim Wild

Through the years, Wild put the best mares that he could personally find in Wapiti's broodmare band. Among his first mares was Tick Tock, a national champion daughter of Double Six Domino. She was followed by Star Mist, a national champion daughter of Star Duster (QH), and Jessie Joke and Joker's Miss Reed, two of the greatest Joker B. daughters.

In short order, he added Love Letter by Peavy Bimbo; Chipeta A. and Rina by Ding Bob II; 17 daughters of Bright Eyes Brother; and Quarter Horse mares by Three Bars (TB), Top Deck (TB), Two Eyed Jack and Spotted Bull (TB).

By the time it was all said and done, the Flying W broodmare band reigned as one of the most genetically powerful ever assembled.

Wild's personal association with Wapiti blossomed into a mutual admiration society at a very early stage. Anyone who ever saw the two together realized that they enjoyed a very special relationship.

"Wap was a great horse to be around,"

"POWDER SMOKE"
"10th RUNNING OF THE WORLD WIDE APPALOOSA FUTURITY"
ALBUQUERQUE, N.M.   SEPT. 17, 1971   B. McNATT, UP
STRIKE UP (2nd)   250 Yds 18.56 AND AWAY WE GO (3)
RALPH HENLEY, OWNER   J.D.ANDERSON, TR.
-----GROSS PURSE $30.842.36 -----

Powder Smoke, a 1969 stallion by Wapiti's Haunta and out of Pinetucky's Hootchie Patchy, won the 1971 World Wide Futurity and was named 1971 ApHC Champion Running Horse.

Courtesy Appaloosa Museum & Heritage Center

Wild says. "He was an intelligent horse and a kind horse, as were all of his foals.

"I used to keep him in a big paddock south of the barn. Any time I'd approach the gate and call to him, he'd come at a dead run. He was easy to handle in the breeding shed; we hand-bred him exclusively. We never did use a breeding dummy or artificial insemination."

By the late 1970s, Wapiti's breeding career was nearing its end. From his next-to-last foal crop, which numbered seven, came Wild Affair and Wapiti's WWF.

Wild Affair, a 1977 stallion out of Love Affair, was bred by Laura Richardson of Zachary, Louisiana, and developed by her into a champion halter horse and sire.

Wapiti's WWF (Worth Waiting For), a 1977 mare out of Peavy B, was bred by Tom and Betty Springer of Wapakoneta, Ohio, and developed by them into a top halter mare.

Wapiti's last foal crop hit the ground in 1978 and numbered but two. By this time, the legendary Peavy-bred stallion had contracted a life-threatening illness.

"Wap had a form of skin cancer," Jim Wild says. "I provided him with the best medical care available. Even with that, we could never get it permanently cured. I swore to myself that I'd do whatever I could to keep him alive as long as he showed that was what he wanted.

"On July 2, 1979, Wap got down and couldn't get up. I called the vet immediately and had him humanely put to sleep.

"We buried Wapiti here on the ranch, in the paddock where he spent so many years," Wild continues. "We also put a monument over his grave with a life-sized horse on the top of it, painted to match his markings.

"Wap was a once-in-a-lifetime horse. We were lucky to have owned him and luckier still to have been able to carry on with his sons and daughters, and their sons and daughters."

Like the team of Mavis Peavy and Peavy Bimbo before them, the team of Jim Wild and Wapiti was a record-setting one. Together, the Missouri pair lived through one of the most exciting and successful periods in Appaloosa history. What's more, they made monumental contributions to it.

Although sired by a registered Quarter Horse and out of a registered Quarter Horse, Wapiti was never a mystery horse or genetic freak. He was a great Appaloosa from a long line of great Appaloosas—outstanding producers every one. He lived up to his heritage.

In recognition of his positive impact on the breed, Wapiti was inducted into the ApHC Hall of Fame in 1988. Jim Wild, his life-long partner, was similarly inducted in 1996.

After Wapiti passed away on July 2, 1979, Jim Wild had a memorial to him built and placed in the paddock where he spent the majority of his life.

Courtesy Jim Wild

Chapter 20

BRIGHT EYES BROTHER
F-3047

Bright Eyes Brother—"In diamonds, it's Tiffany's … In Appaloosas, it's Bright Eyes Brother."—Cecil Dobbin,
Western Horseman *ad, February 1960.*

Courtesy Helen Dobbin

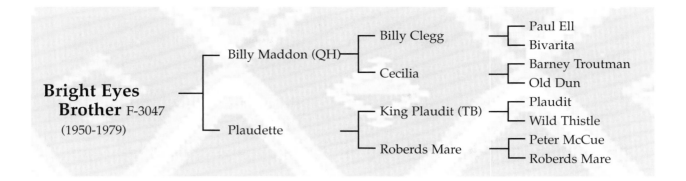

```
                                                 ┌── Paul Ell
                              ┌── Billy Clegg ────┤
             ┌── Billy Maddon (QH)─┤              └── Bivarita
             │                │                   ┌── Barney Troutman
Bright Eyes  │                └── Cecilia ────────┤
  Brother F-3047 ─┤                               └── Old Dun
  (1950-1979)│                                    ┌── Plaudit
             │                ┌── King Plaudit (TB)─┤
             └── Plaudette ───┤                    └── Wild Thistle
                              │                    ┌── Peter McCue
                              └── Roberds Mare ────┤
                                                   └── Roberds Mare
```

At roughly the same time that the Appaloosa descendants of the Old Blue Mare were first making their presence known, a close relative surfaced in New Mexico that would do much to enhance the family name.

Bright Eyes Brother, a 1950 stallion by Billy Maddon (QH) and out of Plaudette, was bred by C. L. "Tess" Maddon of Albuquerque. Although not a descendant of the Old Blue Mare, Bright Eyes Brother owed every bit of his Appaloosa heritage to the same Coke Roberds/Arab line of spotted horses that had spawned her and her storied offspring.

Billy Maddon, a 1944 sorrel stallion by Billy Clegg (QH) and out of Cecilia, was a winning halter horse and a Register of Merit sire.

Plaudette, a 1939 mare by King Plaudit (TB) and out of a Roberds Mare, was an unregistered Appaloosa with enough excess white to make her objectionable to both AQHA and ApHC. Despite this, she was a top match-racing horse and polo pony, and the dam of at least 16 foals including Maddon's Bright Eyes—the "Blue-Eyed Queen of Sprint"—and Bright Eyes Brother.

For the first eight years of his life, "Brother," or "Frosty" as he was initially known, languished in relative obscurity. Then, as luck would have it, he was discovered by a pioneer breeder who turned him into one of the best-known Appaloosa stallions of all-time.

As the mid-1950s dawned and the Appaloosa movement spread eastward, the Rocky Mountain region was one of the first to take up the banner. Cecil Dobbin, a Colorado Springs, Colorado-based auctioneer and horseman, was quick to throw his support behind the breed.

A born promoter, Dobbin worked behind the scenes to gain the breed access to major Rocky Mountain show and sale venues. A personal friend of *Western Horseman* Publisher Don Flint and Editor Dick Spencer III, he also lobbied for increased breed coverage in the magazine.

Dobbin's own involvement with the Appaloosa breed dated back to his purchase of a leopard stallion named Chief Crazy Horse C. T-957 in the early 1950s. Shortly thereafter, he acquired a son of Norell's Little Red named McCardo from Dewey Norell of Collbran, Colorado.

This shot of Bright Eyes Brother as a foal was taken at the C. L. Maddon Ranch near Albuquerque, New Mexico.

Courtesy Jim Wild

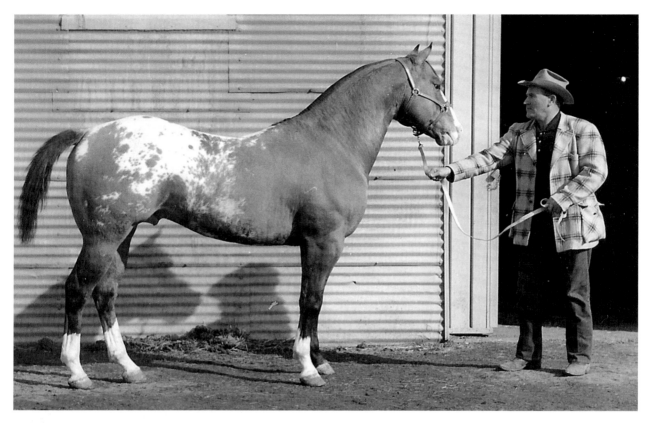

This photo of Bright Eyes Brother was shot right after he had earned Grand Champion Stallion honors at the 1959 National Western Livestock Show in Denver, Colorado. The shot of "Brother," with owner Cecil Dobbin at the lead shank, was taken by Western Horseman *editor Dick Spencer III.*

Courtesy Helen Dobbin

Dobbin was quick to realize that, even though his first two stallions were sufficient to get him established in the Appaloosa business, he was in need of a better-bred and better-built stud. During the course of his auctioneering travels, he began hearing rumors of just such a horse.

Helen Dobbin, Cecil's wife of 35 years, was in on the entire pioneering Appaloosa experience and retains vivid memories of the family's part in it.

"Cecil was at a horse sale in 1956 or 1957," she says, "when he overheard Hank Wiescamp visiting with some men. Hank told them that Bright Eyes—the three-time World Champion Quarter Running Horse—had two half-brothers. One, he said, was an AQHA-registered black stallion and the other was an unregistered dun Appaloosa stallion with a big white blanket. Hank went on to tell the

men that he knew where the Appaloosa was, and he was trying to get him bought.

"To say the least, 'Cec's' curiosity was aroused. But he didn't want to let Hank or any of those men know it, for fear that one of them would beat him to the punch. So he just lay low and quietly began trying to locate the horse."

By the summer of 1958, Dobbin had learned that the mystery stallion was owned by a man who competed off of him in calf roping and team roping at rodeos throughout the Four Corners area of Colorado, New Mexico, Arizona and Utah. Dobbin tasked a close rodeo friend to keep an eye out for the pair, with instructions to get a name and address once a positive I.D. was made.

In the fall of the year, Dobbin's amateur detective furnished him with the information. The horse's owner was Wiley

Donaldson, and he lived on the Apache Indian reservation near Dulce, New Mexico.

"One afternoon, I found Cecil in the bedroom, packing a suitcase," Helen says. " 'What are you doing?' I asked. 'I've found that stud and I'm going after him,' he said."

The story has been oft-repeated about how Cecil Dobbin withdrew all of his and Helen's personal savings to buy the newly discovered Appaloosa. Also well-documented is his trip into town to tell his *Western Horseman* cronies of his intent and Don Flint's offer to provide financial backing.

Helen Dobbin provides some additional insight into the event.

"Cecil left here in his pickup," she says, "with an open-topped, two-horse trailer in tow. Before he got to Dulce, he unhitched the trailer and parked it alongside the road next to some construction equipment. In town, he

found out where Wiley Donaldson's place was and drove out to it.

"When Cec arrived at the Donaldson place, there was no one home. This gave him the chance to locate the stud and look him over. Cec was sitting on the front porch when Wiley showed up.

"'I was just passing through this area,' he told Wiley, 'and I heard that you owned a pretty good Appaloosa stud.

"'I sure do,' Wiley said. 'He's out in the corral. Would you like to go out and take a look at him?'

"'I already have,' Cec said. 'He's the kind of horse that could do me a lot of good. I'd like to buy him from you.'

"'He's not for sale,' Wiley said. 'I rope off of him all the time, and he puts a lot of groceries on the table. On top of that, my wife and little girl love him. They'd never forgive

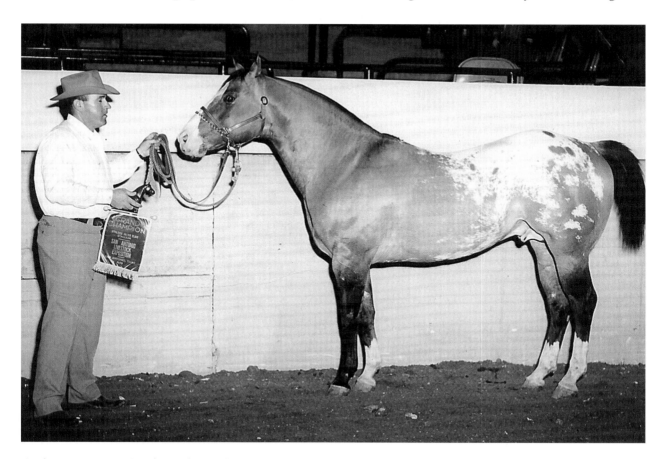

At the 1959 International Appaloosa Show in San Antonio, Texas, Bright Eyes Brother was named the Grand Champion Stallion over a star-studded field of horses that included Rustler Bill, Joker B. and Navajo Britches.

Courtesy Helen Dobbin

me if I sold him.'

"If there was one thing Cecil was really good at," Helen continues, "it was horse trading. If he came upon a horse that he had his mind set on owning, he'd do whatever it took to get the deal done. That's the way it was with that Appaloosa stud. He parlayed with Wiley until the wee hours of the morning and, when it was all said and done, the stud was his."

After negotiating the stallion's purchase, Dobbin cemented the deal.

"At one or two in the morning, after Wiley had agreed to sell," Helen says, "Cecil said to him, 'I'm going to write you a check right now as full payment for the horse. If I go out tomorrow morning to load him and he's dead, he's still my property. From this point

on, there's no backing out of the deal for either of us.'

"Cec knew that Wiley's wife and daughter were going to throw a fit when they found out he'd sold the horse. It'd taken Cec a long time to find the stud, and he didn't want to lose him over any misunderstanding."

Dobbin spent the night at the Donaldson home. Before daybreak, he got up, retrieved his horse trailer and loaded the stud. After securing a brand release from the local brand inspector, he headed north.

Once back home in Colorado Springs, the elated horseman called Spencer to come out and see his new acquisition.

"Dick and his first wife, Jo, came out," Helen Dobbin says. "After looking the stud over, Dick asked, 'What's his name?'

Bright Delight, a 1961 mare by Bright Eyes Brother and out of Peggy's Delight, was the Champion 2-Year-Old Mare and Grand Champion Mare at the 1963 National Show in Boise, Idaho.

Courtesy Appaloosa Museum & Heritage Center

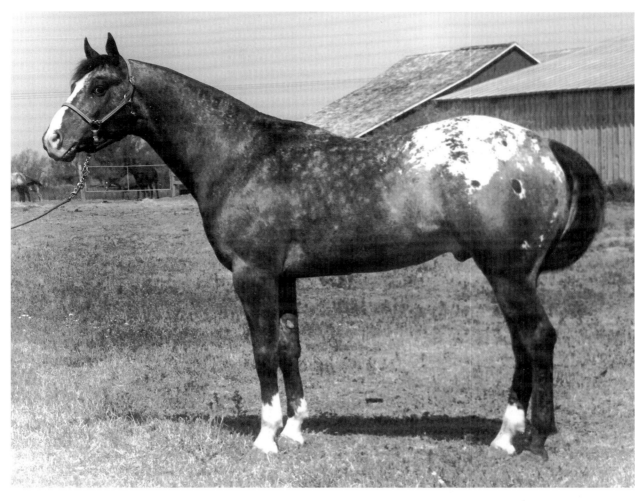

Bright Banner, a 1960 stallion by Bright Eyes Brother and out of All Sugar, was a champion halter horse and top sire.
Photo by Darol Dickinson

"'They call him 'Frosty,' Cec said. 'But I'm going to change that. He needs a better name.'

"'You might as well call him 'Bright Eyes Brother,' Dick said. 'That's who you're going to tell everybody he is.'

"And that's how 'Brother' was named."

Cecil Dobbin introduced Bright Eyes Brother to the horse world in a *Western Horseman* ad that appeared in the December 1958 issue. In it, he announced:

"Over the years, I feel I've been fortunate in having a good battery of Appaloosa studs. I have also carried on a search for one particular stallion; and, now I believe I have found THE ONE. He is BRIGHT EYES' BROTHER, and I believe he will do for the Appaloosa

breed what Bright Eyes did for the Quarter Horse breed. Plaudette, dam of Bright Eyes and Bright Eyes' Brother, was an outstanding Appaloosa mare."

Even prior to introducing Bright Eyes Brother to the world at large, Cecil had begun fitting him for halter competition.

In January of 1959, Appaloosas cracked the color barrier and were shown for the first time at the prestigious National Western Livestock Show in Denver, Colorado. Bright Eyes Brother was exhibited at the show and earned honors as the Champion Aged Stallion and Grand Champion Stallion. Finishing behind him as the second-place aged stallion and Reserve Champion Stallion was Carey's Little Chief.

Next up for Dobbin and Brother was the fourth annual Appaloosa show, held during the San Antonio International Livestock Exposition in San Antonio, Texas.

Once again, Brother emerged the Champion Aged Stallion and Grand Champion Stallion, topping a star-studded field that included Rustler Bill, Joker B., Navajo Britches, Cooterville Echohawk, Quavo B and Vanguard D.

The appearance of the big, blanket-hipped Appaloosa in South Texas almost precipitated a good old-fashioned donnybrook.

"At San Antonio," Helen Dobbin says, "Cec

put Brother up in a nice box stall, with his complete pedigree on a sign hung outside of it. At this time, Bright Eyes was one of the most popular Quarter racehorses of all time.

"Pretty soon, a crowd gathered in front of Brother's stall. It was made up mostly of Quarter Horse people, and they were a little hot under the collar. They didn't see how it could be possible that Bright Eyes and Bright Eyes Brother could be out of the same mare. They just knew that Cecil was making the whole thing up, and they wanted the pedigree sign to come down.

"It got so bad that the AQHA sent one of

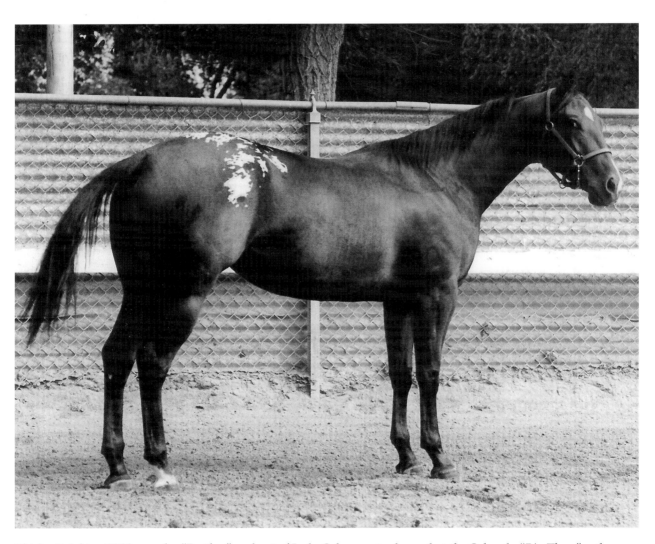

Shirley Bright, a 1966 mare by "Brother" and out of Lady Colorow, stood grand at the Colorado "Big Three"—the National Western Stock Show in Denver, the Colorado State Fair in Pueblo and the Mountain and Plains Appaloosa Horse Club Show in Estes Park.

Photo by Darol Dickinson, courtesy Helen Dobbin

their representatives over to calm the crowd down. He verified that the pedigree was correct. The Quarter Horse folks didn't like it too well, but there wasn't anything they could do about it."

Upon returning home from San Antonio, Dobbin readied Bright Eyes Brother for the 1959 breeding season. He also made a return trip to New Mexico to scour the countryside for any of Brother's get.

Wiley Donaldson had not used Brother as a breeding horse. He had, however, turned him in with the bucking and saddle stock at some of the rodeos he attended. A few "rodeo romances" occurred and Dobbin was able to locate and purchase two top young Bright Eyes Brother prospects.

Both horses—Bright Light, a 1958 mare out of Lady Dulce, and Dusty Rose, a 1959 mare out of Posie—went on to become top show horses.

After the 1959 breeding season was over, Bright Eyes Brother was re-fitted for halter and shown at the Mountain and Plains Appaloosa Horse Club show in Estes Park, Colorado, and the Colorado State Fair in Pueblo. At both shows, he was awarded Grand Champion Stallion honors.

In January of 1960, Dobbin and Brother returned to the National Western Livestock Show. There, for the second year in a row, the big dun stallion was named the Champion Aged Stallion and Grand Champion Stallion. Second place in the aged stallion class and Reserve Champion Stallion honors went to High Hand. He was followed by Hawk Eye, Patchy Jr. and Carey's Little Chief—all of whom were either past or future national champions.

After his back-to-back Denver wins, Bright Eyes Brother was retired from halter and the emphasis on his development was switched to the breeding shed.

Bright Starlette, a 1963 mare by Bright Eyes Brother and out of Deanna Duster (QH), was a champion halter horse, top producer and an ApHC Hall of Fame inductee.
Photo by Darol Dickinson, courtesy Helen Dobbin

Prior to being purchased by Dobbin as an 8-year-old, Brother had sired a total of five ApHC-registered foals. His first foal crop for Dobbin arrived in 1960 and numbered 18. Among its most noteworthy members were Mighty Bright, Bright Banner, Bright Charmer and Bright Robin.

Mighty Bright, a 1960 stallion out of Peggy's Delight, was bred by Lane Hudson and will be discussed in the following chapter.

Bright Banner, a 1960 stallion out of All Sugar, and Bright Charmer, a 1960 mare out of Red Sand, were bred by Dobbin. Both would be developed into top halter horses. In addition, "Banner" would go on to become a leading sire.

Bright Robin, a 1960 mare out of Puss, was bred by Harry Reed of Colorado Springs. She, too, would become a top halter mare and producer.

From Bright Eyes Brother's second crop of 20 foals came the likes of Bright Delight, Bright Doll, Bright Glow, Bright Chip and Bright Luster.

Bright Delight, a 1961 mare out of Peggy's Delight, was bred by Lane Hudson. The Champion 2-Year-Old Mare and Grand Champion Mare at the 1963 National Show in Boise, Idaho, she would go on to become one of the breed's top producers.

Bright Doll, a 1961 mare out of Chipeta Doll, was bred by Jim Wild of Sarcoxie, Missouri. She would go on to become a top halter and Western pleasure horse, and the Champion Produce of Dam winner at the 1978 National Show in Billings, Montana, and the 1978 World Championship Show in Oklahoma City.

Mr. Exclusive, a 1968 stallion by Bright Eyes Brother and out of Dash's Blossom, was sold to Mel and Aggie Marvin of Eaton Rapids, Michigan. "Exclusive" went on to become a top halter horse and sire.

Photo by Mel Marvin, courtesy Mel and Aggie Marvin

Bright Chip, a 1961 stallion out of Chipeta A., was bred by Jim Wild. Sold to Eugene and Doris Sharp of Morgan Hills, California, he went on to become an all-time leading sire and a 1991 inductee into the ApHC Hall of Fame.

Bright Glow, a 1961 stallion out of Star Dream, was bred by Dobbin. The Grand Champion Stallion at the 1965 National Western, he was sold to Bob and Marjorie Acomb of Stafford, New York, and was developed into a promising young breeding horse. Unfortunately, he died after siring only three foal crops.

Bright Luster, a 1961 mare out of Lady Senator, was also bred by Dobbin. Sold to Martin Abrahamsen of Aurora, Colorado, she went on to become a leading broodmare, producing such horses as Dial Bright Too, an all-time leading sire, and My Host Bright, a top race mare.

Brother's third set of Colorado-bred foals, which numbered 19, included such champions as Bright Cash and Miss Love Letters.

Bright Cash, a 1962 gelding out of Puss, was the Grand Champion Gelding at the 1967 National Show in Walla Walla, Washington.

Miss Love Letters, a 1962 mare out of Love Letter, was bred by Jim Wild. Sold to E. J. Plott of Canton, Ohio, she went on to become a top halter mare and producer.

In addition to the above-mentioned horses, there were numerous other noteworthy Bright Eyes Brother get born during his first years in Colorado. Included among them were such horses as Bright Mist, Bright-Esta, Bright Charmer, Bright Plaudette, Carey's Bright Eyes, Bright Streak, Bright Scout, Bright Fan, Star Bright and Bright Rose.

Once he had proven to the Appaloosa world that Bright Eyes

Bright Brand, a 1967 stallion by Bright Eyes Brother and out of Wapiti's Tip Top, was a Texas Appaloosa Horse Club high-point halter horse.

Courtesy Helen Dobbin

AmBright, a 1971 mare by Bright Eyes Brother and out of Wapiti's Tip Top, was a champion halter mare and a top producer.

Courtesy Helen Dobbin

Bright Tribute, a 1971 stallion by "Brother" and out of McCardo's Willie Reese, was one of his sire's most accomplished show get. Sold to Lewis and Marilyn Feuerstein of Creston, California, "Tribute" was a two-time national grand champion stallion.

Photo by Steve DeGino, courtesy Helen Dobbin

Brother was an up-and-coming sire, Dobbin went on to demonstrate how to effectively market the big horse's foals. In September of 1962, he held what would be hailed as one of the industry's top production sales up to that point.

Billed as the Red Carpet Sale, and held in Elbert, Colorado, it saw Bright Banner become the high-seller at $21,000 when purchased by Chuck Singleton of Trowbridge, California. In addition, Bright Tiger, a 1962 stallion out of Pop's Dream (QH), sold for

$8,000 to Tom Petrie of Ramona, California. Bright Knight, a 1961 stallion out of Dry Fly, sold for $4,500 to Paul Johnson of Cascade, Colorado, and Santa Barbara, California.

In articles appearing in *Western Horseman* and *Appaloosa News*, the event was used as a model for how to conduct a successful horse sale.

Over the course of the next 11 years—from 1963 through 1974—Bright Eyes Brother turned out a steady stream of champions. Among his brightest stars during this stage of his life were Bright Starlette and Bright Glitter—both bred by Dobbin.

"Starlette," a 1963 mare out of Deanna Duster, was sold to Barney Waugh of Mitchell, Nebraska. A grand champion halter horse, she also went on to become one of the breed's premier producers. Among her top offspring were the national champion full siblings Skip Bright and Skip's Brightette, and the ApHC Hall of Fame inductee Skip The Color.

As a result of her own contributions to the breed, Bright Starlette was inducted into the ApHC Hall of Fame in 1990.

"Glitter," a 1966 mare out of Lady Senator, was sold to Lewis and Marilynn Feuerstein of Buttonwillow, California. For them, she went on to become Champion Produce of Dam winner at the 1981 National Show in San Antonio, Texas.

In addition to these national and world champion horses, there was a host of other noteworthy Bright Eyes Brother get born during this era. Included among them were such top show and breeding horses as Bright Auctioneer, Shirley Bright, Bright Pro, Bright Brand, Mr. Exclusive and Bright Secret.

By the early 1970s, Brother's career as a breeding horse was drawing to a close. Between 1971 and 1976, he sired only 16 foals. Of these, Bright Tribute and Bright Reflection stand out.

"Tribute," a 1971 stallion out of McCardo's Willie Reese, was sold to the Feuersteins. Developed by them into one of the top halter horses of his day, he was the Champion 2-Year-Old Stallion and Grand Champion Stallion at the 1973 National Show in Salem, Oregon, and the Champion Aged Stallion and Grand Champion Stallion at the 1975 National Show in Santa Rosa, California.

"Reflection," a 1975 stallion also out of McCardo's Willie Reese, was

bred by the Feuersteins and shown by them to earn dual honors as the Champion 2-Year-Old Stallion and the Reserve Grand Champion Stallion at the 1977 National Show in Syracuse, New York. Re-sold to Jack and Glenna Clark of British, Columbia, he was the Champion 3-Year-Old Stallion at the 1978 World Championship Show in Oklahoma City.

In 1976, Cecil Dobbin decided that the Colorado winters were beginning to weigh too heavily on Bright Eyes Brother. In a move designed to get the then-26-year-old situated in a milder climate, he leased him to the Feuersteins in California.

Bright Reflection, a 1975 full brother to Bright Tribute, was the Champion 2-Year-Old Stallion and the Grand Champion Stallion at the 1977 National Show in Syracuse, New York, and the Champion 3-Year-Old Stallion at the 1978 World Championship Show in Oklahoma City.

Photo by Don Shugart, courtesy Todd Henderson

One of the most potent sires of all time, Bright Eyes Brother was imbued with the "look of eagles."
Photo by Darol Dickinson, courtesy Ed Roberts

Brother's last foal crop, numbering four and born in California, hit the ground in 1977. From it came the legendary stallion's final show star.

No Moore, a 1977 mare out of Saucy Time, was bred by the Feuersteins. Shown at the 1980 World Championship Show in Oklahoma City, she was named the Champion 3-Year-Old Mare. Through an administrative entry error, though, she was subsequently declared ineligible and her world crown taken away.

Bright Eyes Brother was retired from breeding at the end of the 1976 season and lived for several years after that. He passed away in 1979 at the age of 29.

When the team of Cecil Dobbin and Bright Eyes Brother appeared on the scene in the late 1950s, the Appaloosa breed was involved in an ambitious effort to spread "spotted fever" throughout the land.

Dobbin and Brother—the consummate promoter and the horse with the "look of eagles"—were quick to throw themselves into the fray. Together, they helped take the Appaloosa show and breeding horse to new heights—not only in the Rocky Mountain region, but nationwide, as well. In recognition of their contributions, both were inducted into the ApHC Hall of Fame in 1988.

Bright Eyes Brother, shown here in action on the Dobbin's Flying N Ranch near Peyton, Colorado, possessed a level of charisma and eye-appeal that endeared him to a legion of fans.

Photo by Darol Dickinson, courtesy Helen Dobbin

Chapter 21

MIGHTY BRIGHT
#9760

Mighty Bright—"If ever a horse was named correctly, it was him."

Courtesy Helen Dobbin

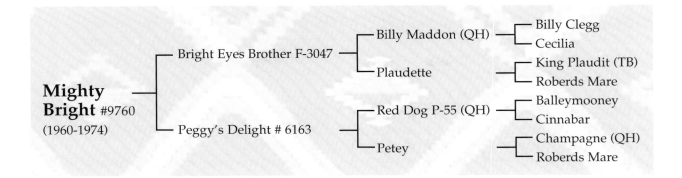

Shortly after Cecil Dobbin acquired Bright Eyes Brother in the fall of 1958, the stallion came to the attention of Lane Hudson, a Denver-based Quarter Horse breeder and cutting horse exhibitor. Beginning in the early 1940s, Hudson had popularized the Sobre line of palomino halter horses, and the Lady's Black Eagle and Star Boarder line of performance horses.

Upon hearing rumors that Dobbin had acquired an Appaloosa brother of the legendary Maddon's Bright Eyes, Hudson made a trip to Colorado Springs to get a first-hand look at the stallion. "Brother" made such a favorable impression on him that he immediately approached Dobbin about breeding a mare.

Dobbin was noncommittal, saying that he would first have to see and approve the mare.

The paths of these three principles crossed again at the 1959 Denver National Western Stock Show. Bright Eyes Brother was named the Grand Champion Appaloosa Stallion there, and Hudson's interest in him increased. All that was needed now was to find just the right Appaloosa mare to cross on him.

A chance conversation at the show with fellow Quarter Horse breeder Al Buckli of Wibaux, Montana, put Hudson on the trail of a mare that he thought might fill the bill. According to Buckli, the mare carried AQHA papers but was in reality a roan Appaloosa. Hudson found out that the mare was either owned by or under the care of Fred Field of Gunnison, Colorado.

Field was exhibiting horses at the stock show, so Hudson located him and asked if he

had such a mare. Field replied that he did and that her name was Peggy's Delight. She was a direct daughter of Jack Casement's famous foundation sire Red Dog P-55.

Hudson knew he was on the right track.

The next morning, Hudson hooked up his trailer and started out for Gunnison. He found that the mare had some age on her and she was still nursing the foal from the year before. The winter had been tough on her, but she still showed evidence of good conformation and breeding.

After several hours of negotiations, Field and Hudson were still $500 apart so Hudson returned home with an empty trailer.

Several months later, Field called Hudson accepting his earlier offer.

Peggy's Delight, a 1944 roan mare, was by Red Dog P-55 and out of Petey by Champagne.

"Peggy's" AQHA papers listed her breeder as Frances "Biddy" Peavy of Westplains, Colorado, and the mare carried the Peavy family's famous "VZ" brand on her left shoulder. In an attempt to find out more about his new acquisition's pedigree, Hudson got in touch with one of the state's best-known Western personalities.

"Mavis Peavy was Biddy's mother," Lane says, "Mavis and I knew each other through the Quarter Horse business, so I dialed her up at her ranch near Padroni to see if I couldn't find out more about the bottom side of Peggy's pedigree."

Mavis was quick to inform Hudson that Petey, his new mare's dam, was of superior breeding. A 1940 bay mare by Champagne

(QH) and out of a Roberds Mare, she was bred by Coke Roberds of Hayden, Colorado. Though she sported AQHA papers, Petey was a marginally colored Appaloosa.

Mavis went on to tell Hudson that her daughter, Frances, had purchased Petey as a yearling directly from Coke, at one of his early sales. She further recalled that the mare had been purchased quite reasonably, due in part to the fact that pre-teen Frances had convinced her father, Marshall Peavy, to let her bid on the yearling filly herself. Most of the other buyers at the sale, it seemed, were reluctant to bid against a youngster.

After he completed the deal on Peggy's Delight and got her home, Hudson found out she wasn't in foal as had been expected. In fact, she was ready for breeding and was

taken immediately to Bright Eyes Brother. Eleven months later, on April 15, 1960, Mighty Bright was foaled.

"Since I had never raised a foal out of Peggy," Hudson says, "and since this was going to be the very first Appaloosa that I had ever raised, I really wanted to be there when she foaled.

"I didn't have any idea what kind of signs she made prior to foaling, though, and to tell you the truth, she just sort of snuck off and had Mighty Bright all by herself. The first inkling I had that he was here was when I stepped off the porch that morning to go do chores and there he stood, in the middle of a lot, staring straight at me.

"At first I wasn't sure what I had," Hudson continued. "He was a light-red dun color,

Peggy's Delight, the dam of Mighty Bright, was the 1960 and 1961 Mountain and Plains Appaloosa Horse Club High-Point Broodmare.

Courtesy Peavy Estate

with a bald face, two blue eyes and four high stockings. At first, I couldn't see any Appaloosa color. Then he turned away from me and I saw that he had a nice white blanket spread over the top of his hips.

"When I got to looking closer at him, I could see that he had a lot of quality and conformation, and I began to think that maybe, just maybe, I was on to something."

It didn't take long for the rest of the horse world to confirm Hudson's suspicions.

Mighty Bright was shown at halter three times as a weanling. He won all three classes and was the 1960 Mountain and Plains Appaloosa Horse Club High-Point Weanling Stallion. Not to be outdone, his then-16-year-old dam was the club's High-Point Broodmare.

At what would turn out to be Mighty Bright's last horse show—the 1960 Colorado State Fair in Pueblo—Lane Hudson received one of the strongest endorsements of the colt's potential worth that he could have hoped for.

"Hank Wiescamp of Alamosa, Colorado, offered me $10,000 for Mighty Bright while we were at the fair," Hudson says. "In those days, that was a lot of money for a baby, but I figured that if a man with Wiescamp's knowledge liked him that much, then maybe I was better off keeping him for awhile."

Later, Wiescamp sent a man to see what it would take to buy the colt, but he still wasn't for sale.

A leg injury Mighty Bright sustained while Lane was preparing him for the 1961 Denver National Western Stock Show ended the young stallion's promising show career. It did not take long, however, for Hudson and the rest of the Appaloosa fraternity to realize that the flashy youngster's true calling was not to be a show horse, but instead to be a sire.

Mighty Bright's first foal crop was born in 1963. It was small, numbering only 12, but

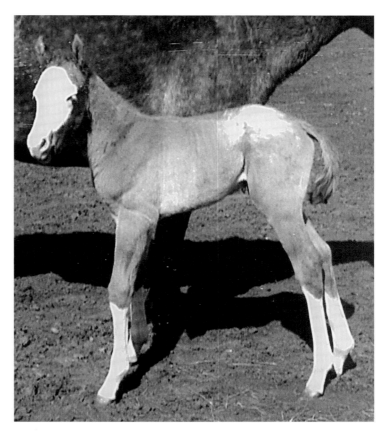

Even as a foal, Mighty Bright evidenced the quality that would see him go on to become a champion halter horse and top sire.
Courtesy Lane Hudson

among that group was an especially promising colt named Mighty Peavy.

Might Peavy was out of Genivieve Peavy by Peavy Bimbo. As noted in Chapter 19, "Genivieve" was the first of several mares that Lane acquired from Mavis Peavy.

Genivieve was a top halter mare and, shown by Hudson, was named the Grand Champion Mare at the 1962 National Show in Springfield, Illinois, and at the 1962 New Mexico State Fair in Albuquerque.

Her son, Mighty Peavy, quickly followed in her footsteps.

Dennis Crist, then of Modoc, Kansas, purchased "Peavy" as a yearling. Crist campaigned the chestnut, blanket-hipped stallion very successfully at halter, with the high point of Peavy's show career coming in 1967 when he was named Grand Champion Stallion at the Denver National Western Stock

Show. He then went on to become a two-time national champion get of sire winner and a multiple national and world champion sire.

Mighty Bright's second foal crop was even smaller than the first, producing only 10 foals. From it, however, came such durable stars as Mighty Paul, Mighty Shiek, Mighty Marshall, Mighty Bounce and Mighty Loma.

Mighty Paul, a 1964 stallion out of Carmen Calypso (QH), was sold to Monte and Linda Heinrich of Yoder, Wyoming, and was developed by them into a top halter horse and a multiple national and world champion sire.

Mighty Shiek, a 1964 stallion out of Genivieve Peavy, was sold to Clarence Danielson of Watford City, North Dakota. He, too, would go on to become a national champion get of sire winner and a multiple national and world champion sire.

Furthermore, when "Shiek" won the 1974 National Champion Get of Sire title, he and Mighty Peavy became the only two full brothers in the history of the breed to share the honor.

Mighty Marshall, a 1964 stallion out of Overdue Peavy (QH), was sold to Roger and

Mighty Peavy, a 1963 stallion by Mighty Bright and out of Genivieve Peavy, was the Get of Sire Champion at both the 1971 National Show in Las Vegas, Nevada, and the 1978 National Show in Billings, Montana.
. Photo by Alfred Janssen III, courtesy Denny Crist

Dixie Klamfoth of Groveport, Ohio. His dam was the second of the Mavis Peavy-bred broodmares to be acquired by Lane Hudson. An exceptionally well-bred mare, she was sired by Ambrose and out of Chipeta by Ding Bob.

Like his grandsire, Bright Eyes Brother, and his half-brother, Mighty Peavy, Mighty Marshall earned honors as the Grand Champion Stallion at the National Western Stock Show.

In addition, he stood grand at the Houston Livestock Exposition in Houston, Texas; the Ak-Sar-Ben Livestock Show in Omaha, Nebraska; and the National All-Breed Show in Columbus, Ohio. Finally, he was the 1971 World Champion Senior Western Pleasure Horse and the 1972 Reserve Grand Champion Stallion.

Hudson consigned Mighty Bounce, a 1964 stallion out of Cherry Cordial (QH), and Mighty Loma, a 1964 mare out of Bar W Bar Bet (QH), to the sale held in conjunction with the 1965 National Show in Sacramento, California.

"Bounce's" dam was the third of the great Peavy mares to be acquired by Lane. Sired by Cherry Bounce and out of Overdue Peavy, she would go on to become one of Hudson's most prolific producers. Mighty Bounce, her first Appaloosa son, set the standard for the full siblings that followed when he topped the 1965 National Sale and then went on to become a highly successful show horse and sire on the West Coast.

Mighty Loma placed second in the yearling filly halter class at the 1965 National Show. After the sale, she went on to become a top halter mare and producer.

From Mighty Bright's third foal crop of 18 youngsters came the likes of Mighty Gunsmoke, Mighty Mona, Mighty High and City Slicker.

Mighty Gunsmoke, a 1965 gelding out of

Mighty Shiek, a 1964 full brother to Mighty Peavy, was the Get of Sire Champion at the 1974 National Show in Shelbyville, Tennessee.
Photo by Darol Dickinson, courtesy Clarence Danielson

Barretta Mount (QH), was sold to Bob and Shirley Allen of Albion, New York. Under their ownership, he was named the Greater Eastern Appaloosa Regional (GEAR) Champion No. 1, and holder of Certificate of Achievement (COA) No. 1 in Western Pleasure.

Mighty Mona, a 1965 mare out of Helen Hudson (QH), was sold to Mrs. A. S. Kelly of Chester, Vermont. Mighty Mona was also an early GEAR Champion and one of the top

Mighty Paul, a 1964 stallion by Mighty Bright and out of Carmen Calypso (QH), was a top halter horse and sire.
Photo by Darol Dickinson, courtesy Helen Dobbin

broken shoulder negated those plans, however. Instead, the stallion was sold to Bernard Selvy of Parker, Colorado, for whom he went on to become a top sire.

The stars of Mighty Bright's next foal crop would have to be Mighty Amy and Spittin' Image.

"Amy," a 1966 mare out of Cherry Cordial, was a beautiful blue grullo with a blazed face, four even white socks and a small white blanket. Purchased by Richard Zimmerman of Ellicott City, Maryland, she dominated the halter scene on the East Coast for several years. Later sold to A. F. Jackson III of Houston, Texas, she was named the Champion Aged Mare at the 1971 National Show in Las Vegas, Nevada. She died a short time after that show, never having produced a foal.

Spittin Image, a 1966 stallion, was so named because he was a duplicate of his famous sire in color. His dam was Miss Mavis—the fourth great Mavis Peavy-bred mare to be acquired by Lane. Sired by Peavy Bimbo and out of Ida Pearl (QH) by Gold Heels, she was both a champion show mare and a great producer.

"Image," her first son, was sold as a youngster to Gene Keefer of Cheyenne, Wyoming. Purchased as a 2-year-old by Lois and Susan Baker of Parker, Colorado, he went on to become one of the top halter and performance horses in the Rocky Mountain region. In later years, he was sold to Joe Stroube of Corsicana, Texas, and Dave and Kim Utke of Sheldon, North Dakota. He made a top sire for both sets of owners.

Mighty Tim, a 1967 stallion out of Cherry Cordial (QH), was the runaway star of Mighty Bright's next foal crop. Purchased as a young horse by Mrs. A.S. Kelly of Chester, Vermont, "Tim" compiled an extensive show record in both halter and performance on the East Coast and throughout the Midwest.

halter mares on the East Coast.

Mighty High, a 1965 gelding out of Cuchara Jewel, was sold to Sherry Alexander of Chillicothe, Ohio. Like his half-siblings, he went on to become a GEAR Champion and a top halter, performance and youth mount.

City Slicker, a 1965 stallion out of Sobre's Helen M (QH), was an especially beautiful Mighty Bright son. A dark bay with a big white blanket full of haloed spots, he was targeted by Lane to be kept as a show horse and junior sire. A freak accident that resulted in a

Mighty Marshall, a 1964 stallion by Mighty Bright and out of Overdue Peavy (QH), was the 1971 World Champion Senior Western Pleasure Horse. Also a top halter horse, "Marshall" is seen here with owner Roger Klamfoth of Groveport, Ohio.

Photo by Johnny Johnston, courtesy Roger Klamfoth

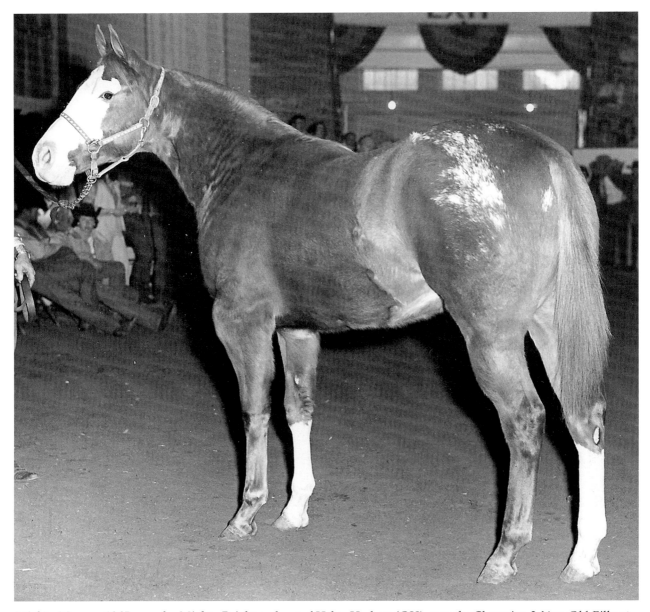

Mighty Mona, a 1965 mare by Mighty Bright and out of Helen Hudson (QH), was the Champion 2-Year-Old Filly at the National Western Stock Show in Denver, Colorado.

Photo by Darol Dickinson, courtesy Helen Dobbin

Later purchased by the Utkes to head their Sheldak Ranch breeding program, he went on to become one of his sire's greatest breeding sons and a multiple national and world champion sire.

Meanwhile, back at the ranch, Lane Hudson and Mighty Bright continued to turn out champion after champion. Also from Mighty Bright's 1967 foal crop came Mighty Marie and Mighty Doc.

"Marie," a 1967 mare out of Wee Marie (QH) by Norell's Little Red, also found her way back East where she won championship after championship. She was often hauled with her famous half-brother, Mighty Marshall, and received her stiffest competition from her half-sisters Mighty Amy and Mighty Mona.

Mighty Doc, a 1967 gelding out of Mandy Murdock (QH), was the Champion Yearling Gelding title at the 1968 National Show in Oklahoma City, Oklahoma

As the 1960s wound down, so, too, did the Lane Hudson portion of the Mighty Bright story.

Eleven Mighty Brights hit the ground in 1969, with the best known of them being Moms Mabley.

Moms Mabley, a 1969 mare out of Tahitian Irene, was sold to John Cavey of Parker, Colorado, and developed by him into a top show mare.

Mighty Bright's last Colorado foal crop hit the ground in 1970. From it came a number of top broodmares, but no noteworthy show horses or sires.

By 1970, Hudson had a pasture full of Mighty Bright daughters and a promising young junior stallion named Mr. Big Wig to breed them to. Because of this, he agreed to lease Mighty Bright to Jack Ryan of Corpus Christi, Texas.

Ryan bred the stallion a little heavier than Hudson had and, in 1971, 19 Mighty Bright foals were born. Among their number were Sweet Pearl and Jackie's Bright Flame.

Sweet Pearl, a 1971 mare out of Cedar Hill Three Leo Girl, went on to earn honors as the 1976 World Champion Senior Western Pleasure Horse. Jackie's Bright Flame, a 1971 mare out of Skip's Flame (QH), went on to become a top Lone Star State halter and cutting horse.

In 1971, Mighty Bright changed hands for the first and last time in his life when Hudson sold the famous sire to Dr. George Gayle and his wife, Jane, of Houston, Texas. From his first foal crop for the Texas couple, born in 1972, came Mighty Gayle and Mighty Go Man.

Mighty Gayle, a 1972 mare out of Little Gold Digger, went on to become the Champion Junior Western Pleasure Horse at the 1975 National Show in Santa Rosa, California, and at the 1976 World Championship Appaloosa Horse Show in

Mighty Amy was one of the most beautiful show mares of all time. A 1966 mare by Mighty Bright and out of Cherry Cordial (QH), "Amy" was the Champion Aged Mare at the 1971 National Show in Las Vegas. Hadley Campbell is seen at the halter.

Photo by Johnny Johnston, courtesy Appaloosa Museum & Heritage Center

Spittin' Image, a 1966 stallion by Mighty Bright and out of Miss Mavis, was so named because of his startling resemblance to his sire. A top halter and performance horse, he went on to become a foundation sire for Dave and Kim Utke's Sheldak Ranch in Sheldon, North Dakota.

Photo by Darol Dickinson, courtesy Kim Utke

Oklahoma City, Oklahoma.

Mighty Go Man, a 1972 stallion out of Go Lady Go, remains one of the most unique Mighty Bright sons of all time. Sold to Russell and Laura Brest of Sidney, Montana, he was developed into a grand champion halter horse and top sire. An amazing color-getter, out of 51 foals he sired 49 colored youngsters for the Brests.

Getting back to Mighty Bright, he was destined to sire only three more foal crops for George and Jane Gayle. From the 1974 crop came Mighty Friday—Mighty Bright's last great show horse.

"Friday," out of Carmen Calypso (QH), was bred by Lane's brother-in-law and sister, Dick and Margie Kirk of Houston, Texas. Under their ownership, Friday was named the 1978 National and World Champion Aged Gelding.

While owned by the Gayles, Mighty Bright was honored as the No. 1 GEAR Supreme Champion Sire of Performance Horses. To earn this award, five of his foals had to win any combination of GEAR Championships or Certificates of Versatility.

The five foals that earned this prestigious award for Mighty Bright—all by being named GEAR Champions—were Mighty Marshall, Mighty High, Mighty Gunsmoke, Mighty Mona and Mighty Amy.

Mighty Bright died in the spring of 1974 at

Mighty Tim, a 1967 stallion by Mighty Bright and out of Cherry Cordial (QH), was also a top halter and performance horse. And, like Spittin' Image, "Tim" went on to become a foundation Sheldak Ranch sire.. **Photo by Darol Dickinson, courtesy Kim Utke**

Mighty Marie, a 1967 mare by Mighty Bright and out of Wee Marie (QH), was yet another top halter horse. The refined dun mare is shown here with Dixie Klamfoth after earning grand champion mare honors at a circa early-1970s Ohio show.

Courtesy Roger Klamfoth

the Gayles' ranch outside of Houston. An autopsy revealed that he died of a heart disorder. Although he was gone, the Lane Hudson-bred stallion's legacy was just beginning.

As noted earlier, Mighty Bright's sons had begun to make their own widespread and significant contributions to the breed years earlier. In addition to those sons already mentioned, such horses as Mighty McCue, Mighty Ute, Mighty Padroni, Road Agent, Mighty Bright Bimbo, Mighty Kentuckian and Mighty Texan all went on to become top sires.

And then there were the Mighty Bright mares. Colored and uncolored, and often-times full sisters to the more-famous show members of the family, the list of Mighty Bright daughters that became renowned as producers is extensive.

Leading that list would have to be Mighty Bimbo and Barretta Bright.

Mighty Bimbo, a 1967 full sister to Spittin' Image, was the 1977 National Champion Produce of Dam winner.

Barretta Bright, a 1968 full sister to Mighty Gunsmoke, went on to become one of Sheldak Ranch's cornerstone mares. Among her top produce are 1996 ApHC Hall of Fame inductee Prince Shannon, as well as King David, Star Of David and Lord David.

But there were other top-producing Mighty Bright mares, as well, including Mighty Thelma, Mighty Flo, Mighty Pauline, Mighty Bars, Mighty Gay GG, Mighty Flaxie GG, Mighty Sugar GG, Mighty Dixie GG, Mighty Dolly GG and Mighty Skipaway.

By some standards, Mighty Bright's life as a breeding horse was short. When the final tally was entered, he sired only 13 foal crops, with some of those being quite small in number.

For a horse like Mighty Bright, however, it was enough.

When he came on the scene in the early 1960s, Mighty Bright helped raise the Appaloosa show and breeding horse standards to higher levels than had ever been seen. His impact was immediate and far-reaching. The quality of his foals and their foals was consistent, and the legacy that he left is still felt in every corner of the industry.

Mighty Bright, his breeder Lane Hudson and his last owner Dr. George Gayle, were all 1988 inductees into the ApHC Hall of Fame.

Mighty Friday, a 1974 gelding by Mighty Bright and out of Carmen Calypso (QH), was bred by Lane Hudson's brother-in-law and sister, Dick and Margie Kirk of Houston, Texas. Under their ownership, the big dun was named the Champion Aged Gelding at the 1978 National Show in Billings, Montana, and the 1978 World Championship Show in Oklahoma City, Oklahoma.

Photo by Johnny Johnston, courtesy Appaloosa Museum and Heritage Center

Chapter 22

HANDS UP
F-2217

Hands Up, the product of a speed pedigree, fashioned an enduring line of all-around Appaloosas.
Photo by Paul Yard, courtesy **Western Horseman**

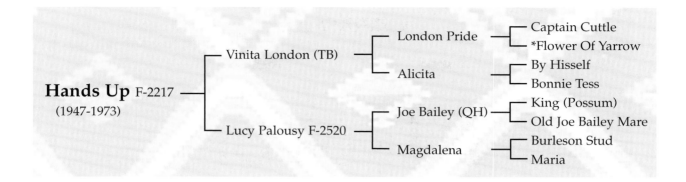

```
                                                            ┌─ Captain Cuttle
                                    ┌─ London Pride ─────────┤
                    ┌─ Vinita London (TB) ─┤                └─ *Flower Of Yarrow
                    │                 │                      ┌─ By Hisself
                    │                 └─ Alicita ────────────┤
Hands Up F-2217 ────┤                                        └─ Bonnie Tess
  (1947-1973)       │                                        ┌─ King (Possum)
                    │                 ┌─ Joe Bailey (QH) ────┤
                    └─ Lucy Palousy F-2520 ─┤                └─ Old Joe Bailey Mare
                                      │                      ┌─ Burleson Stud
                                      └─ Magdalena ──────────┤
                                                             └─ Maria
```

At roughly the same time that the Mansfield's Comanche horses were being discovered on the plains of the Texas Panhandle, a second Appaloosa family was being spawned in the same area.

This was the Hands Up line.

Hands Up, a 1947 stallion by Vinita London (JC) and out of Lucy Palousy F-2520, was bred by Ida Mae McKinley of Texhoma, Texas.

Vinita London, a 1937 stallion by London's Pride and out of Alicita, was bred by Walter Hancock of Vinita, Oklahoma. A blazed-face, stocking-legged sorrel, the stallion was a top "short-distance" match-race horse and an AQHA race Register of Merit sire.

Lucy Palousy, a 1941 blue roan mare, is listed as being by the foundation sire Joe Bailey P-4 (QH) and out of Magdalena. Also a top match-racing mare during the early to mid-1940s, she reportedly met and defeated such top sprinters as Grey Hancock, also known as Grey Eagle.

Retired from the track, "Lucy" went on to become a top producer.

In addition to Hands Up, she was also the dam of the foundation stallion Little Britches K, by Kandyman (QH); and the top show mares Sparkle Plenty, by Hands Up; Lucy's Pride, by Cherokee A.; Joker's Lu Cee, by Joker B.; and Joker's Lucy 2, by Joker B.

Hands Up, a bay, blanket-hipped stallion, was his dam's first known offspring.

Early in his life, Hands Up was acquired by Buddy Heaton of Hugoton, Kansas—one of the most colorful Western characters of his day.

Heaton—born in Ulysses, Kansas, in 1929—is recalled as one of the most-gifted high school athletes to ever come out of the state. A renowned rodeo clown and bulldogging competitor, he was also a self-described "rounder" and Appaloosa fancier.

"I bought Hands Up in 1949, as a 2-year-old," Heaton says. "I got him from Bill John Pugh of Dumas, Texas.

"When I ran across Hands Up, Bill John was match-racing him. He'd got along real well with him and, as a result, I had to pay through the nose to get the horse. He cost me $500 in cash, another horse and a wooden horse trailer.

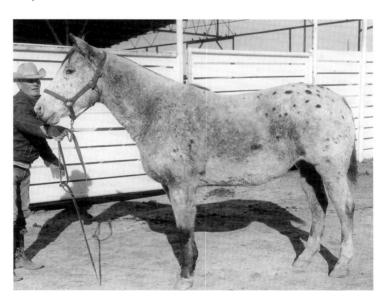

Lucy Palousy, Hands Up's dam, was one of the breed's greatest foundation producers.

Courtesy Marian Alton

Blinded in a freak barnyard accident in the early 1950s, Hands Up was still allowed to roam free with his broodmare band every spring and summer.

*Courtesy **Marian Alton***

"I match-raced Hands Up myself, and even bulldogged off him at some rodeos. In racing, we won a few good ones. Then, one day down at Lubbock, Texas, I got him outrun and didn't have the money to leave town on. So I wound up selling him to Roy G. Wood of Chelsea, Oklahoma, for $1,500 in cash and an Appaloosa-colored mule. I sure hated to part with the stud, but there wasn't much I could do about it at the time."

Riley Miller, pioneer Appaloosa breeder from Justiceburg, Texas, recalls his first glimpse of Hands Up during this part of the foundation stallion's life.

"It was in 1950, at a rodeo in Breckenridge, Texas, that I first saw Hands Up," he says. "Buddy Heaton

Miss Liberal, a 1952 mare by Hands Up and out of Flying Flag (QH), was one of the top show mares of her era. The Lucy Palousy look-alike is seen here with owner Dorothy Bowling at the 1961 National Show in Fort Worth, Texas. ApHC President Howard Poor is presenting the Jo Warren mink stole award to Dorothy for being the show's high-point lady exhibitor.

*Courtesy **Western Horseman***

was one of the rodeo clowns working the show. He also had a trick horse act with a palomino named El Roco.

"At the beginning of his act, Buddy rode Hands Up into the arena at a dead gallop. He was whoopin' and hollerin' and puttin' on quite a show. He didn't really have Hands Up do any tricks, just rode him around at a dead run.

"But the horse was still a showstopper. He was a good-looking, loud-colored Appaloosa—pretty-headed and necked, with a bald face, two blue eyes and a big, spotted blanket. Folks around that part of the country had just never seen a horse like him before.

"Several years later," Miller continues, "I was visiting with Ace Hooper of Plainview, Texas, when the talk got around to Hands Up.

"Ace—who bred and owned Top Hat H. and High Stakes—told me that he'd first seen Hands Up in 1949, at Dumas, Texas. Bill John Pugh was running him there and had won two races on consecutive days—against what Ace called 'some real good racehorses.'

"Ace approached Bill John and asked him if Hands Up was for sale. Bill said he was—for $650. Ace wanted to buy him but didn't have the money. So he hurried back home to Plainview, Texas, to gather it up.

"Ace got the cash together and hunted Bill John up. By the time he did, though, Buddy Heaton had beaten him to the punch."

Although Buddy Heaton was successful in purchasing Hands Up, as mentioned earlier, fate decreed that he would not keep him long. When possession of the loud-colored racing and bulldogging stallion passed from Heaton to Roy Wood in 1950 or 1951, the pioneer breeder registered him with ApHC as Hands Up T-184 (later F-2217).

Although he no longer owned Hands Up,

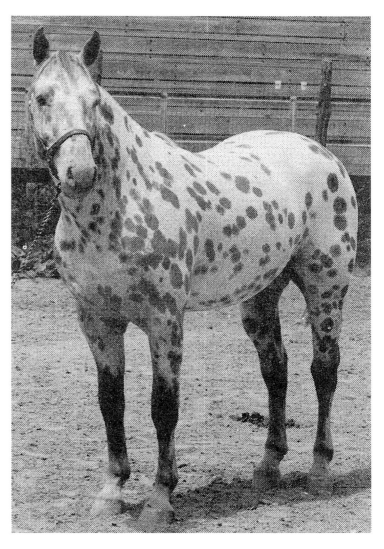

Golden King, a 1958 stallion by Fiesta and out of Winema, was a Hands Up grandson who positively impacted the breed. A champion halter horse in his own right, he founded the Bandido/Cowboy Justice line of top leopard show horses.

Photo by Chuck Bearden

Heaton still figured prominently in the production of the stallion's best-known son and best-unknown daughter.

"In 1951," he says, "I hauled two Quarter Horse mares down to Roy Wood's to be bred to Hands Up. One mare, Deacon Bess, was mine. The other mare, Flying Flag, belonged to Dr. G. L. Blackmer of Hooker, Oklahoma.

"The next spring, Deacon Bess foaled a bald-faced, sorrel, blanket-hipped colt that I named High Hand (see following chapter).

" 'Doc'—who was a close personal friend of

Arrow Chief, a 1956 stallion by Hands Up and out of Lane's Red Sorrel, is seen here being ridden by Marion Alton of Claremore, Oklahoma, in a circa late-1960s 100-mile endurance race. The duo is at the 75-mile mark and showing no signs of wearing down.

Courtesy Marian Alton

mine—sold Flying Flag to a horse trader named C. E. Brose of Liberal, Kansas. In the spring of 1952, the mare produced a cracker jack of a bald-faced, roan, blanket-hipped filly.

"For some unknown reason, when that filly was registered, she was listed as being by Comanche. But I'm here to tell you that I know for a fact that Hands Up was that filly's real sire. And they named her Miss Liberal."

Miss Liberal, listed on ApHC records as a 1952 roan mare by Comanche and out of Flying Flag (QH), was sold by Brose to John Albright of La Veta, Colorado. Albright, in turn, sold her to John Bowling of Colorado Springs, Colorado. Shown primarily by Bowling's daughter, Dorothy, Miss Liberal went on to make a considerable splash in the show ring.

Among the versatile mare's many wins were Grand Champion Mare honors at the 1959 Mountain and Plains Appaloosa Horse Club Show in Estes Park, Colorado, the 1959 Colorado State Fair in Pueblo and the 1961 National Western Stock Show in Denver, Colorado.

In addition, she was the Champion English Pleasure Horse at the 1960 National Show in South Sioux City, Nebraska; the Champion Ladies Costume Horse and High-Point Ladies Performance Horse at the 1961 National Show in Fort Worth, Texas; and the Champion Ladies Costume Horse at the 1962 National Show in Springfield, Illinois.

Returning to Hands Up—the head of the clan—shortly after being pur-

Sparkle Plenty, a 1958 mare by Hands Up and out of Lucy Palousy, was a top Texas show mare.

Courtesy Western Horseman

Miles' Stormy Day, a 1955 gelding by Hands Up and out of Susie Q. by Mansfield's Comanche, was a top North Country halter and cutting horse. He's seen here in action at the 1968 Montana Winter Fair in Bozeman.

Courtesy Marian Alton

Vanguard D., a 1958 stallion by Hands Up and out of Jingle Bell, was the Champion 2-Year-Old Stallion and Grand Champion Stallion at the 1960 National Show in South Sioux City, Nebraska.

Courtesy **Western Horseman**

chased by Wood, the flashy Appaloosa came to the attention of a young Claremore, Oklahoma, girl. That chance encounter precipitated a life-long relationship that was so intense and so loyal that from that point on the girl became part of the stallion's story.

"In 1951, when I was 13 years old," Marian Alton says, "I was riding in a parade in Tulsa, Oklahoma. Roy Wood was also in the parade and he was mounted on Hands Up. I had never seen such a beautiful horse. I dismounted on the spot and snapped a picture with a camera I had slung around my neck.

"I was so enamored with Hands Up that I later talked my parents into hauling me out to the Wood Ranch south of Claremore to get a closer look. That was the beginning of my friendship with Roy and my dedication to the Hands Up line."

After being acquired and registered by Wood, Hands Up was shown at three hallmark Appaloosa events.

Exhibited at the 1952 National in Quincy, California, he placed second to the legendary Apache in the 1/8- and 1/4-mile races. Finishing behind him in both events were Blossom and Patchy. Entered in the 1/2-mile race, he finished fourth behind Apache, Patchy and Blossom.

In 1953, an organization known as the American Appaloosa Association (AAA) was formed. Headed by King Parsons of Boulder, Colorado, the association was in existence for only two years. Nevertheless, in the summer of 1953 AAA sponsored an Appaloosa show in Claremore, Oklahoma. Shown by Wood, Hands Up was named the event's champion aged stallion.

On July 5, 1954, the first all-Appaloosa show ever held in the state of Texas took place in Belton. Exhibited at the watershed event, Hands Up earned honors as champion aged stallion and grand champion stallion.

Shortly after these two shows, Hands Up suffered a severe setback due to a barnyard accident.

Although accounts of when and how the accident occurred vary, the general consensus is that the stallion was inadvertently sprayed with a toxic "barn spray" instead of fly spray and was rendered completely blind. However it happened, the mishap put a sudden halt to Hands Up's show career. For the rest of his

Chief Many Mile, a 1957 stallion by Hands Up and out of a Quarter mare, was the Champion Rope Race Horse at the 1965 World Champion Playoffs in Scottsdale, Arizona.
Courtesy Appaloosa Museum & Heritage Center

After getting his first glimpse of Hands Up while at a gas station, renowned Western artist Orren Mixer asked permission to do an oil portrait of him.

243

"RAY'S PRINCESS II"

"THE TEXAS APPALOOSA ALLOWANCE"

SUNLAND PARK, N.M.   MAY 8, 1971   J. NICODEMUS, UP
VANDY'S VI (2nd)   440 Yds :21.93   STAR DIVER (3)
JAMES A. ROWAN, OWNER   CHARLES W. CASCIO, TR

Ray's Princess II, a 1966 mare by Hands Up and out of Phyllis Lady, was one of the top Appaloosa racehorses of the 1970s. Here, she wins the 1971 Texas Appaloosa Allowance over Vandy's Vi and Star Diver.

Courtesy Marian Alton

life, he was relegated to duty as a breeding stallion.

As serious as Hands Up's handicap was, it did not prevent Marian Alton from getting to know him even better.

"Beginning in my early teens," she says, "I spent a lot of time out at the Wood Ranch. Even though Hands Up had been blinded by this time, Roy would turn him out every summer with his mares. And he'd let me go out with just a halter and lead, and hop up on him and ride him around.

"I can't remember ol' Hands Up ever taking a wrong step with me. One day, while I was up on him, the mares and foals took off at a dead run for the barn. I thought, 'Oh no, I'm in for it now. This blind horse is going to get all upset and we're going to have us a real train wreck.' But he never got riled at all. He and I just moseyed on back to the barn like nothing had happened. That's the kind of disposition he had."

Just as he had done as a race and show horse, Hands Up excelled as a sire.

Among the many champions he contributed to the breed during the Wood era of his life were Fiesta, Miles' Stormy Day, Guapo, Chief Many Mile, Vanguard D. and Sparkle Plenty.

Fiesta, a 1954 stallion out of Amarillo Blanca, was bred by Lewis Igleheart of Miami, Oklahoma. Sold to first to Roy Wood and then to Charles White of Kenedy, Texas, he went on to become a top sire. Through his son Golden King—a 1958 stallion out of Winema—he also founded the Bandido/Cowboy Justice line of top leopard show horses.

Miles' Stormy Day, a 1955 gelding out of Susie Q (the dam of Kelley's Sonny Boy), was bred by Woods. Sold to Lew Ferguson of Helmville, Montana, he went on to become a top halter and cutting horse.

Guapo, a 1957 stallion by Hands Up and

Lightning Bug B, a 1980 stallion by Bugs Alive In 75 (QH) and out of the Hands Up granddaughter Shezadier, was a medallion-winning racehorse and a top sire.
Courtesy the Bennett family and Helen McDaniel

out of Muffins, was bred by Francis Johnson of Hutchinson, Kansas. A champion halter and race horse, Guapo sired such top get as Snap Up, the Champion Aged Stallion and Reserve Grand Champion Stallion at the 1968 National Show in Oklahoma City, and Sure Shot, the Champion Weanling Gelding at the 1970 National Show in Huron, South Dakota.

Chief Many Mile, a 1957 stallion out of a Quarter mare, was bred by Edgar Prine of Blue Jacket, Oklahoma. Sold to Cleatys Oliver of Oak Grove, Missouri, he was the Champion Rope Race Horse at the 1965 World Champion Playoffs in Scottsdale, Arizona.

Hands Up was 25 years old when this shot of he and owner Nolan Hutcheson was taken in 1972.

Photo by Marian Alton

Vanguard D., a 1958 stallion by Hands Up and out of Jingle Bell, was bred by Roy Wood. Sold to E. H. Lynch of Tulsa, Oklahoma, he was named the Champion 2-Year-Old Stallion and Grand Champion Stallion at the 1960 National Show in South Sioux City, Nebraska.

Sparkle Plenty, a 1958 mare out of Lucy Palousy, was also bred by Wood. Sold to Carl Miles of Abilene, Texas, she was developed by him into a grand champion halter mare.

In 1960, Hands Up—the head of the family—was first leased and then sold by Wood to Nolan Hutcheson of Houston, Missouri, for a reported $12,500. Hutcheson's Indian Creek Ranch would be the famous stallion's final home.

The fact that he was now located a little far-

ther away did not stop Marian Alton from staying involved with him.

"I graduated from high school in 1956," she says, "and my parents gave me a choice. I could breed a mare to Hands Up or be given a new, red "98" Oldsmobile to take to college. I chose to raise a foal and that was the start of my life-long dedication to the bloodline."

Beginning in 1957 and continuing for the next 15 years, Marian bred a host of mares to Hands Up. By her own account, she hauled 22 mares to Missouri to be bred. In addition, she owned several more Hands Up sons and daughters. Included in that number were such horses as Arrow Chief, a 1956 stallion out of Lane's Red Sorrel, and Feather Up, a 1973 mare out of Feather Too by Arrow Chief.

In 1977, Marian bred Feather Up, a double-bred Hands Up, to Mr Duplicate (QH). Mr. Duplicate Hand, a U.S. and Canadian National Champion halter horse, was the resulting foal.

As far as the overall Nolan Hutcheson/Hands Up era is concerned, it was one marked by unparalleled prosperity.

"Appaloosa racing was on the rise in this part of the country in the late 1960s and early 1970s," Marian Alton says. "Realizing that Hands Up came from running blood on both sides of his pedigree, Nolan began assembling some top speed-bred Quarter Horse and Thoroughbred mares to breed to him. The resulting foals were not only speedy but had top halter conformation, as well."

Among the brightest Hands Up racing stars to be born during the Indian Creek era were Ray's Princess II, Strike Up and Lightning Bug B.

Ray's Princess II, a 1966 mare out of 19 Phyllis Lady, was bred by Ray Green of Rogers, Arkansas. Raced under Green's banner, she was one of the top competitors of the early 1970s and officially AAA-rated.

Strike Up, a 1969 gelding out of Pansa Deeds (QH), was bred by Greg Simon of Colwich, Kansas. Raced under Simon's banner, he was AAA-rated and 1971's leading money-earning race gelding.

Lightning Bug B., a 1980 stallion by Bugs Alive In 75 (QH) and out of the Hands Up granddaughter Shezadier, was bred by John Ferris of Russellville, Kentucky. The winner of the 1982 Cricket Bars Futurity at Blue Ribbon Downs in Sallisaw, Oklahoma, the medallion-earning racehorse is now owned by Steve Bennett and Helen McDaniel of Independence, Kansas.

The Indian Creek years were among Hands Up's most prolific. From 1962 through 1972, 203 of his 302 registered foals were born.

Hands up passed away on March 23, 1973, at the age of 26, and was buried on the ranch. In 1996, construction of a new highway made it necessary to exhume Hands Up's remains. One year after that, those remains were re-interred on Marian Alton's ranch near Claremore, Oklahoma.

As one of the first noteworthy stallions to be born in the Texas panhandle, Hands Up paved the way for those of his breed that would follow. Owned first by one of the industry's most colorful figures, and later by two of its most prominent pioneer breeders, his contributions as a breeding horse were of great import.

He remains, to this day, one of the breed's most colorful personalities and greatest foundation sires.

Here's a compelling shot of Hands Up, standing in the doorway of his private shed on Hutcheson's Indian Creek Ranch near Houston, Missouri.

Photo by Marian Alton

Chapter 23

HIGH HAND

F-3366

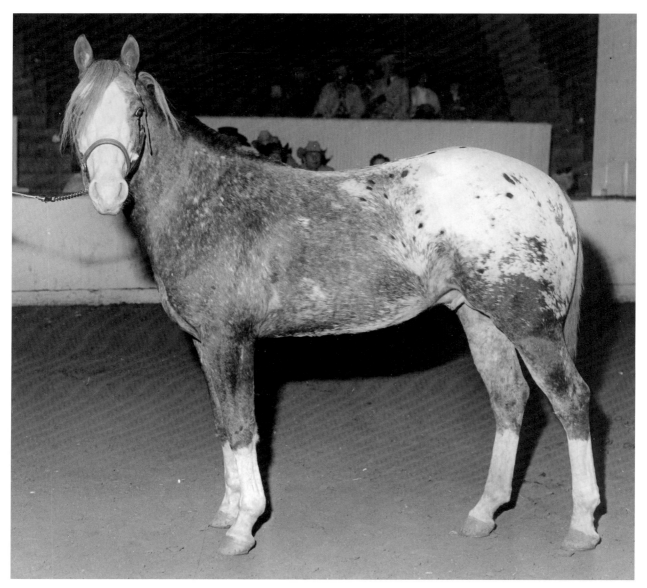

High Hand, one of the breed's most unique personalities, and a 1988 ApHC Hall of Fame inductee.

Courtesy Appaloosa Museum & Heritage Center

At maturity, High Hand stood 14 hands tall and weighed around 1,000 pounds. He was not a big horse, but measured in terms of what he contributed to the Appaloosa breed—both as an individual and as a sire—he was a giant.

Buddy Heaton of Hugoton, Kansas, bred High Hand, and that was just as it should have been. As a pair of colorful characters, they were an even match.

Heaton—rodeo cowboy, rodeo clown, race-horse man and all-around free spirit—hauled his AQHA mare Deacon Bess to the Chelsea, Oklahoma, ranch of Roy Wood to be bred to Hands Up in the spring of 1951. He was hoping to get a stud colt with at least a little color and chrome. What he got was High Hand.

"High Hand was born on May 13, 1952, in a pasture that was about a half-mile from the house," Heaton recalls. "My wife and mother were driving past the pasture right as the mare was having the foal.

"They came and got me just as fast as they could, and I was so excited to see what she had that I jumped right up and cut down there. She'd already had him, and there he was—a sorrel with a big white blanket, bald face and four stocking legs. I just picked that little son-of-a-gun up and carried him the half-mile to the house with his mama a-followin'. "

That his loud-colored youngster showed promise from the day he was born came as no surprise to his breeder—the colt had a license to.

Hands Up, his sire, was one of the breed's great foundation stallions (see preceding chapter).

Deacon Bess, High Hand's dam, was a royally bred mare, sired by Dick McCue and out of Kansas Ginger. Dick McCue was a grandson of Peter McCue, and Kansas Ginger was a daughter of Nicky P-291, the great Matador Ranch stallion. Nicky was, in turn, by Sheik P-11, the great Coke Roberds-bred foundation sire.

"High Hand was a character from the day he was born," Heaton says. "What with me being in the rodeo business and clowning and all that, it was just natural that I would try to teach him some tricks.

"That little horse was just so doggone smart that he took to being a trick horse

Shown at the 1954 American Appaloosa Association show in Mineral Wells, Texas, High Hand was the Champion 2-Year-Old Stallion.

Courtesy Buddy Heaton

about like a duck takes to water. He'd lie down, sit up, reach around and pull his saddle blanket off, walk on his hind legs, count and bite you on the rear—just hit you with his nose, really.

"He'd throw his lip up and smile, he'd march and he'd jump straight up in the air when I put my hand on his withers. Now, I stood about 6-foot, 4-inches, and High Hand only stood about 14 hands, and it would look like I was jerkin' him plumb off the ground. The crowds just went wild."

As they traveled around the country during the early 1950s with their rodeo clown and trick horse act, Heaton and High Hand developed an act of a slightly different nature that began to pay some handsome dividends.

"I knew High Hand could run a lick," Heaton says, "but when we were anywhere in public, I wouldn't ride him much—just do my trick-horse thing with him. I'd be in my clown getup, and I'd pull my drunk act and start trying to match-race him against any of those old boys' ropin' or doggin' horses.

"When it come time to run, I'd insist that I was the only one who could ride High Hand, so whoever was running at me had to match my weight, and that was over 200 pounds.

"Now, think about it a minute. Who wouldn't want to take a big ol' dumb rodeo clown who was a-ridin' a little Appaloosa trick horse to the cleaners?

"But I'm here to tell you that High Hand was one tough, fast little son-of-a-gun, and before we was done, we made a lot of believers out of a lot of rodeo cowboys."

One of High Hand's most memorable match-races took place at the famed Calgary Stampede in Calgary, Alberta, Canada.

"I was friends with a lot of those boys up in Canada who played professional football," Heaton says. "Now, I never could figure out

Utilized by owner Buddy Heaton of Hugoton, Kansas, as a rodeo trick horse and match-racing mount, High Hand attracted a legion of fans. The 6-foot-4-inch Heaton is seen up on High Hand in this shot taken at the Cheyenne Frontier Days in Cheyenne, Wyoming.

Courtesy Buddy Heaton

250

Although he was not campaigned heavily in the event, High Hand was known to be a top-notch cutting horse. In this photo, he is seen is at John Albright's place near La Veta, Colorado, being ridden by Jack Ryberg.

Courtesy Ed Roberts

who was the toughest up there—the football players or the chuck wagon relay-race cowboys. But I come damn close to finding out one time.

"One of those football players who I was really good friends with was a boy by the name of Roy Jensen. Roy and I and a bunch of Roy's football buddies matched High Hand for $15,000—that was a lot of money then—against any relay racehorse that those chuck wagon boys wanted to throw at us. Now, they had 750 to 800 head to choose from, but I wasn't worried. Jensen was a-holdin' the money and he was a foot-racin' son-of-a-gun.

"I told him that if High Hand got beat, to take the money and run, and the football boys was gonna start a fight with the chuck wagon boys, and by the time the dust settled, we'd be halfway back to Kansas.

"I never did find out which bunch was the toughest. We won that race by right at four lengths."

By this time, Heaton had to wonder just how many other hidden talents his diminu-

tive spotted stallion possessed, and it didn't take long for High Hand to let him know.

"It was January of 1957, and I was rodeoing up in Denver at the National Western Stock Show," Heaton recalls. "I had been bulldogging off of Willard and Benny Combs' great little mare, Baby Doll. If she wasn't available, I'd use Roy Duvall's horse.

"Anyway, Baby Doll turned up sick or lame or something, and Duvall was supposed to be there but he never showed. So there I was about ready to make my run with no horse to make it on.

"I hollered at old Frank—he was the fella who took care of the saddle horses—to bring me High Hand. Now, I had never bulldogged off of High Hand before. He had never even been behind the barrier. But I rode him right in there like I knew what I was doing. He backed up and they popped at him and tripped the barrier. Well, that rascal like to jerked both my arms out at the sockets, but we planted that steer in 6.7 seconds and won the day money!

"After that, everybody wanted to use him. I

went on and bulldogged off him a lot, but I never did let hardly anybody else ride him."

In 1958, fate and a friend of Heaton's intervened to change High Hand's ownership and the direction his life would take from that point on.

"Dr. G. L. Blackmer of Hooker, Oklahoma, was a good friend of mine and one of the finest men God ever put on this earth," Heaton says. "I had kind of a talent for getting into trouble in those days, and 'Doc' was always a-savin' my bacon.

"One day, he decided it was time for me to sober up and settle down, and he talked me into selling High Hand so I could go to auc-

tioneering school up in Billings, Montana."

And so it was that High Hand was auctioned on October 18, 1958, at the local sale barn in Hugoton.

Harold Calhoun of Byers, Colorado—a man who would later figure prominently in High Hand's life—took the bid on the colorful stallion all the way to $10,000, but that wasn't quite good enough. Blackmer bid $10,500 and became the horse's second owner.

That same fall, Blackmer sold High Hand to John Albright of LaVeta, Colorado. Albright, Blackmer's son-in-law, promptly placed the stallion into reining and cutting training with Jack Ryberg.

DOCTOR JUDGE
"FIRST RUNNING OF WORLD WIDE APPALOOSA DERBY"
NEW MEXICO STATE FAIR   SEPT 16, 1963   BOBBY HARMON, UP
DOUBLE HANCOCK (2nd)   440 Yds 23.4   CHARLO (3rd)
WALTER M. ANDERSON, OWNER   JACK PATTON, TRAINER

Doctor Judge, a 1960 stallion by High Hand and out of Pinkey, was the winner of the 1963 World Wide Futurity in Albuquerque, New Mexico.

. Courtesy Appaloosa Museum & Heritage Center

Although he was not shown much, High Hand was named Reserve Champion Appaloosa Stallion at the 1960 Colorado State Fair in Pueblo. He stood Reserve Grand Champion Stallion at the 1960 and 1961 Denver National Western Stock Shows. With Ryberg in the saddle, High Hand won the novice cutting in Pueblo in 1960 and the Appaloosa reining at the Colorado State Fair in 1961.

And he began to attract attention as a potential breeding stallion.

One of the first horsemen to bring a top-notch mare to High Hand's court was Walter "Judd" Anderson of Turpin, Oklahoma.

"Judd Anderson was quite a race-horse man," Heaton recalls. "He had a stud by the name of Snip Raffles that was pretty well-known in this part of the country.

"Anyway, Judd, Doc Blackmer and I were playing poker one night down at the sale barn. Doc had been pestering Judd for quite some time to breed a good mare to High Hand.

"Finally, Judd says to Doc that he's tired of hearing about that blankety-blank Appaloosa stud, and if he'll breed a mare to the horse, will Doc quit badgerin' him? Doc swears he will, so Judd brings a scorpion of a little mare by the name of Pinkey (QH)—an own daughter of Snip Raffles—to High Hand in 1959.

"Well, Judd likes the colored stud colt that he gets from that cross so well that he brings the mare back the next year, and that's how Doctor Judge and Ipana Maid came to be."

After initially putting Doctor Judge and Ipana Maid in cutting training early in 1963, Anderson heard that there was to be a futurity and derby for Appaloosa racehorses that fall in Albuquerque, New Mexico. He quickly changed the training venue on the two youngsters and had them prepared for the track.

Doctor Judge took to the change well enough to win the inaugural running of the World Wide Derby, and Ipana Maid won her

Ipana Maid, a 1961 full sister to Doctor Judge, placed second in the 1963 World Wide Futurity. The talented sprinter then went on to become one of the breed's greatest speed producers.
Courtesy Appaloosa Museum & Heritage Center

futurity time trial and finished second to Boogie Britches in the finals.

Doctor Judge became one of High Hand's first all-around champions—winning as a racehorse, a halter horse and a cutting horse. Retired to stud, he sired such notable get as Hoddy Doc, the 1972 National Champion Senior Cutting Horse; Judge-Me-Not, a AAA racehorse and halter and performance champion; That's Judd, high-point Michigan halter champion; and Miss Judge Bar and Judd's Image, both race winners in Colorado.

Making up for her second-place finish in the 1963 World Wide Futurity, Ipana Maid went on to produce back-to-back winners of the race with Zepana Bull in 1974 and Dervish Maid in 1975.

With the successes of Doctor Judge and Ipana Maid, High Hand's popularity as a breeding horse began to grow. More and better mares found their way to the ex-trick horse.

One of these, an Albright-owned mare named Miss Connie Kay (QH). Bred to High Hand in 1960, she produced a colt named Cuchara Pat Hand the following year.

To establish a market for his High Hand get, Albright consigned "Pat Hand" as a

Hoddy Doc, a 1967 stallion by Doctor Judge and out of Hoddy Bee Bee, was the Champion Senior Cutting Horse at the 1972 National Show in Columbus, Ohio.

Courtesy Appaloosa Museum & Heritage Center

yearling to the fall edition of the Heart of the Rockies Appaloosa Sale in Greeley, Colorado. The colorful youngster topped the sale at $8,000, with the high bidder being A. T. McDannald of Houston, Texas.

Pat Hand won his halter class the following spring at the Houston Livestock Exposition and followed that with a highly successful show career in the halter ring and cutting arena. Retired to stud, he sired Pat Hand Jr., the Champion Aged Gelding and Grand Champion Gelding at the 1969 National in Baton Rouge, Louisiana.

Rebred to High Hand in 1961, Miss Connie Kay presented Albright with a marginally colored filly named Patty Hand in 1962. Harold Calhoun, the Byers, Colorado, farmer whose interest in High Hand had never wavered, purchased Patty Hand from Albright and developed her into a durable, two-way champion.

Calhoun haltered and raced Patty Hand throughout the 1960s. In racing shape, she would win or place at halter at such prestigious shows as the Denver Stock Show and the New Mexico and Colorado State Fairs. In halter shape, she placed in the 2-year-old filly class and won the 350-yard race for 2-year-olds at the 1964 National in Albuquerque, New Mexico.

Back in Albuquerque the following fall, she won the World Wide Derby over a star-studded field of early-day race champions that included Ghost of Comanche, Gimpy's Wimpy, War Don, Double Patch, Nava Star, Miss Hoop and Active Duty.

Meanwhile, back at the Albright ranch, High Hand and Miss Connie Kay weren't quite through yet. In 1963, they produced a third full sibling named Cuchara High Connie.

Sold to the Saddle and Surrey Ranch of

Dallas, Texas, as a yearling, "Connie" was named as the Champion Yearling Filly at the 1964 National. Retired to the broodmare band, she produced Special Wonder, the Champion Men's Western Pleasure Horse at the 1982 World Championship Show in Oklahoma City.

Although the High Hand/Miss Connie Kay cross was probably the most successful single one made during the John Albright "Cuchara" era of High Hand's life, there were several other noteworthy sons and daughters that came into being during this time.

Trammell XV, a 1959 blanket-hipped, bald-faced son of High Hand, was the 1964 National Champion Calf Roping Horse.

Cuchara High Hand, a 1963 son, stood grand at Denver in 1966 and was also a winner in racing and cutting. Purchased by Dr. Woodrow Campion of Liberal, Kansas, the stallion returned to the land of his famous sire to found his own family of champions.

High Hand Man, foaled in 1962, became a tremendously versatile and durable halter and performance champion for C. J. Jackson of Rifle, Colorado, and an excellent sire in his own right.

Cuchara Money Hand, Joan's Hand, Cuchara Peppy Hand, Carey's High Hand and Granville's Glori Hand were all born during this time and all were big-time halter, race and performance champions.

In 1963, one of High Hand's most notable offspring, the great CGM Mighty High, was born.

"Mighty High" was bred by John Braddy of Greeley, Colorado, and was out of his champion Appaloosa cutting mare, Ayoka. Sold as a youngster to Carl Gene Miller of Morton, Illinois, the filly was promptly turned over to Illinois trainer Lloyd Donley. The rest, as the say, is history.

In 1966, Mighty High and Donley won the hackamore reining at the 19th National Show in Syracuse, New York. In 1967, Mighty High stood first in the aged mares class and was named the Grand Champion Mare at the National Show in Walla Walla, Washington.

In 1969, she was the Reserve Champion Performance Horse at the National Show in Baton Rouge, Louisiana. At this show, Jack Hennig rode her in calf roping and John Brown was aboard her in heading and heeling.

In 1970, with Donley back in the saddle, Mighty High was the high-point performance horse at both the 23rd National Show in Huron, South Dakota, and the 10th World Championship Appaloosa Performance Show in Sweetwater, Texas. At the World, she qualified for and was entered in 10 of the 12 events.

By now, Mighty High's sire was regarded as one of the leading all-around Appaloosa

Judge-Me-Not, a 1966 stallion by Doctor Judge and out of Marcy Marie (TB), was a champion halter, performance and racing horse.
Courtesy Laura Brest

255

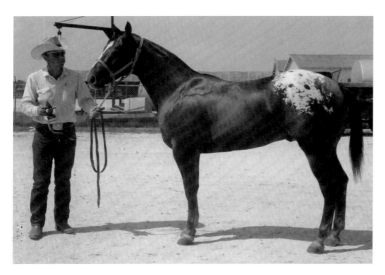

Cuchara Pat Hand, a 1961 stallion by High Hand and out of Miss Connie Kay (QH), was a top show horse and sire.
Courtesy Appaloosa Museum & Heritage Center

sires of the day. As such, he was a highly desirable piece of property, and in 1962, Dwight Parks of Meridian, Texas, made Albright an offer for High Hand that resulted in the stallion's fourth change of ownership.

Parks kept him for three years and then sold him in a dispersal sale to Charlie Walker of Amarillo, Texas. Walker had to have a dispersal sale of his own a short six months later, and as would be expected, High Hand was its feature attraction.

At the Walker Dispersal, held April 2, 1966, in Amarillo, a trio of Colorado horsemen—Dean Davis, Martin Abrahamsen and Harold Calhoun—were determined to own High Hand. With Walker as a fourth

Patty Hand, a 1961 mare by High Hand and out of Miss Connie Kay (QH), won the 1964 World Wide Derby over a star-studded field.
Courtesy Appaloosa Museum & Heritage Center

GCM Mighty High, a 1963 mare by High Hand and out of Ayoka, was the Champion Aged Mare and Grand Champion Mare at the 1967 National Show in Walla Walla, Washington.
Photo by Johnny Johnston, courtesy Appaloosa Museum & Heritage Center

partner, they formed a syndicate and made the front page of the Amarillo Sunday News-Globe the next day when they bought the 14-year-old Appaloosa stallion for the unheard-of price of $60,500.

In time, Abrahamsen and Calhoun bought out the other two partners and became High Hand's sole owners. Under their management, he experienced rejuvenation as a sire. High Hand was the get-of-sire champion for the Mountain and Plains Appaloosa Horse Club for nine straight years—from 1967 to 1975. Some of his greatest sons and daughters came into their own at this time.

America Girl, a Walter Anderson-bred daughter, was the 1970 National Grand Champion Mare. Rabbitt's High Hand, a gelded son, was a three-time National- and World Champion cutting horse. Mr High Bar,

a big, 15-3-hand cherry red sorrel stallion who was probably 20 years ahead of his time as far as halter horses go, stood grand in Denver.

All-around champions like Cybill Bar, Accelerate, Lee Hands, Jaguar Hand, High Hand Jag, High Hand II, High Hand Heidi, High Pocketts, Miss Denver, Breeze Hand, Lan-A-Hand and a host of others were a threat to win it all every time they walked in an arena or set foot on a racetrack. High Hand rewrote the book as a consistent sire of the true "triple-threat" Appaloosa.

But as the 1980s neared, High Hand became an old horse. There was some talk of retiring him from stud—even talk of reserving a space for him to be buried at the Horse Hall of Fame in Lexington, Kentucky.

A young man named Teddy Kemper came

America Girl, a 1966 mare by High Hand and out of Miss Espy Bar, was the Champion Aged Mare and Grand Champion Mare at the 1970 National Show in Huron, South Dakota.

Photo by Johnny Johnston, courtesy Appaloosa Museum & Heritage Center

to Byers, Colorado, around this time and fell in love with High Hand. While Abrahamsen and Calhoun refused to sell him, they did agree to let Kemper take him to Kentucky to live out his life. On the way, however, High Hand got sick and Kemper halted the journey in Oklahoma for awhile. He boarded the stallion at several places, including Mary Hummel's Circle H Bar H Ranch in Yukon.

This went on over the winter, and by the following spring it became apparent to the group of people who had followed his trail that High Hand had nowhere to go.

Dr. Harbord Cox of Pampa, Texas, was one of those people, and when asked by another member of the group to provide a last home for the aging stallion, he replied simply that, "it would be an honor to keep him."

Cox was true to his word and High Hand

was retired to a life of luxury on the West Texas plains not too terribly far from the country he had grown up in. He was accorded his own Spanish-style box stall, his own lot, his own shade tree and even his own pal—a Saint Bernard dog named Mindy.

He remained a character to the very end, exhibiting little idiosyncrasies in his retirement such as always sleeping with his head to the north and always facing east when he stood under his shade tree. Once, during a grooming session with Cox's wife, Dolores, he suddenly performed one of his old tricks, taught to him by Buddy Heaton more than a quarter of a century before. She never did figure out what she did to trigger the response.

In October of 1982, Martin Abrahamsen passed away and Harold Calhoun became High Hand's sole legal owner. A lot of water had passed under the bridge from the day some 25 years earlier when Calhoun had sat in the sale ring in Hugoton and tried to out-bid Doc Blackmer.

"In July of 1983," Calhoun says, "Dr. Cox and his veterinarian called me and said that they had discovered cancer in High Hand. They wanted to put him to sleep and asked for my permission. I asked them not to do anything until I could see him. My daughters and I piled into the car the next morning and drove down to Pampa.

"He was in good shape, and the more I thought about it, the more I decided that they were probably right. There was no need to prolong the inevitable, no need to let the horse suffer and go downhill. I told them to do what they thought was best and headed home. I think they put him to sleep the next day."

High Hand's passing truly marked the end of one of the most colorful chapters in the Appaloosa breed's history. He was a champi-on, a trick horse, a match-race horse, a rodeo horse, a halter horse and a cutting horse. He sure enough was a sire.

But, to a struggling breed that was fighting its way back from near oblivion, he was much more than all that.

High Hand was an individual. He had color, he had charisma and he had style. First, he attracted people with his gaudy color and then he won their hearts with his tremendous ability. In doing so, he won die-hard fans to a breed that needed all the support it could get.

How can you adequately describe a horse like High Hand? How can you quantify and put into perspective what he did for the breed? Maybe you don't have to go any further than Buddy Heaton did as he reminisced about the flashy Appaloosa stallion who he had helped bring into this world.

"I'll give this to High Hand," he said quietly. "He was the biggest little horse I ever did see."

High Hand and owner Harold Calhoun of Byers, Colorado, are seen in this candid shot taken in July of 1983, the day before the then-32-year-old living legend was humanely put to sleep.
"He was the biggest little horse I ever did see."—Buddy Heaton

Chapter 23

ABSAROKEE SUNSET
#7322

Absarokee Sunset, seen here as a 2-year-old, was a top performance horse and sire.
Courtesy Appaloosa Museum & Heritage Center

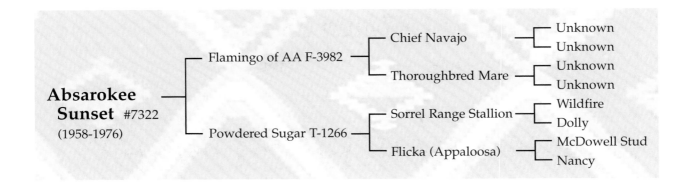

```
                                                          ┌─ Unknown
                                        ┌─ Chief Navajo ───┤
                                        │                  └─ Unknown
                  ┌─ Flamingo of AA F-3982 ─┤
                  │                     │                  ┌─ Unknown
                  │                     └─ Thoroughbred Mare ─┤
  Absarokee       │                                        └─ Unknown
  Sunset  #7322 ──┤
  (1958-1976)     │                     ┌─ Sorrel Range Stallion ─┬─ Wildfire
                  │                     │                  └─ Dolly
                  └─ Powdered Sugar T-1266 ─┤
                                        │                  ┌─ McDowell Stud
                                        └─ Flicka (Appaloosa) ─┤
                                                          └─ Nancy
```

Just as Apache and Chief of Fourmile were among the top Appaloosa performance horses of their era, so was Absarokee Sunset among the top performance horses of his.

"Sunset," a 1958 stallion by Flamingo of AA and out of Powdered Sugar, was bred by Gwen McKittrick of Ashland, Montana.

Flamingo of AA F-3982, a 1953 stallion by Chief Navajo F-1970 and out of a chestnut mare with Thoroughbred conformation, was bred by Wyatt Haskell of Wyola, Montana. A champion cutting horse at 10 years of age, "Flamingo" was nevertheless known to have an independent spirit and be prone to buck.

Although Chief Navajo's exact breeding is unknown, pioneer Montana breeders and exhibitors such as Eunice Grewell, Laura Brest and Betty Springer maintained that he was from a line of horses bred by Bert Babcock of Three Forks, Montana, during the 1920s and 1930s.

Powdered Sugar T-1266, a 1950 mare by a sorrel range stallion and out of Flicka, was bred by Grewell, who lived in Selisia, Montana. This mare was also endowed with an independent personality and was never broke to ride.

Like Chief Navajo, much of Powdered Sugar's pedigree is unknown. The sorrel range stud, for instance, is listed as being sired by Wildfire, a "registered Quarter Horse." This leads to a very interesting and plausible conjecture.

There was, in fact, a registered

Quarter Horse named Wildfire in Montana in the 1930s and 1940s. A 1928 palomino by Saladin and out of Papoose, he was registered with the National Quarter Horse Breeders Association as NQHBA-8024.

Bred by Marshall Peavy of Clark, Colorado, this stallion was from the same Old Blue Mare family of Appaloosas that produced Norell's Little Red, Peavy Bimbo and Wapiti (see Chapters 16-19).

However Powdered Sugar was bred, one thing remains evident. She carried enough desirable genes to produce one of the breed's all-time greats.

Shown by owner Don Mecklenburg of Bayfield, Colorado, Sunset was the Reserve Champion Stallion at the 1961 New Mexico State Fair in Albuquerque.

Photo by Alexander, courtesy Appaloosa Museum & Heritage Center

McKittrick, a forest ranger in the foothills of the Absaroka Mountains, was responsible for naming Absarokee Sunset. "Absarokee" is the Indian word for "crow," and Absarokee, Montana, was once home to the headquarters of the Crow Indian Reservation.

In June of 1960, McKittrick sold Absarokee Sunset to Don Mecklenburg, a ranger friend from Bayfield, Colorado. It was Mecklenburg who broke Sunset to ride. In later years, he would remember the young stallion as being "a little cold-backed and apt to buck every time he was saddled."

Realizing that Sunset had tremendous potential, Mecklenburg turned to veteran trainer Bob Hankla of Pueblo, Colorado, for help.

Hankla, who had lost one hand and severe-ly damaged the other in a 1946 electrical accident, logged time on Sunset in the summer of 1960. Mecklenburg took the stallion back home in August and returned him to Hankla the following June.

In the late summer of 1961, Hankla and Sunset competed in their first show together—the Mountain and Plains Appaloosa Horse Club (MPApHC) show in Estes Park, Colorado. Although not in show shape, Sunset placed third at halter and was the reserve champion performance horse.

Next up was the Colorado State Fair in Pueblo and the New Mexico State Fair in Albuquerque. In Pueblo, the 3-year-old stallion was the champion performance horse. In Albuquerque, he was the reserve champion performance horse.

Shown by trainer Bob Hankla of Pueblo, Colorado, Sunset was the Grand Champion Stallion and High-Point Performance Horse of the 1964 Houston Livestock Show and Rodeo.
Photo by Jim Keeland, courtesy Appaloosa Museum & Heritage Center

Beginning in 1962, Hankla arranged to lease Sunset from Mecklenburg and bear the cost of showing the stallion himself. The move proved to be a shrewd one.

Absarokee Sunset was shown 15 times that year, and was named grand champion stallion and high-point performance horse 13 times. Over the course of the five years that Sunset and Hankla were a team, they put together a show record the likes of which the breed had never seen.

To begin with, Sunset was named the Champion of Champions (high-point halter and performance horse) at the Colorado State Fair for five years in a row—1961-1965.

He was named the Champion Aged Stallion and Grand Champion Stallion at the 1962 and 1963 National Western Livestock Shows in Denver, Colorado; and he was the 1962, 1963 and 1964 MPApHC Champion Aged Stallion and Grand Champion Performance Horse.

He was the 1962 and 1963 New Mexico Appaloosa Horse Club High-Point Performance Horse; the 1963 high-point performance horse at the Southwestern Livestock Exposition and Fat Stock Show in Fort Worth, Texas; and the Grand Champion Stallion and High-Point Performance Horse at the 1964 Houston Livestock Show and Rodeo in Houston, Texas.

On the national scene, Sunset was the Champion Rope Race Horse at the 1961 World Champion Performance Playoffs in Sedalia, Missouri; the Champion Senior Western Pleasure Horse at the 1962 World Champion Performance Playoffs in Sedalia; and the winner of the matched pairs class (with Absarokee Sun) at the 1964 National Show in Albuquerque.

All told, Sunset and Hankla won more than 250 trophies during their five-year run.

As good as he was as a show horse, Absarokee Sunset's true calling was as a sire.

Sunset was often ridden in ladies Western pleasure classes by Marie Mass, Miss Rodeo America for 1961. This photo was taken following the pair's win of that event at the 1963 New Mexico State Fair in Albuquerque.

Courtesy Appaloosa Museum & Heritage Center

His first foal crop, which numbered four, hit the ground in 1961. From it came his first show ring superstar.

Absarokee Sun, a 1961 stallion out of Senator Louise (ID), was bred by Hankla. Beginning in 1962, Sunset and "Sun" were hauled together and often wound up competing against each other for grand and reserve champion stallion honors.

In 1964, Absarokee Sun earned honors as the Champion 3-Year-Old Stallion and Grand

263

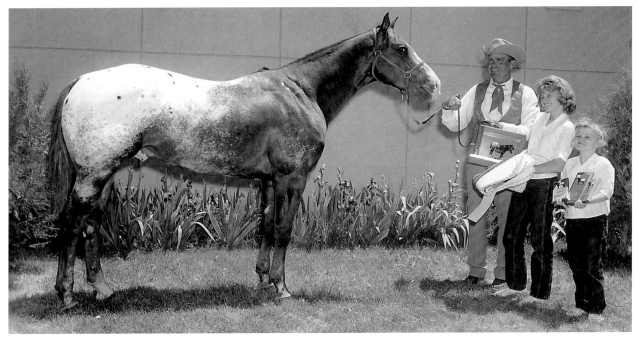

Absarokee Sun, a 1961 stallion by Absarokee Sunset and out of Senator Louise, was the Champion 3-Year-Old Stallion and Reserve Champion Stallion at the 1964 National Show in Albuquerque.

Courtesy Appaloosa Museum & Heritage Center

Absarokee Blue Light, a 1962 mare by Absarokee Sunset and out of Miss Blue Light (QH), was a top halter, roping and cutting horse. She is seen here with Sunny Jim Orr of Pueblo, Colorado, after being named Grand Champion Mare at the 1967 National Western Livestock Show in Denver, Colorado.

Photo by Darol Dickinson, courtesy Western Horseman

Champion Stallion at the National Western Livestock Show and the Colorado State Fair. He was also named the Champion 3-Year-Old Stallion, Reserve Champion Stallion and winner of the aforementioned matched pairs class with Absarokee Sunset at the 1964 National Show.

Sun won between 45 and 50 grand and reserve championships before he was put to sleep on October 6, 1965, due to a severe foot injury.

Absarokee Blue Light, a 1962 mare by Absarokee Sunset and out of Miss Blue Light (QH), was the next member of the line to excel in the show ring.

Bred by Mecklenburg, she was traded to Hankla for Senator

After Bob Hankla's death in December of 1965, Absarokee Sunset was purchased by Dr. R. H. Dunham of Kansas City, Missouri. The pair is seen here in front of the show arena Doc built in honor of his new stallion.

Courtesy Eric and Pam Dunham

Absarokee Jokette, a 1967 mare by Sunset and out of Joker's Tango Lady, was a top youth and speed event competitor. Eric Dunham—Doc's youngest son—is in the saddle.

Courtesy Eric and Pam Dunham

Absarokee Scooter S., a 1970 stallion by Absarokee Sunset and out of Scooter's Nessel (QH), was shown by Lloyd Donley to Reserve Champion Weanling Stallion honors at the 1970 National Show in Huron, South Dakota.

Photo by Johnny Johnston, courtesy Eric and Pam Dunham

Louise—Absarokee Sun's dam. A top halter, roping and cutting horse, "Blue Light" earned honors as the Grand Champion Mare at the 1964, 1965 and 1966 National Western Livestock Shows.

Absarokee Sunset sired a number of other champions during the Bob Hankla years, including Absarokee's Sunshine, Absarokee's Slim and Naja Chief.

Absarokee's Sunshine, a 1963 mare out of Lee's Sunup Sunshine, was one of the top youth mares in the Midwest in the late 1960s and early 1970s.

Absarokee's Slim, a 1964 gelding out of Red Flame, was the Champion Senior Western Pleasure Horse at the 1971 National in Las Vegas, Nevada; and Naja Chief, a 1965 gelding out of Christy Star (QH), was the

Champion Senior Reining Horse at the 1973 World Champion Performance Playoffs in Jackson, Mississippi.

In the fall of 1965, Don Mecklenburg decided to sell his famous stallion and advertised him in the Western Livestock Journal for $24,000.

Hankla was loath to part with Sunset but lacked the funds to buy him outright. In need of a partner, he contacted Dr. R. H. Dunham, a friend and fellow Appaloosa fancier from Kansas City, Missouri.

Hankla was in the process of finalizing the transaction when he was killed in a car wreck on Christmas Eve of 1965 while en route to the Dunhams' to spend the holidays.

Dr. Dunham decided to go ahead with the deal and, in March of 1966, purchased Sunset outright.

Dunham had been in the Appaloosa business for a number of years prior to acquiring Sunset and had owned and stood Appaloosa sons of Toby II, Mansfield's Comanche and Joker B.

After he took possession of Sunset, the Kansas City physician immediately placed him at the head of a broodmare band that included daughters of such famous Appaloosa sires as Wapiti, Joker B., Peavy Bimbo, Little Britches K., Bright Eyes Brother and Colida; and such well-known Quarter Horse sires as Sugar Bars, Triple Chick, Three Chicks, Diamond Charge and Go Man Go.

In addition, Dunham constructed a first-class show arena. Dubbed "Sunset Arena," it was the scene of top Appaloosa shows throughout the 1970s and 1980s.

Dunham also continued to show Sunset on a limited basis at halter, and the 8-year-old stud was the 1966 Missouri Appaloosa Horse Club High-Point Aged Stallion. At the conclusion of the 1966 show season, he was retired.

Now a full-time breeding stallion, Sunset turned out a host of Midwestern champions. Among his initial Dunham-era winners were Absarokee Wisey and Absarokee Scamp.

Absarokee Wisey, a 1968 mare out of Smutty Scoot (QH), was the 1973 National Champion Camas Prairie Stump Racing Horse, and Absarokee Scamp, a 1968 gelding out of Poco Pendaries (QH), was the 1970 National Champion 2-Year-Old Gelding and Champion Junior Gelding.

Although Absarokee Sunset and many of his get showed before the ApHC implemented the medallion award system in 1974, no less than 15 of the stallion's get qualified for bronze medallions. They include:

- Absarokee Too Much, a 1971 mare out of Pokeylo Revenue (QH)—1976 National Champion Senior Reining.
- Absarokee's Rebel, a 1967 gelding out of Ginchie (QH)—1977 competitive trail riding winner.
- Absarokee Wise Guy, 1972 gelding out of Smutty Scoot (QH)—1977 National Champion Aged Gelding.
- Absarokee's M.G., a 1966 mare out of an unknown mare—1977 World Champion Nez Perce Stake Race.
- Absarokee Sunny, a 1973 stallion out of Senator Louise (ID)—1977 World Champion Junior Reining.
- Absarokee Dodger, a 1970 gelding out of Delicate Dodger (QH)—1978 World Champion Senior Cutting.
- Absarokee Wisebuy, a 1976 gelding out of Smutty Scoot (QH)—1979 World Champion

Donley also showed Absarokee Scamp, a 1968 gelding by Sunset and out of Poco Pendaries (QH), to the Champion 2-Year-Old Gelding title at the same show.

Photo by Johnny Johnston, courtesy Eric and Pam Dunham

Represented by Absarokee Too Much, Absarokee Nikita and Absarokee Sugbar, Sunset was the Reserve Champion Get of Sire winner at the 1972 National Show in Columbus, Ohio. That's Doc Dunham at "Sugbar's" head.

Photo by Dalco, courtesy Eric and Pam Dunham

Western Riding and 1986 National Champion Senior Western Riding.

- Absarokee Tico, a 1975 stallion out of Just Plain Jane (ID)—1979 National Champion Junior Reining.
- Absorakee Candy Bar, a 1971 gelding out of Revenue Bay (QH)—1980 World Champion Nez Perce Stake Race.
- Absarokee Do-Rite, a 1973 gelding out of Smutty Scoot (QH)—1981 World Champion Western Riding.
- Absarokee Wiseoff, a 1974 gelding out of Smutty Scoot (QH)—1986 World Champion Senior Western Riding.
- Sudden Death, a 1976 mare out of Bendi Charge—1981 Year-End High-Point Camas Prairie Stump Race and 1982 World Champion Nez Perce Stake Race.
- Absarokee Jodie, a 1976 mare out of Jodie Bess (QH)—1981 Year-End High-Point Rope Race.

- Absarokee Smutt, a 1971 gelding out of Smutty Scoot (QH)—1982 National Champion All-Ages Western Riding.

In addition to these national and world champions, Absarokee Sunset sired a host of regional champions. Included among their number were such stars as Absarokee Jokette, Absarokee's Revie, Absarokee Honeygirl, Absarokee's Sheba, Absarokee Sunup, Absarokee Sugbar, Absarokee Nikita, Absarokee Scooter S. and Leo Sunset.

In due time, Sunset began to receive sire awards every bit as prestigious as those he earned as a show horse. He was named the Greater Eastern Appaloosa Regional's (GEAR) fifth Premier Sire. The award came about as a result of the earnings of GEAR champions Absarokee Wisey, Absarokee Joe, OK Wapiti Sunnie, Absarokee Wise Guy and Absarokee Smutt.

In 1975, Sunset was named the first Mid-

Con Champion Sire for having sired the Mid-Con Champions Absarokee Too Much, Absarokee Dodger and Absarokee Blaze.

He was awarded an ApHC Bronze Medallion Plaque for having sired the earners of 12 or more bronze medallions.

Again, while many of Sunset's get compiled their show records before the advent of the ApHC national point system, club records reveal that the legendary stallion sired 64 performers that earned 51 halter and 2,165 performance points, 10 superior performance awards and one versatility championship.

Absarokee Sunset passed away on October 19, 1976, apparently of colic.

Born in the wilds of Montana and bequeathed by his sire and dam with a double-dose of independence, Sunset was one of the top competitors of his day. He then founded an enduring family of strong-willed and able competitors that raised the bar as performance horses.

In recognition of his many accomplishments as both a show horse and a sire, Absarokee Sunset was inducted into the ApHC Hall of Fame in 1988.

Absarokee Sunshine, a 1963 mare by Absarokee Sunset and out of Lee's Sunup Sunshine, was owned and shown by Rick Olsen of Valparaiso, Indiana. "Sunshine" was a top youth mount, earning seven trophy saddles.
Photo by Johnny Johnston, courtesy of Eric and Pam Dunham

Chapter 25

COLIDA
7681

Colida, the breed's great mystery horse, made a name for himself.

Courtesy Bill Cass

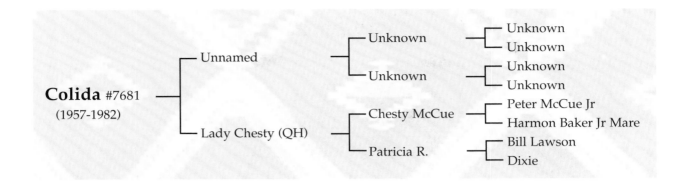

Colida #7681
(1957-1982)
— Unnamed
  — Unknown
    — Unknown
    — Unknown
  — Unknown
    — Unknown
    — Unknown
— Lady Chesty (QH)
  — Chesty McCue
    — Peter McCue Jr
    — Harmon Baker Jr Mare
  — Patricia R.
    — Bill Lawson
    — Dixie

Colida, the breed's great "mystery horse," has long been the subject of discussion and conjecture. Despite decades of investigation by breeders and historians alike, details of the colorful Appaloosa stallion's origins remain cloaked in speculation and secrecy.

For the record, Colida was foaled on April 13, 1957. Sired by an unnamed stallion and out of Lady Chesty (QH), he was bred by the Rhodes Brothers of Kit Carson, Colorado.

Lady Chesty, a 1947 mare by Chesty McCue and out of Patricia R., was also bred by the Rhodes Brothers and registered by them with AQHA in November of 1949. She remained in the Rhodes' possession until April 18,

1957, when her ownership was transferred to Harold Cox of Chatham, Illinois.

Cox did not purchase Lady Chesty directly from the Rhodes Brothers, but rather from Cletus Hulling of Freeport, Illinois. Hulling was the largest horse trader east of the Mississippi and was constantly scouring the outlying areas of the West in search of horses to buy and re-sell.

If, as the rumors persist, Colida was sired by a Colorado Quarter Horse stallion with an Appaloosa skeleton in his closet, then Hulling would have been a perfect conduit for getting both the mare and foal out of the country.

Shown by Bill Cass at the 1963 Houston Livestock Show and Rodeo, Colida was named Reserve Champion Stallion.
Photo by Jim Keeland, courtesy Bill Cass

The high point of Colida's show career came when he earned dual honors as the Champion Aged Stallion and Grand Champion Stallion at the 1963 National Show in Boise, Idaho.

Courtesy Western Horseman

Whoever his sire was and whatever the circumstances were that found him in Illinois as a foal, from this point on Colida's life becomes easier to track.

Bill Cass of Welch, Oklahoma—Colida's owner for most of his life—is able to shed some light on Colida's earliest days.

"I bought Colida in 1960," he says. "Several years later, I made a trip to Illinois to visit Harold Cox.

"Harold was a farrier and a calf roper. In 1956, his top roping mare got bred by accident. She had a foal in 1957 and Harold was not too happy about it. Looking to find a surrogate mother, he contacted Cletus Hulling about the possibility of buying a mare that was nursing a newborn foal.

"Cletus sold him Lady Chesty and her Appaloosa colt.

"Now, Harold's plan was to see if he could get Lady Chesty to accept his mare's foal. If she would, he was going to knock the Appaloosa colt in the head. Lady Chesty wouldn't have anything to do with his mare's foal, though, so he sold her and the colt to Russell Marcussen of Riverton, Illinois.

"That's how close Colida came to never making it at all."

Marcussen took possession of Lady Chesty and her colt in the late spring or early summer of 1957. Lady Chesty was officially transferred to his ownership in August of 1957.

In 1959, Marcussen registered his then-2-year-old Appaloosa stallion with ApHC as Colida T-7681 (later #7681). Although the registration application is undated, the accompanying photo of Colida is stamped May 1959. The stallion's name was reportedly derived from parts of two words—"Col," for the state of his birth, and "Ida," for the home of ApHC.

It has been stated that Marcussen test-bred Colida to a group of solid mares in 1959 and that the result was a surprisingly colorful crop of foals. That assertion notwithstanding, only one of those foals was ever registered.

MS Miss Kitty, a 1960 mare out of Carlita Dowdy (QH), was bred by Marcussen and went on to become a top halter horse and a race winner at distances ranging from 220 to 880 yards.

MS Little Brother, a 1961 full brother to "Miss Kitty," was the only member of Colida's second foal crop to be registered. Shown on a limited basis, "Little Brother" was a high-point state halter horse.

Sometime between the fall of 1959 and the spring of 1960, Marcussen

Colida's Buck, a 1964 gelding by Colida and out of Buck's Flapper (QH), was the Champion 3-Year-Old Gelding at the 1967 National Show. Owner John Diediker of Parsons, Kansas, is at the halter.
Photo by Johnny Johnston, courtesy Bill Cass

Flying Star, a 1964 stallion by Colida and out of Patsy Hull (QH), was the Champion 3-Year-Old Stallion and Grand Champion Stallion at the 1967 National Show in Walla Walla, Washington.
Photo by Johnny Johnston, courtesy Bill Cass

Colida was a two-time national champion get of sire winner. Represented by Flying Star, Porter C. and Colida's Buck (top), he took the 1967 title. Represented by Trusty's Colida, Cotrim and Co-Lauri (bottom), he took the 1972 award.
Top photo by Johnny Johnston, bottom photo by Dalco, courtesy Bill Cass

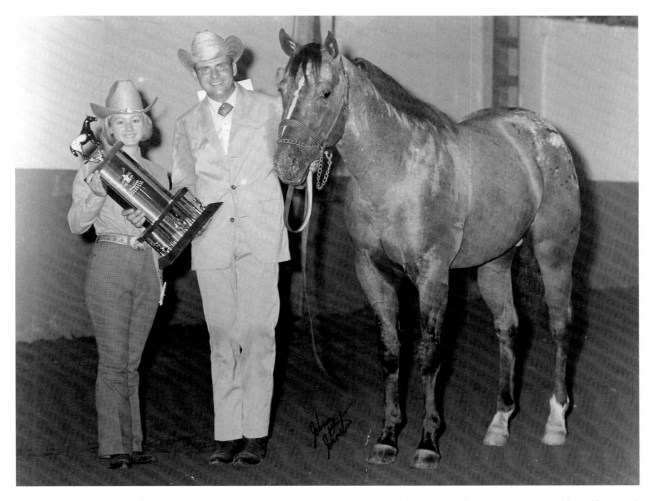

Cofleet, a 1966 stallion by Colida and out of Peggy Norfleet, was the 1969 National Champion 3-Year-Old Stallion and Reserve Champion Stallion.

Photo by Johnny Johnston, courtesy Bill Cass

took Colida to a local horse trainer named Orvil Nottingham, to be schooled as a cutting horse. The trainer was reportedly very hard on the young stallion—so hard that it got to the point where he could no longer enter the stallion's stall. His wife had to go in, halter Colida and tie him up.

Nottingham would then enter the stall, work Colida over and saddle him up for the day's training session. The stallion refused to be cowed however, and turned into a border-line outlaw instead.

In the fall of 1960, fearing that Colida would hurt someone, Marcussen took him to a Fort Smith, Arkansas, sale. It was at this point in the colorful stallion's life that Bill Cass entered the picture.

"Up until the late 1950s," Cass says, "I was a dyed-in-the-wool Quarter Horse man. I grew up around people like 'Uncle' John Dawson of Talala, Oklahoma; Ronald Mason of Nowata, Oklahoma; and Art Beal of Broken Arrow, Oklahoma. These men had horses like Oklahoma Star P-6, Old Red Buck P-9 and Waggoner's Rainy Day P-13.

"One day, Marvin Snodderly, a local kid, said to me, 'I'd like to raise me some Appaloosas.'

"I said, 'So would I, but I'm afraid I'd scare off my Quarter Horse customers if I tried to raise both breeds. If you want to run the business, we'll go 50-50 on 'em.' And that's what we did.

"We bought an Appaloosa son of Buttons B.

Co-Stephanie, a 1970 mare by Colida and out of Reno Zanti (QH), was the 1974 National Champion Junior Western Pleasure Horse. In winning the coveted title, "Stephanie" bested a field of 224 entries.
Photo by Johnny Johnston, courtesy Appaloosa Museum & Heritage Center

named Beau Lightning and started showing him. Within a couple of years, Marvin and I had accumulated 150 head of horses."

In January of 1960, the Appaloosa partners decided to take in the Fort Smith, Arkansas, horse sale.

"I was standing around at the sale," Cass says, "when Marvin came up to me and said, 'There's a horse coming through back there. He don't amount to nothing; he's sired by an unknown horse and out of a Quarter Horse mare. But we ought to buy him for a pasture-breeding horse.'

"So I said, 'Let's go back and look at him.'

"Well, I looked at the horse ... and then I looked at Marvin ... and then I looked back at the horse. I thought Marvin was puttin' me on. When you look at a horse with that much quality, you ought to be able to see it.

"I said, 'Hell, Marvin, let's turn the show horse out to pasture and show the pasture horse.'

"Stanley Lewis was at the sale," he continues. "He was from up around Sarcoxie, Missouri, and was working for Jim Wild. Stanley had showed Tick Tock and Jessie Joke to national championships out in Santa Barbara, California, the year before. He was the only guy from our part of the country who had ever done that.

"Marvin said, 'Let's buy the horse and let Stanley in on the deal. He can show him for us.' So that's what we done. We bought Colida and gave Stanley half-interest in him. Marvin and I split the remaining half.

"Now, when we bought the horse he had a needle mark in his neck. They claimed he'd just been vaccinated for sleeping sickness. Hell, that wasn't it at all. They'd tranquilized him."

Even though Colida proved difficult to handle, he was shown to a limited degree by his new owners.

"In 1961," Cass continues, "Stanley and Marvin took Colida down to the National Show in Fort Worth, Texas.

"They couldn't get along with him. It took both of 'em—one on either side—to lead him. And then he was pretty unmanageable in the ring. He wouldn't set up or anything.

"Still, they placed fifth with him in a class of 79 aged stallions.

"Stanley was managing Jim Wild's Flying W Stables at the time," he says, "so he kept Colida up there for the first year-and-a-half. The deal was not working out too well for me. I was havin' to haul my mares up there to get 'em bred, and I came to feel like I didn't have any say as to how the stud was being managed.

"By 1961, Marvin and I had split up. He got away with all of Beau Lightning and half of the other horses. I got his quarter-interest in Colida and the other half of the horses.

"Then I made the decision that I was either going to own all of Colida or none of him. After ironing out a few difficulties between Stanley and me, the partnership was dissolved."

As soon as he got Colida home, Cass went to work on the 4-year-old stallion's attitude.

"When I got him," he says, "Colida was still 'on the prod.' He'd rear and he'd strike out with his foot. He didn't think too much of men. It took awhile, but I got him to come around. I rode the hell out of him. I used him. I gained his confidence."

In the fall of 1962, Colida and Cass took to the road.

"The first show I took Colida to," he says, "was the 1962 Tulsa State Fair. Ben Johnson of Grand Junction, Colorado, was the judge, and he named Colida grand champion over Vanguard D. and Navajo Britches. And they were both national champions.

"Next, we went to McKinney, Texas, and he was grand there over Top Hat H. Harry Reed was showing Top Hat, and he said to me, 'Why don't you follow me down to the Big 'D' show in Dallas. I'll beat you there. And he did. Top Hat was the grand champion stud and Colida was reserve.

"And that was pretty much it for that year."

The following year, Cass and Colida got serious.

Colida's Bill Hancock, a 1972 stallion by Colida and out of Oak Bow (QH), was the 1976 World Champion Senior Cutting Horse.
Courtesy Bill Cass

"Our first show in 1963 was the Southwestern Livestock Exposition at Fort Worth," he says. "J. D. Kraft from Whitesboro, Texas, was the judge and he buried me. We got a third. Then, low and behold, here Kraft and another ol' boy from Texas come. They made the trip all the way up from Texas to Welch, Oklahoma, just to try to buy my horse.

"I told 'em, 'No way in hell....' "

From Fort Worth, it was on to Houston.

"The day before the Houston show," Cass says, "I spent from sunup to sundown on Colida, gatherin' cattle. There'd come a little thaw and the top of the ground was pretty sloppy. By the time we got done, the only clean spot on the horse was where the cinch fit.

"But I went to work cleanin' him up that night and we headed south.

"Come the morning of the halter classes, I was all duded up in a suit and tie. Colida was clean and shiny, so I just hopped on him bareback and rode him up to the end-gate.

"There we was … him with just a halter and me all decked out in a suit … watching the halter classes.

"Ray Davis, the field man for *Western Horseman* magazine, was perched up on the fence, watching the classes, too. Pretty soon, he jumped down off the rail and sidled up to us.

" 'Is that horse who I think he is?' he asked.

" 'Beats me,' I answered. 'Who do you think he is?'

" 'Is he that 'Col-i-dee' horse?'

" 'That's him,' I said.

" 'Would you mind if I took a little closer look at him?' he asked.

" 'Help yourself.'

"So he stepped a little closer and fanned one of the horse's eyes. And then he fanned the other one.

" 'Thank you,' he said, and walked off.

"Ray had seen Colida at the Fort Worth National, when he was so out of control. He couldn't believe that I'd calmed the horse down that much. He thought I had him doped.

"After he left, I noodled off the horse and led him into the ring. He was reserve champion stud that day."

After returning home from Houston, Cass turned his attention to the Oklahoma Appaloosa show circuit. Between March and December of 1963, he hauled Colida to 20 Sooner State shows. The big, blanket-hipped stud was grand or reserve at all 20, and was named the Oklahoma High-Point Halter Stallion.

Halfway through the 1963 show season, Cass hauled Colida to the 16th National Show in Boise, Idaho. There, he was named Champion Aged Stallion and Grand Champion Stallion.

On the way back to Oklahoma, Cass decided to pay the stallion's breeder a visit.

"From the very get-go," he said, "I made every effort to find out who Colida's sire was. So, after the National, I made a little detour to Kit Carson, Colorado.

"I pulled into the Rhodes Brothers' Ranch and introduced myself to Bill Rhodes. And then I unloaded Colida.

"I explained the whole deal about Lady Chesty and the Illinois connection to him, and then asked him if he could tell me who Colida's sire was.

" 'I wouldn't know anything about that,' he said. 'But that sure is a nice horse you've got there. Not knowing how he's bred, I don't suppose he's worth much. But I'll tell you what I'll do. I'll just buy him from you.'

" 'No you won't,' I said. 'I don't care how he's bred. He's the best Appaloosa I've ever seen and he's not for sale.'

"That man knew who Colida's sire was. He just wasn't offerin' it up."

Later, at an American Quarter Horse Association (AQHA) convention in Denver, Colorado, Cass again came tantalizingly close to solving the mystery.

"Monsieur Moore of Dewey, Oklahoma, was a good friend of mine," he says. "He was also a long-time director and past-president of AQHA. One year, he took me with him to an AQHA convention in Denver.

"Monsieur introduced me around and then

Colida Will, a 1972 stallion by Colida and out of Miss Tulsa Will (QH), was bred and owned by Bill and Ethelyn Cass. He was the 1977 National Champion Aged Stallion.

Photo by Johnny Johnston, courtesy Bill Cass

he and I sat down at a table with Jack Casement, an early-day Quarter Horse breeder from Colorado, and Nelson Nye, a Quarter Horse historian from Arizona.

"The conversation got around to Colida and who his sire might have been.

" 'I can finger the horse right now,' Casement said. 'But I'm not going to do it. It would cost me a friendship.'

"And, of course, he and the Rhodes brothers had been friends for years.

"So, that's about as close as I ever got to getting Colida's sire named by the people who were in the know.

"There was nothing left to do but just go on with it."

And go on with it Bill Cass and Colida did.

The last show of the 1963 season was the Tulsa State Fair. Colida stood grand there, and was retired.

Beginning in 1964, Cass hit the road with a new string of show horses. Included in it were such top Colida get as Porter C., Flying Star and Colida's Buck.

Porter C., a 1962 stallion out of Beau Nika, was bred by Dr. Joe Cochran of Paul's Valley, Oklahoma, and named after Bill Cass's father. Campaigned primarily by John Diediker of Parsons, Kansas, he was a top regional halter and performance horse, and the Reserve Champion Aged Stallion at the 1967 National Show in Walla Walla, Washington.

Post Haste, a Colida grandson, was the 1974 National Champion Men's Western Pleasure Horse. Trainer Chet Bennett is in the saddle.

Photo by Johnny Johnston, courtesy Bill Cass

Flying Star, a 1963 stallion out of Patsy Hull (QH), was bred by Cass. One of the top halter stallions of his day, he was the Champion Aged Stallion and Grand Champion Stallion at the 1967 National Show.

Colida's Buck, a 1964 gelding out of Buck's Flapper (QH), was also bred by Cass. Given to John Diediker in return for showing Porter C., "Buck" was the Champion 3-Year-Old Gelding at the 1967 National Show.

Represented by the above-named trio, Colida was the Champion Get of Sire winner at the 1967 National Show.

In short order, the list of Colida national and world champions began to mushroom. It included:

• Cofleet, a 1966 stallion out of Peggy Norfleet (ID)—1969 National Champion 3-Year-Old Stallion and Reserve National Champion Stallion.

• Trusty's Colida, a 1967 stallion out of Trusty Miss (QH)—1972 National Champion Aged Stallion and National Grand Champion Stallion, 1974 National Champion Rope Race.

• Co-Stephenie, a 1970 mare out of Reno Zanti (QH)—1974 National Champion Junior Western Pleasure.

• Colida Will, a 1972 stallion out of Miss Tulsa Will (ID)—1977 World Champion Aged Stallion.

• Colida's Bill Hancock, a 1972 stallion out of Oak Bow (QH)—1976 World Champion Junior Cutting Horse.

- Colida's Joy, a 1971 mare out of Oak Bow (QH— Champion Broodmare at the 1979 World Championship Show in Oklahoma City, Oklahoma.

Represented by Trusty Colida, Co Trim and Co Lauri, Colida was named the 1972 National Champion Get of Sire winner.

In addition to the above national and world champions, Colida get that included Co Flight, Co-Tone, Colida's Wildfire, Co Aleen, Co-Lauri, Co-Lady, Coleta, Coalice, Co-Dixie, Co-Regent, LA Colt 45 and Snow-Deer Annie were top regional champions.

North of the border, Colida Bartender, Jo-Lida, Colida's Lynn and Colida's Twister were all Canadian national champions.

In 1974, Colida earned honors as Greater Eastern Appaloosa Regional (GEAR) Supreme Sire No. 3.

And the second- and third-generation Colidas were just as good as the first.

Colida's Happiness, a Colida daughter, produced the earners of 13 bronze medallions; MS Miss Kitty, a Colida daughter, produced Post Haste, the 1974 World Champion Performance Horse; and Ima Copino, a Colida son, sired Ima Copino II, the earner of seven bronze medallions.

Colida's Bobbie, a Colida granddaughter, produced Co Cowboy, the 1978 National and World Champion Yearling Stallion; and Frosty Will, another granddaughter, produced DM Sure Will, a gold medallion winner.

By the early 1980s, Colida was a living legend. The sire of more than 500 registered foals, he paid for the Cass Ranch and put three Cass boys through college.

Bill Cass remained intensely loyal to his "rouge stallion." During the 20-plus years they were a team, Cass taught Colida to swim on command and carry him without saddle or bridle. Exhibited on special occasions at horse shows and sales throughout the U.S. and Canada, the stallion delighted thousands with his "feel good" antics.

Colida passed away on July 8, 1982, of old age. It seemed only fitting that he should do so while the National Appaloosa Horse Show was in progress.

Bill and his wife, Ethelyn, were in attendance at the Louisville, Kentucky, event. A special tribute was hastily arranged and the couple was presented a dozen red roses and a plaque.

From a stallion of unknown parentage that was almost destroyed when only a few weeks old, to one of the breed's most colorful characters and greatest sires, Colida lived a full and prosperous life. The Appaloosa community will always be the richer for giving him the chance to prove that the best identity of all is the one you carve out for yourself.

In recognition of their many accomplishments, Colida and Bill Cass were inducted into the ApHC Hall of Fame in 1998 and 2002, respectively.

"That's All Folks…" Colida at home, feeling good.

Courtesy Bill Cass

PHOTO INDEX

ApHC Hall of Fame inductee Elvin Blevins of Wynnewood, Oklahoma, poses with his foundation stallions Buttons B. (left) and Quavo B.   **Courtesy Appaloosa Museum & Heritage Center**

AUTHOR'S PROFILE

FRANK HOLMES has been penning horse-related feature articles and historical books for more than 35 years. His interests have always been centered on the historical aspects of the western horse breeds, and his broad-based knowledge of the origins of the Quarter Horse, Paint, Appaloosa and Palomino registries have established him as one of the pre-eminent equine historians of all time.

As a former staff writer for *Western Horseman* magazine, Frank co-authored volumes 2 through 5 of the immensely popular Legends book series and authored *The Hank Wiescamp Story*.

As the award-winning Features Editor of *The Paint Horse Journal* he contributed a steady stream of top-notch personality profiles, genetic studies, and historical overviews.

From early 2001 on, Frank has devoted the lion's share of his journalistic efforts to the research and writing of historical books designed to capture the West's rich history and pass it on in a way that both enlightens and entertains. Among the books he has previously authored are *Wire to Wire—the Walter Merrick Story* and *More than Color*.

Now living in Falcon, Colorado, he and his wife Loyce, have three sons, Eric, Craig and Morgan.

For more information on the Appaloosa Horse, contact:

Appaloosa Horse Club
The International Breed Registry for Appaloosa Horses
2720 W. Pullman Rd.
Moscow, ID 83843
(208) 882-8150
FAX (208) 882-5578

www.appaloosa.com